The Baseball Book

THE
BASEBALL
BOOK

Revised Edition

Edited by Zander Hollander

A ZANDER HOLLANDER SPORTS BOOK

Random House  New York

Cover photograph credits: FRONT (clockwise from top left): Ozzie Smith (John McDonough/Focus on Sports); Babe Ruth (Focus on Sports); Frank Viola (Michael Ponzini/Focus on Sports); Jose Canseco (Mitchell B. Reibel/Sportschrome East/West); Joe DiMaggio (UPI); Nolan Ryan (Mitchell B. Reibel/Sportschrome East/West); Josh Gibson (UPI); Rickey Henderson (Focus on Sports).
BACK (clockwise from top left): Bo Jackson (Mitchell B. Reibel); Tom Seaver (Mitchell B. Reibel/Sportschrome East/West); Ty Cobb (Sports Photo Source); Hank Aaron (Focus on Sports); Roger Clemens (Mitchell B. Reibel/Sportschrome East/West); Willie Mays (Jerry Wachter/Focus on Sports); Carlton Fisk (Ron Vesely/Focus on Sports).

Text photograph credits: All the photographs in this book are from United Press International with the exception of the following: AP/Wide World Photos, viii, 52, 70, 76, 86, 96 (bottom), 107, 113, 156, 157, 172; Baseball Hall of Fame/Sports Photo Source, 105; Clifton Boutelle, 96 (top); CBS-TV, 100 (bottom); Cincinnati Reds/Sports Photo Source, 38; Tom DeFeo, 29, 42 (top); Malcolm W. Emmons, 9, 81, 83, 164; George Gojkovich, 33 (bottom), 63, 69 (top), 84, 154; Ira Golden, 45, 125; Vic Milton, frontispiece, 40 (top), 65, 67, 129 (top), 147, 161, 168; Milwaukee Braves/Sports Photo Source, 92; Milwaukee Brewers/Sports Photo Source, 95; Ronald C. Modra, 130; NBC-TV, 163; Richard Pilling, 28, 32, 42 (bottom), 64, 80, 98, 116 (bottom), 148; Ken Regan, 36; Mitchell B. Reibel, 23, 27 (top), 35, 47, 68, 82, 93, 97, 108, 138, 139, 141, 143 (top and bottom), 144, 153; John Rogers/Sports Photo Source, 17; San Diego Padres/Sports Photo Source, 142; Carl Skalak, Jr., 160; Sports Photo Source, 66, 78, 100 (top), 124 (top).

Some of the material included here originally appeared in *The Encyclopedia of Sports Talk*, edited by Zander Hollander, copyright © 1976 by Associated Features, Inc.

Library of Congress Cataloging-in-Publication Data

The Baseball book / edited by Zander Hollander. — Rev. ed.
       p. cm.
      "A Zander Hollander sports book."
      Includes index.
      Summary: An alphabetically arranged reference book of baseball's great moments, stars, teams, techniques, language, and anecdotes.
      ISBN 0-679-81055-2 (pbk.) — ISBN 0-679-91055-7 (lib. bdg.)
        1. Baseball—United States—Dictionaries, Juvenile.
[1. Baseball—Dictionaries.] I. Hollander, Zander.
GV867.5.B37 1990
796'.03—dc20   90-38060

Manufactured in the United States of America   10 9 8 7 6 5 4 3 2 1

Acknowledgments

Granted the role of individual stars, baseball is a team game. The editor acknowledges with appreciation the team that contributed to the original edition and this revised edition of *The Baseball Book:* Jim Armstrong, Howard Blatt, Hal Bock, Eric Compton, Red Foley, Cathy Goldsmith, Dave Kaplan, Phyllis Hollander, Frank Kelly, Dennis Lyons, Amy Mayone, Phil Pepe, Bill Roeder and Debbie Zwecher.

Play Ball!

It's time for a trip into the fascinating world of baseball.

All *aboard* for a visit to the *Hot Corner*, the *Phantom Infield*, the *Hall of Fame*, the *Grapefruit League* and the *World Series*. Along the way you'll get to meet *Dizzy and Daffy*, the *Green Monster*, *Iron Mike*, the *Iron Man*, the *Mop-up Man*, the *Gashouse Gang* and *Casey at the Bat*.

You'll be offered a *Can of Corn*, a *Tater*, a *Hot Dog* and a *Meat Hand*—and also the *Split-Finger Fastball*—but you won't need an *Aspirin Tablet*. Be advised to avoid the *Duster* as well as *Murderers' Row*.

There'll be time for the *Seventh-Inning Stretch* before you put your *Foot in the Bucket*, get *Sent to the Showers* and wind up at the *Victory Party*.

These are only a few of the more than 400 entries—from Hank Aaron and Dwight Gooden to Babe Ruth and Robin Yount—that you'll find on your journey through *The Baseball Book*. The goal of this revised and updated edition is to touch all the bases: to tell the stories of the superstars, the great moments and the teams; to define the colorful language of the game; and to provide the records and award winners on which baseball legends are built.

Whether you play it or watch it at the ballpark or on television, whether you're new to the sport and want to learn about it or are a seasoned fan, this book is designed to answer your questions while giving you a laugh or two along the way.

Since the entries are alphabetical, you can easily look things up. If you're following a particular player or team, check the index at the back, because many names appear in more than one entry. And, of course, you can simply browse through the pages and discover why baseball is our national pastime.

—Zander Hollander

This was the swing by Hank Aaron that made baseball history on April 8, 1974. Aaron and umpire David Davidson watch the flight of the ball. Behind Aaron is Dodger catcher Joe Ferguson.

AARON, HANK. With a seeming sense of the dramatic, Hank Aaron of the Atlanta Braves finished the 1973 season with 713 career home runs, just one short of one of baseball's most cherished records, the 714 hit by the immortal Babe Ruth.

All winter the anticipation grew. Finally, the 1974 season began, with the Braves playing in Cincinnati on April 4. In his very first time at bat, against Jack Billingham, Aaron hit a sinking fastball over the left-center-field fence to tie the Babe.

Four days later in Atlanta, at exactly 9:07 P.M., on an overcast, windy, cool evening, before 52,780 screaming fans who had come hoping to see history, Henry Louis Aaron slugged a fastball delivered by Los Angeles Dodger left-hander Al Downing. The ball soared over the left-center-field fence, and Hank had his record-smashing 715th.

When Hank Aaron hit his 715th home run, it was a blow heard round the baseball world.

This homer by Aaron, who was inducted into the Hall of Fame in 1982, has been voted by fans as baseball's "Most Dramatic Moment."

Two years later Aaron ended his fabulous 23-year career, finishing with a record total of 755 home runs. Less well known is the fact that Aaron also finished as the all-time leader in runs batted in with 2,297, as No. 2 in runs scored with 2,174 and as No. 2 in hits with 3,771. (Pete Rose would later surpass Aaron and also Ty Cobb, who had been the leader with 4,191.)

Aaron was born on February 5, 1934, in Mobile, Alabama, and came to the majors in 1954 as an outfielder with the Milwaukee Braves. He was slender and did not look like a power hitter. But he had developed the ability to snap his wrists as he swung, and those fast wrists would get him his record number of home runs.

Aaron won two batting championships, led the league in RBIs four times, and was the home-run king four times. And his good hitting was continuous. Eight times he hit 40 or more homers, and 11 times he drove in over 100 runs. He was the greatest power hitter of his time and finished with a .305 career batting average.

ABOARD. On base. When a team has a man on base, it is said to have a man aboard. So a team may have nobody aboard (bases empty) or it may have one, two or three runners aboard.

AGENT. Someone who negotiates a contract for players for a fee. The agent (often a lawyer) is the bargainer between the ballclub and the player, and his fee is usually a percentage of the contract.

Among established stars the agent may also negotiate commercials for the player. So when you see Bo Jackson on television doing sneaker commercials or Orel Hershiser telling you why he uses a certain shampoo, be assured that the athlete is being well paid for his effort, and also that an agent is getting his share of the fee.

ALL-STAR GAME. In 1933 Arch Ward, sports editor of the Chicago *Tribune*, seeking to add a baseball flavor to Chicago's hundredth birthday celebration, had the idea that fans would like to see a game between the best players from the National League and the best from the American League. So on July 6, 1933, the first All-Star Game was played at Chicago's Comiskey Park. The American League won the game on a two-run home run by Babe Ruth. Lefty Gomez of the New York Yankees was the winning pitcher.

Connie Mack *(left),* of the American League, and John McGraw, of the National League, were the opposing managers in the first All-Star Game in 1933. Mack's team won, 4–2.

All-Star Game in the beginning, winning the first three and 12 of the first 16. But the National League won 30 of the next 37 to take a commanding lead in the series. The American League rebounded in the late 1980s, winning both the 1988 and 1989 contests—for the first time since 1957–58 the AL was able to win consecutive games. In 1990 the AL made it three in a row.

The most memorable All-Star Game occurred in 1934 at New York's Polo Grounds. Pitching in his home park, Carl Hubbell, a New York Giant left-hander, struck out— one after the other—the mighty Babe Ruth, Lou Gehrig, Jimmie Foxx, Al Simmons and Joe Cronin.

The Dodgers' Don Drysdale, throwing in the 1968 All-Star Game, holds the record for the most innings pitched in All-Star Game history (19).

The All-Star Game became an annual attraction and has been played every year since 1933, except for 1945, when the game was called off because of World War II. In 1959 the players of both leagues voted to play two All-Star Games and did so until 1963, when, realizing they were making the game less appealing, they went back to one game a year.

Part of the earnings from the All-Star Game goes to the players' pension fund, which is one reason players have no objection to playing on what would otherwise be a day of rest. Another reason is the honor that goes along with being selected. Stan Musial, Willie Mays and Hank Aaron share the record of having played in the most All-Star Games—24.

The American League dominated the

AMERICAN LEAGUE. This is the younger of baseball's two major leagues (the other is the National League). It was first thought of in 1892, although it was not formed until nine years later.

In 1892 Charles Albert Comiskey, player-manager for the Cincinnati Red Stockings, and Byron Bancroft (Ban) Johnson, baseball columnist for the Cincinnati *Gazette,* began to grow unhappy with the old-fashioned and cumbersome 12-team National League and started thinking of forming a league of their own.

Comiskey talked up the idea of bringing back the old Western Association, an earlier league, with a new name, to compete with the National League. Interest was great among owners, and Comiskey recommended Johnson as president of the new league.

Even with the imaginative and energetic Johnson at the head, however, the new league moved slowly until 1899, when the National League dropped four teams. Johnson added the four teams to his league and changed the name from the Western Association to the American League. On April 24, 1901, the American League began operations with a gala opening game in which Cleveland played Chicago in Chicago.

Charter members of the American League were Chicago (which went on to become the first American League champion), Boston, Detroit, Philadelphia, Baltimore, Washington, Cleveland and Milwaukee.

The next year Milwaukee was replaced by St. Louis, and in 1903 John McGraw, one of the owners of the Baltimore club, sold his share of the team and went back to the National League to head the New York Giants. Johnson's reply was defiance. He moved the Baltimore franchise to New York in direct competition with the Giants, despite politicians' threats to run city streets through his ballpark.

The eight teams that made up the American League in 1903 were to remain in the same cities until the 1954 season, when the St. Louis Browns asked for and received permission to move to Baltimore. The following year the Philadelphia Athletics moved to Kansas City.

In 1961 the American League voted to expand to 10 teams. To achieve this, the Washington Senators moved to the twin cities of Minneapolis–St. Paul and became the Minnesota Twins, and new franchises were awarded to Los Angeles and Wash-

ington. Players for the two new teams were taken from a pool established by the eight existing teams. Each team submitted a list of available players, and the Los Angeles Angels and the new Washington Senators could then purchase players to stock their teams. The season schedule was increased from 154 games to 162.

In 1965, after a dispute with their National League neighbors, the Dodgers, the Angels moved out of Los Angeles. The Angels had been tenants of Dodger Stadium and considered the rental much too high. They constructed a new stadium in nearby Anaheim (site of Disneyland) and opened the 1966 season in their new home. To create broader appeal, the Angels changed their name from the Los Angeles Angels to the California Angels.

In 1968 the Kansas City club moved to Oakland. And in 1969 the American League expanded to 12 teams, with a new franchise in Kansas City and another in Seattle. The league was split into two divisions, East and West, with the winning team of each division playing for the league championship. The winner of these playoffs wins the AL pennant and represents the league in the World Series.

The Seattle franchise was moved to Milwaukee in 1970, and the Washington, D.C., club moved to Texas two years later. Eventually the Eastern Division consisted of Baltimore, Boston, Cleveland, Detroit, Milwaukee and New York. California, Chicago, Kansas City, Minnesota, Oakland and Texas made up the Western Division. Toronto (Eastern Division) and a new Seattle team (Western Division) joined the league in 1977.

Under the guidance of Ban Johnson the American League thrived once it had gotten off the ground, but failure to get along with baseball commissioner Kenesaw Mountain Landis caused Johnson to resign in 1927. He was succeeded by Ernest S.

Barnard, who reigned until his death in 1931 (the same year Ban Johnson died). On Barnard's death, Will Harridge was promoted from American League secretary to league president. Harridge resigned after the 1958 season, and in 1959 Joe Cronin became the American League president. In 1973 Cronin became chairman of the board of the American League and was succeeded as president by Leland (Lee) MacPhail.

MacPhail served for 10 seasons before retiring, with former Yankee third baseman Dr. Bobby Brown taking over in 1984.

APPEAL. A claim by a member of the defensive team of a violation of the rules by the offensive team when such a violation is not automatically penalized. Example: If a batter bats out of turn or a runner fails to touch a base, the batter or runner cannot be called out unless the defensive team appeals to the umpire.

AROUND THE HORN. A double play completed from the third baseman to the second baseman to the first baseman. The expression originated from the fact that it is the longest way to make a double play, just as the route around Cape Horn at the tip of South America is the longest way from the Atlantic Ocean to the Pacific Ocean (and was the only route until the Panama Canal was built).

ARTIFICIAL TURF. Also called Astroturf, carpet, synthetic grass or rug. First developed in 1964, when the Houston Astros found that they could not grow real grass under the roof of the Astrodome, artificial turf quickly caught on not only with baseball teams but also with football teams.

Owners liked the fact that artificial turf cut down on the number of rainouts, since it could absorb more water than grass and also be vacuumed dry by a machine. By the late 1980s, artificial turf was in use in 10 of 26 major-league parks.

ASPIRIN TABLET. A slang expression that hitters use to explain what a ball thrown by a fastball pitcher like Nolan Ryan (at nearly 100 miles per hour) looks like when it comes up to the plate. It's not difficult to swallow, but it sure is tough to hit.

ASSIST. Official credit given in the scoring of a game to a player who throws or deflects a batted or thrown ball so that a putout results, or would have resulted except for an error on the play. In the case of a deflection, the player must slow the ball down or change its direction to rate an assist.

Assists by infielders are common; they are relatively uncommon by outfielders, since it means throwing a runner out while he is trying to take an extra base or throwing a man out to complete a double play after an outfield catch.

The record for most outfield assists in one season is 44, set in 1930 by Chuck Klein of the Philadelphia Phillies. The record for most outfield assists in one game is four and is held by many players. The record for most outfield assists in one inning is two and is also held by many players.

AT-BAT. An official turn at hitting charged to a player except when he receives a base on balls, is hit by a pitched ball, makes a sacrifice hit, or is interfered with by the catcher.

ATLANTA BRAVES. Winding up his third World Series victory with his 24th shutout inning in a row, Lew Burdette gave the Milwaukee fans something special to celebrate in 1957. Five years after leaving Boston and 43 years after the last world championship in the franchise's history, the Braves had defeated the Yankees in a seven-game World Series.

But the following year a Braves team led by pitchers Burdette and Warren Spahn and batters Hank Aaron and Eddie Mathews blew a 3–1 Series lead to the Yankees and lost in seven games. And in 1959 the Braves lost a three-game pennant playoff to the Dodgers.

By 1966 the love affair between the Braves and the city of Milwaukee was over, and the club moved to Atlanta. Apart from division-winning seasons in 1969 and 1982 (when the Braves set a major-league record by winning their first 13 games), the team's fans have had little to cheer about—other than the hitting exploits of home-run king Aaron.

The Miracle Braves of 1914, who were in last place halfway through the season but who wound up winning the pennant by 10½ games, rode the hitting of Joe Connolly, the fielding of Rabbit Maranville and the pitching of Dick Rudolph and Bill James to a Series sweep of the Philadelphia

The Braves' Lew Burdette threw a 1–0 no-hitter against the Phillies on August 18, 1960.

Athletics. In the four games Philadelphia scored a total of six runs.

In 1948, sustained by the pitching of Spahn and Johnny Sain, the Braves won a pennant, but lost the World Series in six games to Cleveland.

The only pitcher who has brought back memories of Spahn, Burdette and Sain during the Braves' more recent history is Phil Niekro, who knuckleballed his way to 318 career victories, all but 50 of them with the Braves.

AUTOMATIC STRIKE. This is a pitch delivered with a count of three balls and no strikes. The pitcher simply tries to get the pitch over, and the batter is usually under orders not to swing on the chance that either it will be a ball or the pitcher is unlikely to throw two more strikes in a row. It is considered "automatic" because the pitcher is deliberately aiming for the strike zone without using his most effective pitch. The pitcher does this because he knows that the batter will probably not swing. Also called a cripple.

BACKSTOP. The catcher. Also, a screened structure behind home plate to stop foul balls from going into the stands.

BAIL OUT. When a pitch comes too close for comfort and the batter pulls away

quickly to escape being hit, it is called bailing out. If a batter bails out unnecessarily too often, it shows he is afraid of being hit, and pitchers will work on that weakness to keep him away from the plate.

BALK. Pitchers enjoy freedom of movement on the mound. They can make any move they want, including wheeling toward a base, pretending to throw or even charging toward a runner. All of it is perfectly legal—until the pitcher toes the pitching rubber. Then his moves are limited by the balk rule.

For a long time, balks were rarely called by the umpires. But in the 1987 World Series, St. Louis manager Whitey Herzog complained that Minnesota pitchers were violating the balk rule by failing to come to a complete stop in their motion with runners on base. American League umpires had long ignored the letter of the law on the full stop. The next season, however, they did not. In the season's first two weeks, the Milwaukee Brewers and Oakland A's each had a record six balks called against them in one game. For the season, Oakland set a record with 76 balks, 16 of them—another record—against Dave Stewart. It hardly deterred the A's, though. They still won the pennant.

The balk language was changed the following year, permitting umpires wider latitude in determining whether pitchers were making the required stop.

There are 13 different ways to commit a balk, but in actual practice only three types of balks are common: The pitcher checks himself illegally, breaking his delivery when he is already committed to the pitch; the ball slips out of his hands while his foot is on the rubber; or, as Dave Stewart learned in 1988, he fails to come to a full stop with a runner on base.

The late Tommy Holmes, a baseball

writer, used to say that every fan should be presented with a copy of the balk rule on entering the park. That would help reduce the cries of "Balk!" that come ringing from the stands whenever the pitcher makes a false move, or what looks like one. But the rule itself is no model of clarity. When calling balks, umpires tend to rely more on custom and experience than on the fine print of the law. (*See also* Catcher's balk.)

BALL. Called by many other names, including horsehide, apple, onion, pill, pea and sphere. The rules state that the ball must be a sphere formed by yarn wound around a small core of cork and rubber that is then covered with two strips of white horsehide tightly stitched together. It must weigh not less than 5 or more than 5¼ ounces and measure not less than 9 or more than 9¼ inches around.

Suspicions that baseballs were being made out of different materials, making for a livelier ball, have been common since 1919, when a marked increase in distance hitting was first noticed. In the period 1920–23 almost three times as many home runs were hit in the major leagues as in 1916–19. The rate kept going up until it leveled off in the 1950s, but baseball officials have never admitted to any change in the composition of the ball.

In baseball's early years, hitting a baseball was rather like hitting a rock. The ball lacked resiliency, and as a result home runs were a rare commodity. Frank Baker of the Philadelphia Athletics was nicknamed "Home Run" for his long-ball proficiency in 1911, a year when he led the league with all of 11 home runs. In the dead-ball era, that was a lot. Baker was the game's top homer hitter for the next three years as well, with 10, 12 and 9. Not long after that, things began to change.

When home runs started flying out of major-league parks at a record rate in 1987, many pitchers complained that, the ball had been juiced up. But when home runs returned to a normal level the following season, the complaints stopped.

A core of cork mixed with rubber is covered with a layer of black rubber and a layer of red rubber, and is then wound with 121 yards of rough blue-gray wool, 45 yards of white wool, 53 yards of fine blue-gray wool, and 150 yards of fine white cotton. After all this is coated with rubber cement, the cover is sewn by hand—two figure 8–shaped pieces of white horsehide are joined by 108 double stitches of red thread.

Balls used in the two leagues are identical except that each has the signature of its own league president stamped on the cover. A. G. Spalding & Brothers was the exclusive manufacturer of major-league baseballs from the time the leagues began until 1976, when the contract was awarded to the Rawlings Company. Production costs have risen sharply in recent years, and all the baseballs used in the major leagues are now manufactured in Haiti.

In 1965 it was claimed that the Chicago White Sox stored a number of balls in a cold spot before using them in a game. The purpose of the freezing was to deaden the baseballs and keep them from being hit for long distances. This was believed helpful to the White Sox, a team with little hitting ability and a lot of pitching. The charge was denied by Chicago and never proved by the accusers. If the White Sox did, indeed, try such shenanigans, it did them no good. They still failed to win the American League pennant.

BALL HAWK. An outfielder, especially one who is very fast and good at chasing down fly balls—and catching them.

BALLS AND STRIKES. A pitch outside a prescribed zone is called a ball, four of which allow the batter to move to first base. A pitch that passes through the zone without being hit is a strike, as is a pitch swung at and missed, a pitch fouled with less than two strikes, or a pitch bunted foul no matter what the count. Three strikes make an out.

The umpire behind the plate is the unquestioned judge (in theory, if not in practice) of whether a pitch is a ball or a strike. He keeps track of how many balls and strikes a batter has by means of an indicator, a pocket-sized scoreboard with dials for balls, strikes and outs.

In announcing the count (number of balls and strikes a batter has), it is proper to give the balls first, the strikes second. So a count of three and two means three balls and two strikes.

The Orioles, with American League Triple Crown winner Frank Robinson *(right)* and Brooks Robinson, swept the Dodgers in the 1966 World Series.

BALTIMORE ORIOLES. If one word sums up the history of the Orioles, it is pitching. From their 1966 world championship to the start of the 1980s, the Orioles boasted numerous 20-game winners who kept them in contention almost every year.

The Orioles' astonishing sweep of the Dodgers in the 1966 World Series should have served as an indication that the O's were establishing a pitching dynasty. In that Series young hurlers Jim Palmer, Wally Bunker and Dave McNally helped hold the Dodgers to a total of two runs in four games.

From 1970 through 1980 the Orioles had 19 pitchers who won 20 games or more, including three in their world championship year of 1970, and four (Palmer, McNally, Mike Cuellar and Pat Dobson) the following season, when they won the pennant.

There was no sign in the Orioles' early history that the team would establish any sort of dynasty. Originating in Milwaukee in 1901 and becoming the St. Louis Browns in 1902, the franchise finished in the first division only 12 times and won its only pennant in 1944, a war year, when many of the game's stars were in military service.

After the war ended, the team finished in the second division for eight straight years. Attendance dropped, and not even the promotional stunts of owner Bill Veeck could save the team. Veeck finally sold out to a Baltimore group, and the club began a new life in Maryland in 1954.

It wasn't until 1960 that the Orioles became a contender. Led by young third baseman Brooks Robinson and the "Baby Birds" pitching staff, which featured Milt Pappas, Steve Barber and Chuck Estrada, the O's started their rise to respectability. In 1966 a trade that brought Frank Robinson from Cincinnati set into gear the Orioles' drive to the championship.

Ironically, it was Frank Robinson who brought the Orioles a taste of their glory days when he returned to Baltimore as manager in 1988. Although they finished that year in last place, Robinson guided them in 1989 to within two games of a division title in the American League East.

The Orioles finished the 1989 season with 87 wins—33 more than the year before—and Robinson was an overwhelming choice as Manager of the Year.

BANJO HITTER. A weak hitter who seems to lightly strum the ball, as one would a banjo. It is a term of disparagement, but any player will say that even a banjo hit is music to his ears.

BANKS, ERNIE. Only 5,264 fans were at Chicago's Wrigley Field on May 12, 1970, the day 39-year-old Ernie Banks

Mets' Banner Day at Shea Stadium in Flushing, New York.

joined one of baseball's most select fraternities, the 500 Club. In the second inning, the man known as "Mr. Cub" cracked a 1–1 pitch from the Braves' Pat Jarvis into the left-field bleachers. It was his third homer of the season and the 500th homer of his career.

The first homer ever hit by Banks in the majors came on September 30, 1953, two days after the Cubs bought him from the Kansas City Monarchs. By the time he unloaded his last, No. 512 in 1971, his 19th and final season, Banks was regarded as a god on the north side of Chicago.

Born on January 31, 1931, in Dallas, this lanky right-handed slugger began his career as a shortstop. He was converted into a first baseman in 1962. No matter what his position, he was always a force in the Cubs' lineup.

Banks captured back-to-back National League Most Valuable Player awards in 1958 and 1959, won NL home-run titles in 1958 (47) and 1960 (41) and led the NL in RBIs in 1958 (129) and 1959 (143). He drilled more than 40 homers in a season five times. He played in 11 All-Star games.

The career numbers that led to his 1977 induction into the Hall of Fame were overwhelming—2,528 games, 512 homers and 1,636 RBIs. But even more memorable than any of his statistics was the pure, boundless "Let's play two" joy this sweet-tempered man brought to playing a boys' game.

BANNER DAY. One of baseball's many promotions (others include Camera Day, Old-Timers' Day, Senior Citizens' Day and Ladies' Day) designed to create spectator participation and increase attendance. Banner Day had its origin with the New York Mets in the old Polo Grounds and came about purely by accident. Fans began carrying signs and banners to the ballpark to cheer their personal heroes, make known

their grievances, support their favorite team or simply show off their cleverness.

They used bedsheets, cardboard and rolled-up pieces of paper. At first the slogans were simple statements in crayon, pen or pencil, but soon the banners evolved into works of art, and the slogans read like sophisticated advertising campaigns.

Finally the Mets' promotion department decided to run a competition for creator of the best banner, and among the winners were the following banners:

WHO SAYS A GOOD BASEBALL TEAM
HAS TO WIN?

WE'RE IN THE CELLAR
BUT WE'RE NOT IN THE DUMPS.

TO ERROR IS HUMAN,
TO FORGIVE IS A METS FAN.

BARNSTORMING. Taken from the political and theatrical term that originally meant to appear briefly in small country towns, where barns served as gathering places. In the past, baseball teams used to barnstorm in the spring, hopping from town to town on their way home from training camp. In addition, star players would often assemble into barnstorming units in the fall, after the regular season was over, playing not only in the United States but occasionally on foreign soil as well. This postseason practice is relatively rare nowadays, although in recent years all-star teams of major leaguers have played games in Japan.

The first foreign tour dates back to 1874, when members of the Boston Red Stockings and the Philadelphia Athletics of the National Association went to Ireland and England to play 14 baseball games and seven cricket matches.

Five years later Frank Bancroft took a

Yankee stars Lou Gehrig *(left)* and Babe Ruth *(right),* with promoter Christy Walsh, were a sight to see wherever they barnstormed.

barnstorming team to Havana, Cuba. In 1888 A. G. Spalding gathered a group of 20 players, mostly from the Chicago National League team, and made the first around-the-world baseball tour, playing in such faraway places as New Zealand, Austria, Ceylon, Egypt, Italy, France, England and Ireland.

In 1908 the Reach All-America team made the first tour of Japan, and later there were additional visits. In 1931 many of the top stars of the day played four games in Japan and drew the staggering total of 250,000 admissions. Soon after that tour the Japanese developed professional teams for the first time. One of the players on the 1931 trip was Lefty O'Doul, who made five more trips to Japan and became the second greatest sports idol in that country, the first being Babe Ruth, who played on the 18-game Japanese tour headed by Connie Mack in 1934. In 1955 the New York Yankees went to Japan as a unit to play exhibitions. Since then many teams have played there.

Still, it was mainly through the appearances of Babe Ruth and Lefty O'Doul that the Japanese took to the game of baseball to such a degree that today they are as fanatical about the sport as we are in the United States.

BASE. Also called bag, sack, cushion. Any of the four objects to be touched or occupied by a member or members of the team at bat. Home base is usually called the plate or the dish and is the starting and finishing point of a trip around the bases, which results in the scoring of a run. First, second and third bases are white canvas bags 15 inches square, not less than 3 or more than 5 inches in thickness, filled with soft material and securely attached to the ground. They differ from home base, which is a 5-sided slab of whitened rub-

ber. It is 17 inches square with two of the corners filled in so that one edge is 17 inches long, two are 8½ inches, and two are 12 inches. It is set in the ground so that the 17-inch edge faces the pitcher. All bases, including home base, are in fair territory. The bases are 90 feet apart. Runners run from one base to the next in a counterclockwise direction.

BASEBALL CARDS. Baseball cards have been around almost as long as the game itself, appearing as early as the 1880s in cigarette and tobacco packages. Following World War I, candy manufacturers used

WAGNER, PITTSBURG

Baseball cards go a long way back, including this Honus Wagner card, which, in mint condition, sold for $110,000 in 1988. Note that the card manufacturer couldn't spell Pittsburgh.

cards to lure purchasers of such goodies as caramels, toffee, mints and milk cocoa.

By the 1930s the chewing gum companies had begun packaging pictures of the stars with biographical data or playing tips on the back side.

From the beginning, collecting baseball cards has been a favorite hobby of countless Americans of all ages. Collectors now assemble at conventions, auctions and club meetings, and are kept up-to-date on what's available through books, magazines and newsletters. Aside from deriving pleasure from sorting, trading and assembling, collectors can find monetary rewards for a particular rare card.

In recent years baseball cards have become a billion-dollar business, with five companies producing seven sets of cards each year. Card shows throughout the United States attract dealers and collectors, and on a busy weekend at a big show there may be transactions worth hundreds of thousands of dollars.

BASEBALL'S ORIGINS. As far as organized baseball is concerned, Abner Doubleday is the father of the game. It may well be, however, that one Alexander J. Cartwright dreamed up the sport as we know it and that baseball is keeping alive a myth by crediting Doubleday.

During the Depression of the 1930s the major leagues, trying to stir up lagging interest in the game, came on a 30-year-old report by A. G. Mills, who had been commissioned to look into the origins of baseball. Mills stated, without a particle of proof, that baseball had been invented in 1839 in Cooperstown, New York, by Doubleday, a West Point cadet who later became a Union general—as well as a close friend of Mills. The major leagues seized on the report, set up a centennial celebration for 1939, and made Cooperstown the site of an official baseball museum and Hall of Fame.

Most baseball historians consider the Mills report a work of fiction, preferring

These baseball cards from 1887 show players from the Washington, D.C., team of the National League.

This is an artist's rendering of *The Second Great Match Game for the Championship,* played in Philadelphia in 1866. The Philadelphia Athletics defeated the Brooklyn Atlantics, 31–12.

to believe that the sport evolved from old English games, notably rounders, and that Cartwright should have been given credit for formalizing it. Cartwright, a surveyor, laid out the field with the bases 90 feet apart and drew up rules (including three strikes and three outs) for the first game played between organized teams, in Hoboken, New Jersey, in 1846.

BASELINES. The boundary lines within which a base runner must stay when running between the bases. The baseline is a direct line between two bases, 90 feet in length and extending three feet on either side. Between home plate and first base, and between third base and home plate, the baselines are *not* the foul lines—they run parallel to the foul lines. Whether or not a runner has stayed within the boundary of the baseline is a source of many heated disputes between players and umpires because, since the action is so fast, the decision is up to the umpire, who has the last word.

BASE ON BALLS. A batter is allowed to go to first base after receiving four pitches that are outside the strike zone. Also called a walk. This is the play that managers detest more than any other in baseball, because there is no defense against a base on balls—the batter is given a free ticket to a base. Enough free tickets will soon prove to be very damaging.

Frankie Frisch was a player and manager turned radio broadcaster for the New York Giants, and not a day would pass that he would not deplore the base on balls. "Oh, those bases on balls" became a Frankie Frisch trademark.

The record for receiving the most bases on balls in a single season is 170 by Babe Ruth in 1923. The National League record is 148, shared by Eddie Stanky of the Brooklyn Dodgers in 1945 and Jim Wynn of the Houston Astros in 1969. Ruth's record was based on pitchers' fears of his great ability as a hitter, while Stanky's was a tribute to his ability to distract pitchers into throwing balls. He did this by constantly fouling pitches that would have been strikes and by moving around and crouching in the batter's box so that he was a difficult target. Eddie Yost, who was nicknamed the Walking Man, walked 151 times in 152 games for the Washington Senators in 1956.

Among current players, Wade Boggs and Jack Clark of the Red Sox, Rickey Henderson of the A's and Will Clark of the Giants are noted for their ability to draw walks, each often reaching base this way more than 100 times a season.

BASE RUNNER. Any player of the team at bat who occupies a base.

BASES LOADED. When first base, second base and third base are all occupied by runners. Also called bases full, bags bulging and the ducks are on the pond.

BAT. A smooth, rounded stick not more than 2¾ inches in diameter at its thickest part and not more than 42 inches long. The rules state that a bat must be one piece of solid wood or formed from a block of wood consisting of two or more pieces of wood bonded together with an adhesive in such a way that the grain of each piece runs in essentially the same direction as the length of the bat. Any such laminated bat may contain only wood and adhesive, except for a clear finish.

Bat nicknames have survived long usage. Some of the more enduring ones are lumber, wood, wand, willow, war club, stick, hickory. A bat is still called a hickory because it used to be made of that hardwood, although white ash has long since proved more satisfactory.

Thanks to Babe Ruth, bats are much lighter than they were in the days when Babe himself swung a 54-ounce club. Other hitters, going for distance to keep up with Ruth, found they couldn't get the bat around fast enough.

These days the average weight of a bat used by major leaguers is 32 ounces. Kevin Mitchell of the Giants wields the heaviest bat—35 ounces—with Dave Parker of the Brewers next at 34½. The Padres' Tony Gwynn, 30 ounces, and the Cardinals' Ozzie Smith, 31, swing the lightest bats.

Most professional bats are made by Hillerich & Bradsby. Their Louisville Slugger, in production since 1894, is still the favorite big-league bat. It comes in any number of models, and most players have bats manufactured to their own specifications, so that each player has his own bat model almost from the time he first joins a major-league team.

On the amateur level, from Little League to high school to the colleges, aluminum bats or bats made of metal compounds are the standard. Unlike wooden bats, they rarely break, so in the end they're not as costly. Nothing short of a revolution would bring an aluminum bat to professional baseball, however.

There is a legend that if a player hits the ball on the trademark of the bat, the bat will break, but that story was born on the sandlots and is not true. During the 1958 World Series, Hank Aaron of the Milwaukee Braves came to bat, and New York Yankee catcher Yogi Berra noticed that the trademark was down.

"Hank," Yogi said, "you'd better turn the trademark around so you can read it. Otherwise, you'll break your bat."

"Yogi," Aaron replied, "I came up here to hit, not to read."

BAT AROUND. When all nine batters of one team come to bat in the same inning before there are three outs.

Joe Carrieri was batboy for six world championship Yankee teams. He later became a lawyer.

BATBOY. A young man, usually a teenager, who assists a team by handing each player his bat, picking up the bat after the player has hit and generally caring for and keeping equipment neat and tidy during a game. The batboy also keeps the umpire supplied with baseballs during the game. It is a job that boys want because they get to rub shoulders with their heroes, the players, and are usually on a first-name basis with them. Another attraction is the opportunity to make one road trip with the team. Batboys are paid a small fee by the team and depend on tips from the players for additional income.

Teams also employ ballboys (and ballgirls) who gather up foul balls during the game. A ballboy does not work in close association with the players, but he can work his way up to batboy.

BATTER. An offensive player who takes his position in the batter's box for purposes of hitting the ball. Traditionally, play is in progress when the home-plate umpire shouts, "Batter up!"

BATTER'S BOX. The area within which the batter stands during his time at bat. It is a rectangle six feet long and four feet wide, with boundaries outlined by chalk lines. The batter is supposed to take his position within these boundaries and stay there, although many stretch that rule, positioning themselves as far back in the box as possible, sometimes with their back foot actually over the line. Hitters often "dig in" when they come to bat, pawing at the dirt with their spikes to create a comfortable anchor spot from which to swing.

BATTERY. The pitcher and the catcher. The name has a military origin and dates to Civil War days when a battery was a group of cannons. Just as the cannons did, the pitcher and catcher start all of the fireworks in a baseball game.

BATTING AVERAGE. A way of measuring a player's batting ability. It is the number of hits divided by official times at bat and carried to three decimal places. The batting average is an outgrowth of the box score, first kept by Henry Chadwick, the pioneer of all baseball writers, in 1853.

At present a batting average of .300 (3 hits for every 10 times at bat) is considered excellent. In modern times (since 1900) there have been just eight players who batted .400 or higher for a full season, including Ty Cobb of the Detroit Tigers and Rogers Hornsby of the St. Louis Cardinals, who each did it three times, and George Sisler of the St. Louis Browns, who did it twice. The others are Shoeless Joe Jackson of the Cleveland Indians, who hit .408 in 1911; Harry Heilmann of the Detroit Tigers, who batted .403 in 1923; Bill Terry of the New York Giants, who batted .401 in 1930; and Ted Williams of the Boston Red Sox, the last major leaguer to do it when he hit .406 in 1941.

The highest batting average in modern times for a single season was .424 by Hornsby in 1924 (536 at-bats, 227 hits). The highest batting average for an entire career belongs to Cobb, who batted a remarkable .367 over 24 years—covering 3,033 games and including 4,191 hits in 11,429 at-bats. (See pages 19–20.)

BATTING CAGE. A metal device on wheels that is used during batting practice, but not during the game, to keep balls from rolling behind home plate or going into the stands, where they would, undoubtedly, remain.

BATTING ORDER. The order in which the players on a team must come to bat. Also called the lineup. If a player bats out of turn, deliberately or otherwise, he is out—provided the team in the field realizes the error and appeals to the umpire immediately after the illegal batter has finished his time at bat. The only way the batting order can be changed is by the use of a substitute batter (a player not already in the game). Once a player has been substituted for, he is no longer permitted to remain in the game.

The batting order is made out in triplicate by the manager on a form provided by the league. The manager keeps one copy for his use and gives one copy to the opposing manager and another to the home-plate umpire.

Many years ago a team would almost always finish with the same nine players that it started with. In recent years baseball has become much more specialized, and the use of substitutes has become so widespread that it is rare that a team finishes a game with the same nine men who started it.

BATTING PRACTICE. The players' favorite pastime. A given amount of time, usually an hour, set aside before each game so that hitters can practice hitting. The poor hitters need it the most but get it the least, because most of the time is taken up by the regulars, who are protective of their allotted time.

BEANBALL. A pitch suspected of having been aimed at a batter's head. Pitchers, according to pitchers, never throw beanballs. Quote: "It slipped," or "I was just brushing him back" (throwing close to the batter to keep him from digging in at the plate). Such explanations are often re-

Batting Champions

NATIONAL LEAGUE

Year	Player, Club	Avg.	Year	Player, Club	Avg.
1900	Honus Wagner, Pittsburgh Pirates	.380	1946	Stan Musial, St. Louis Cardinals	.365
1901	Jesse Burkett, St. Louis Cardinals	.382	1947	Harry Walker, St. Louis Cardinals–	
1902	C.H. Beaumont, Pittsburgh Pirates	.357		Philadelphia Phillies	.363
1903	Honus Wagner, Pittsburgh Pirates	.355	1948	Stan Musial, St. Louis Cardinals	.376
1904	Honus Wagner, Pittsburgh Pirates	.349	1949	Jackie Robinson, Brooklyn Dodgers	.342
1905	J. Seymour Bentley, Cincinnati Reds	.377	1950	Stan Musial, St. Louis Cardinals	.346
1906	Honus Wagner, Pittsburgh Pirates	.339	1951	Stan Musial, St. Louis Cardinals	.355
1907	Honus Wagner, Pittsburgh Pirates	.350	1952	Stan Musial, St. Louis Cardinals	.336
1908	Honus Wagner, Pittsburgh Pirates	.354	1953	Carl Furillo, Brooklyn Dodgers	.344
1909	Honus Wagner, Pittsburgh Pirates	.339	1954	Willie Mays, New York Giants	.345
1910	Sherwood Magee, Philadelphia Phillies	.331	1955	Richie Ashburn, Philadelphia Phillies	.338
1911	Honus Wagner, Pittsburgh Pirates	.334	1956	Hank Aaron, Milwaukee Braves	.328
1912	Heinie Zimmerman, Chicago Cubs	.372	1957	Stan Musial, St. Louis Cardinals	.351
1913	Jake Daubert, Brooklyn Dodgers	.350	1958	Richie Ashburn, Philadelphia Phillies	.350
1914	Jake Daubert, Brooklyn Dodgers	.329	1959	Hank Aaron, Milwaukee Braves	.328
1915	Larry Doyle, New York Giants	.320	1960	Dick Groat, Pittsburgh Pirates	.325
1916	Hal Chase, Cincinnati Reds	.339	1961	Roberto Clemente, Pittsburgh Pirates	.351
1917	Edd Roush, Cincinnati Reds	.341	1962	Tommy Davis, Los Angeles Dodgers	.346
1918	Zack Wheat, Brooklyn Dodgers	.335	1963	Tommy Davis, Los Angeles Dodgers	.326
1919	Edd Roush, Cincinnati Reds	.321	1964	Roberto Clemente, Pittsburgh Pirates	.339
1920	Rogers Hornsby, St. Louis Cardinals	.370	1965	Roberto Clemente, Pittsburgh Pirates	.329
1921	Rogers Hornsby, St. Louis Cardinals	.397	1966	Matty Alou, Pittsburgh Pirates	.342
1922	Rogers Hornsby, St. Louis Cardinals	.401	1967	Roberto Clemente, Pittsburgh Pirates	.357
1923	Rogers Hornsby, St. Louis Cardinals	.384	1968	Pete Rose, Cincinnati Reds	.335
1924	Rogers Hornsby, St. Louis Cardinals	.424	1969	Pete Rose, Cincinnati Reds	.348
1925	Rogers Hornsby, St. Louis Cardinals	.403	1970	Rico Carty, Atlanta Braves	.366
1926	Bubbles Hargrave, Cincinnati Reds	.353	1971	Joe Torre, St. Louis Cardinals	.363
1927	Paul Waner, Pittsburgh Pirates	.380	1972	Billy Williams, Chicago Cubs	.333
1928	Rogers Hornsby, Boston Braves	.387	1973	Pete Rose, Cincinnati Reds	.338
1929	Lefty O'Doul, Philadelphia Phillies	.398	1974	Ralph Garr, Atlanta Braves	.353
1930	Bill Terry, New York Giants	.401	1975	Bill Madlock, Chicago Cubs	.354
1931	Chick Hafey, St. Louis Cardinals	.349	1976	Bill Madlock, Chicago Cubs	.339
1932	Lefty O'Doul, Brooklyn Dodgers	.368	1977	Dave Parker, Pittsburgh Pirates	.338
1933	Chuck Klein, Philadelphia Phillies	.368	1978	Dave Parker, Pittsburgh Pirates	.334
1934	Paul Waner, Pittsburgh Pirates	.362	1979	Keith Hernandez, St. Louis Cardinals	.344
1935	Arky Vaughan, Pittsburgh Pirates	.385	1980	Bill Buckner, Chicago Cubs	.324
1936	Paul Waner, Pittsburgh Pirates	.373	1981	Bill Madlock, Pittsburgh Pirates	.341
1937	Joe Medwick, St. Louis Cardinals	.374	1982	Al Oliver, Montreal Expos	.331
1938	Ernie Lombardi, Cincinnati Reds	.342	1983	Bill Madlock, Pittsburgh Pirates	.323
1939	Johnny Mize, St. Louis Cardinals	.349	1984	Tony Gwynn, San Diego Padres	.351
1940	Debs Garms, Pittsburgh Pirates	.355	1985	Willie McGee, St. Louis Cardinals	.353
1941	Pete Reiser, Brooklyn Dodgers	.343	1986	Tim Raines, Montreal Expos	.334
1942	Ernie Lombardi, Boston Braves	.330	1987	Tony Gwynn, San Diego Padres	.370
1943	Stan Musial, St. Louis Cardinals	.330	1988	Tony Gwynn, San Diego Padres	.313
1944	Dixie Walker, Brooklyn Dodgers	.357	1989	Tony Gwynn, San Diego Padres	.336
1945	Phil Cavaretta, Chicago Cubs	.355	1990	Willie McGee, St. Louis Cardinals	.335

Batting Champions

AMERICAN LEAGUE

Year	Player, Club	Avg.	Year	Player, Club	Avg.
1901	Napoleon Lajoie, Philadelphia Athletics	.422	1946	Mickey Vernon, Washington Senators	.353
1902	Ed Delahanty, Washington Senators	.376	1947	Ted Williams, Boston Red Sox	.343
1903	Napoleon Lajoie, Cleveland Indians	.355	1948	Ted Williams, Boston Red Sox	.369
1904	Napoleon Lajoie, Cleveland Indians	.381	1949	George Kell, Detroit Tigers	.343
1905	Elmer Flick, Cleveland Indians	.306	1950	Billy Goodman, Boston Red Sox	.354
1906	George Stone, St. Louis Browns	.358	1951	Ferris Fain, Philadelphia Athletics	.344
1907	Ty Cobb, Detroit Tigers	.350	1952	Ferris Fain, Philadelphia Athletics	.327
1908	Ty Cobb, Detroit Tigers	.324	1953	Mickey Vernon, Washington Senators	.337
1909	Ty Cobb, Detroit Tigers	.377	1954	Bobby Avila, Cleveland Indians	.341
1910	Ty Cobb, Detroit Tigers	.385	1955	Al Kaline, Detroit Tigers	.340
1911	Ty Cobb, Detroit Tigers	.420	1956	Mickey Mantle, New York Yankees	.353
1912	Ty Cobb, Detroit Tigers	.410	1957	Ted Williams, Boston Red Sox	.388
1913	Ty Cobb, Detroit Tigers	.390	1958	Ted Williams, Boston Red Sox	.328
1914	Ty Cobb, Detroit Tigers	.368	1959	Harvey Kuenn, Detroit Tigers	.353
1915	Ty Cobb, Detroit Tigers	.370	1960	Pete Runnels, Boston Red Sox	.320
1916	Tris Speaker, Cleveland Indians	.386	1961	Norm Cash, Detroit Tigers	.361
1917	Ty Cobb, Detroit Tigers	.383	1962	Pete Runnels, Boston Red Sox	.326
1918	Ty Cobb, Detroit Tigers	.382	1963	Carl Yastrzemski, Boston Red Sox	.321
1919	Ty Cobb, Detroit Tigers	.384	1964	Tony Oliva, Minnesota Twins	.323
1920	George Sisler, St. Louis Browns	.407	1965	Tony Oliva, Minnesota Twins	.321
1921	Harry Heilmann, Detroit Tigers	.393	1966	Frank Robinson, Baltimore Orioles	.316
1922	George Sisler, St. Louis Browns	.420	1967	Carl Yastrzemski, Boston Red Sox	.326
1923	Harry Heilmann, Detroit Tigers	.403	1968	Carl Yastrzemski, Boston Red Sox	.301
1924	Babe Ruth, New York Yankees	.378	1969	Rod Carew, Minnesota Twins	.332
1925	Harry Heilmann, Detroit Tigers	.393	1970	Alex Johnson, California Angels	.329
1926	Heinie Manush, Detroit Tigers	.377	1971	Tony Oliva, Minnesota Twins	.337
1927	Harry Heilmann, Detroit Tigers	.398	1972	Rod Carew, Minnesota Twins	.318
1928	Goose Goslin, Washington Senators	.379	1973	Rod Carew, Minnesota Twins	.350
1929	Lew Fonseca, Cleveland Indians	.369	1974	Rod Carew, Minnesota Twins	.364
1930	Al Simmons, Philadelphia Athletics	.381	1975	Rod Carew, Minnesota Twins	.359
1931	Al Simmons, Philadelphia Athletics	.390	1976	George Brett, Kansas City Royals	.333
1932	David Alexander, Detroit Tigers– Boston Red Sox	.367	1977	Rod Carew, Minnesota Twins	.388
			1978	Rod Carew, Minnesota Twins	.333
1933	Jimmie Foxx, Philadelphia Athletics	.356	1979	Fred Lynn, Boston Red Sox	.333
1934	Lou Gehrig, New York Yankees	.365	1980	George Brett, Kansas City Royals	.390
1935	Buddy Myer, Washington Senators	.349	1981	Carney Lansford, Boston Red Sox	.336
1936	Luke Appling, Chicago White Sox	.388	1982	Willie Wilson, Kansas City Royals	.332
1937	Charlie Gehringer, Detroit Tigers	.371	1983	Wade Boggs, Boston Red Sox	.361
1938	Jimmie Foxx, Boston Red Sox	.349	1984	Don Mattingly, New York Yankees	.343
1939	Joe DiMaggio, New York Yankees	.381	1985	Wade Boggs, Boston Red Sox	.368
1940	Joe DiMaggio, New York Yankees	.352	1986	Wade Boggs, Boston Red Sox	.357
1941	Ted Williams, Boston Red Sox	.406	1987	Wade Boggs, Boston Red Sox	.363
1942	Ted Williams, Boston Red Sox	.356	1988	Wade Boggs, Boston Red Sox	.366
1943	Luke Appling, Chicago White Sox	.328	1989	Kirby Puckett, Minnesota Twins	.339
1944	Lou Boudreau, Cleveland Indians	.327	1990	George Brett, Kansas City Royals	.329
1945	Snuffy Stirnweiss, New York Yankees	.309			

garded with a certain amount of skepticism, especially by batters. In recent years umpires have been given greater power to punish a pitcher thought to be deliberately throwing a beanball (whether he connects or not). With a warning comes an automatic $50 fine. Repeated violations can lead to ejection from a game, a larger fine, and, finally, suspension from baseball.

In 1920 Carl Mays, a pitcher with the New York Yankees, hit Ray Chapman, a shortstop for the Cleveland Indians, in the head with a pitch. Chapman was rushed to New York's Knickerbocker Hospital, where he died the following morning. Because it was fatal, this incident has been regarded as the most famous, or infamous, of all beanings. But there is no evidence that it was intentional.

In the early 1950s Branch Rickey, then president of the Pittsburgh Pirates, instructed all of his players to wear a specially constructed plastic helmet to protect their heads when batting. The practice soon became widespread, and now a batter must go to the plate with a protective helmet on.

BEAT OUT.   To hit safely by beating an infielder's throw to first base. Most commonly used in connection with a bunt: A player beats out a bunt.

BENCH.   Applies not only to the seating facilities reserved for players, substitutes and other team members in uniform in the dugout, but also to a team's substitutes as a group. Thus the saying, "A team is only as strong as its bench."

To bench a player means to remove him from the starting lineup for playing poorly. A player who does not play frequently is said to be riding the bench or is referred to as a bench-warmer. He is a substitute

or utility player, sometimes called a scrub or, in modern jargon, scrubeenie. Frank Torre, when he played for the Milwaukee Braves, used the expression "Vitalis" for a scrub—"because," as he put it, "he would get only a sixty-second workout." This was inspired by a popular television hairtonic commercial of the day.

In bygone days a bench-warmer or scrub was a much-sneered-at player who rarely got into a game because he was not considered good enough to play. In recent years, however, with the advent of the specialist, the bench has become a vital part of any team. Casey Stengel, when he managed the Yankees, made popular the use of the bench. He would have almost two complete offensive teams, a right-handed team to bat against left-handed pitchers and a left-handed team to bat against right-handed pitchers—although certain players, such as Joe DiMaggio, were not replaced by bench-warmers. Stengel also made use of defensive specialists, who made their appearance late in games in which the Yankees had a lead.

In 1954 Dusty Rhodes of the New York Giants gave the bench-warmer added stature. Rhodes rarely started a game, but, used mostly as a pinch hitter, he batted .341 for the season. In the World Series against Cleveland, Rhodes came off the bench in each of the first three games to deliver an important hit and help the Giants sweep the Series. Rhodes's three-run, pinch-hit home run in the 10th inning won the first game, 5–2.

BENCH, JOHNNY.   The ball jumped off Johnny Bench's bat with the familiar crack that said "Home run!" It soared toward the left-field seats in Cincinnati's Riverfront Stadium—Bench Country.

As it disappeared over the fence, Bench took a step toward first base and then

Johnny Bench had a 17-year Hall of Fame career with the Reds. He's tagging out John (Blue Moon) Odom of Oakland in Game 5 of the 1972 World Series.

son in a row. The only other man to accomplish that was Bill Dickey, another Hall of Famer.

Born on December 7, 1947, in Oklahoma City, Bench was just 19 when he caught his first major-league game in 1967. It was the start of an awesome career that included three RBI championships, two Most Valuable Player awards and 10 consecutive Gold Gloves for his defensive play. Bench was inducted into the Hall of Fame in 1989, his first year of eligibility.

BERRA, YOGI. It was a standard picture, repeated, it seemed, every October. In it Yogi Berra, the squat, square catcher of the New York Yankees, would go leaping into the arms of a pitcher, celebrating still another pennant or world championship.

jumped in the air, celebrating the shot that put him in the record book. It was July 15, 1980, the Reds were playing the Expos and the home run was Bench's 314th as a catcher, breaking the mark established by Hall of Famer Yogi Berra.

During the 1970s Bench established himself as the game's most productive hitter, driving in 1,013 runs. Bench also blasted 290 home runs over that period, trailing only Willie Stargell (296) and Reggie Jackson (292).

By the time he decided to retire in 1983, Bench had established himself as Cincinnati's all-time leader in RBIs (1,376) and home runs (389). He hit 327 of his home runs as a catcher, which remained the all-time record until Carlton Fisk broke it in 1990.

Bench put together his brilliant batting numbers while playing at one of baseball's most demanding positions. He tied a National League record in 1980, catching 100 or more games for the thirteenth sea-

The throw comes too late for the Yankees' Yogi Berra to get his man, Washington's Eddie Robinson, in a 1949 game.

Berra's career as one of baseball's star catchers is entwined with the Yankee dynasty years—an awesome stretch from 1947 to 1963 during which New York played in 14 of a possible 17 World Series. Berra set Series records for games, at-bats, hits and singles and played in 30 Series games in a row without committing an error. When he retired in 1964, the Yankees made him their manager, and he took them into yet another Series. Berra also managed the New York Mets into the 1973 Series, becoming one of the few men in baseball history to pilot pennant winners in both leagues.

Like his longtime manager, Casey Stengel, Berra became one of America's most recognizable and beloved characters. His occasionally fractured sayings charmed listeners. For example: "If people don't want to come to the ballpark, how are you gonna stop them?" Or: "We made too many wrong mistakes." But there was nothing funny about his performance. He was a quality catcher and one of the best hitters of his time. His 313 career home runs was a record for catchers until Johnny Bench broke it in 1980. Overall, Berra had 358 homers.

Berra, born on May 12, 1925, in St. Louis, was the American League's Most Valuable Player three times and was named to the All-Star team 15 times. In 1972 he was elected to the Hall of Fame.

BETWEEN THE LINES. The field, foul line to foul line. Players often say, "It's what happens between the lines that counts"—meaning that what a player does in the game is what matters, not his off-field activities.

BLEACHERS. Inexpensive seats beyond the outfield fence. In early ballparks, the bleachers were uncovered, and the occupants were often bleached by the sun.

BLEEDER. A lucky one-base hit, sometimes called a scratch hit. Usually a bleeder is a grounder that is hit softly and trickles through the infield, or takes a bad hop or rolls dead in front of a charging infielder.

BOGGS, WADE. In recent years, the name Boggs has become almost synonymous with the American League batting title. In Boston his extraordinary command of the strike zone has prompted

No player in Red Sox history—not even Ted Williams—has won as many American League batting titles as Wade Boggs (five).

comparisons with the most celebrated of Red Sox greats, Ted Williams.

Born June 15, 1958, in Omaha, Wade Boggs has collected American League batting crowns the way some people collect stamps. Almost impossible to strike out, he was the AL's leading hitter five times in a seven-year stretch starting in 1983, including four straight from 1985 to 1988 during which his lowest average was .357.

His smooth left-handed stroke was recognized as special from the time he broke in by hitting an AL rookie-record .349 in 1982. Between 1983 and 1989 the Red Sox third baseman had an AL-record seven straight years with 200 or more hits and seven years with 100 or more runs scored. And his .346 career batting average (after nine years) was the highest among active players.

A six-time All-Star, Boggs is known for his superstitions and his all-chicken diet.

BONER. A foolish error, known also as a bonehead play, a skull or skuller or a rock. A classic baseball boner was Fred Merkle's failure to touch second base when a teammate drove in the winning run for the New York Giants late in the 1908 season. Johnny Evers of the Chicago Cubs called for the ball, touched second base and had Merkle declared out, nullifying the run. The Cubs won the pennant on the last day of the season, and Merkle went down in history as the man responsible for the Giants' not winning it.

Another classic boner occurred in 1926, when three Brooklyn Dodgers wound up at third base at the same time after a line drive landed safely in right field. One player thought the ball would be caught, while the other two did not, thus the mix-up.

The most famous boner of recent times occurred in 1986, when the Yankees had two runners thrown out at the plate on the

same play against the Chicago White Sox. The second runner ran through the coach's stop sign at third base, only to be tagged out by Chicago catcher Carlton Fisk, who had already tagged the lead runner.

BOSTON RED SOX. Though the Red Sox have had limited success through the years, they have provided their adoring fans with some of the most dramatic moments in baseball history.

In 1967 the Red Sox fought their way to the American League pennant after finishing ninth the year before. On the final day of the season, as a capacity Fenway Park crowd went wild, Jim Lonborg nailed down the team's first pennant in 21 years.

Eight years later Carlton Fisk sent another Fenway crowd into delirium when his home run in the 12th inning gave Boston a victory over Cincinnati in the sixth game of the World Series. But the Red Sox lost the seventh game, as they had in 1946 and again in 1967.

The ultimate heartbreak for the Red Sox and their fans came in the sixth game of the 1986 World Series, when they blew a two-run lead with two out in the bottom of the 10th inning, allowing the New York Mets to battle back and take a 6–5 victory that tied the Series at three games each. The Red Sox then lost the seventh game, blowing a 3–0 lead.

In both 1988 and 1990 the Red Sox won the American League East but fell in four straight to the Oakland Athletics in the playoffs.

Since 1918 Boston has won only four pennants, while finishing last 11 times. At one time, though, the team dominated the league. In 1903 it won the pennant and the first World Series ever played. The Red Sox won the World Series four times between 1912 and 1918, but made a costly mistake in 1920, when owner Harry Frazee, needing money, sold Babe Ruth to the Yankees. After the Babe left, the Red Sox finished in the second division 15 straight years—while the Yankees won seven pennants.

Boston revived in the 1940s, as new owner Tom Yawkey developed stars like Bobby Doerr, Dom DiMaggio and the incomparable Ted Williams. Williams, called by many the best pure hitter the game has

ever produced, is the last man to bat .400 in a season (.406 in 1941).

The Red Sox have had their superstars since then, most notably Carl Yastrzemski—the only man in American League history to accumulate 3,000 hits and 400 home runs—Wade Boggs, who won five batting titles in the 1980s, and Roger Clemens, the fastball pitcher who swept all honors in 1986.

BOTTOM. The second half of an inning, when the home team is at bat.

BOX SCORE. A standardized table that shows, at a glance, the batting order, po-

Boston's Carl Yastrzemski homers off Joe Hoerner of the St. Louis Cardinals in Game 2 of the 1967 World Series. The catcher is Tim McCarver.

sition of the player, at-bats (ab), runs (r), hits (h), runs batted in (bi). After the batting summary there is a line score showing

Fourth Game, 1989 World Series

ATHLETICS 9, GIANTS 6

Oakland	ab	r	h	bi	San Francisco	ab	r	h	bi
R. Henderson lf	6	2	3	2	Butler cf	5	1	3	1
Lansford 3b	4	1	2	1	Oberkfell 3b	3	0	0	0
Canseco rf	4	1	2	0	Thompson 2b	1	0	1	1
McGwire 1b	5	0	1	0	Bedrosian p	0	0	0	0
D. Henderson cf	3	2	1	0	Clark 1b	4	1	1	0
Steinbach c	4	1	1	3	Mitchell lf	4	1	1	2
Phillips 2b	5	0	1	1	Williams ss-3b	4	0	1	0
Weiss ss	3	1	0	0	Kennedy c	3	1	0	0
Moore p	3	1	1	2	Litton 2b-3b	4	1	1	2
Phelps ph	1	0	0	0	Nixon rf	3	0	0	0
Nelson p	0	0	0	0	Robinson p	0	0	0	0
Honeycutt p	0	0	0	0	LaCoss p	1	0	0	0
Burns p	0	0	0	0	Bathe ph	1	0	0	0
Parker ph	1	0	0	0	Brantley p	0	0	0	0
Eckersley p	0	0	0	0	Downs p	0	0	0	0
					Riles ph	0	0	0	0
					Maldonado ph	1	1	1	0
					Lefferts p	0	0	0	0
					Uribe ss	1	0	0	0
Totals	**39**	**9**	**12**	**9**	**Totals**	**35**	**6**	**9**	**6**

Oakland	130	031	010—9
San Francisco	000	002	400—6

E—None. DP—None. LOB—Oakland 10, San Francisco 4. 2B—D. Henderson, Moore, Phillips, Butler. 3B—Steinbach, R. Henderson, Maldonado. HR—R. Henderson, Mitchell, Litton. SB—Canseco.

Oakland	IP	H	R	ER	BB	SO
Moore W, 2-0	6	5	2	2	1	3
Nelson	1/3	1	2	2	1	0
Honeycutt	1/3	3	2	2	0	0
Burns	1 1/3	0	0	0	0	0
Eckersley S, 1	1	0	0	0	0	0
San Francisco						
Robinson L, 0-1	1 2/3	4	4	4	1	0
LaCoss	3 1/3	4	3	3	3	1
Brantley	1/3	3	1	1	0	0
Downs	1 2/3	0	0	0	0	1
Lefferts	1/3	1	1	1	1	0
Bedrosian	1 2/3	0	0	0	2	0

Umpires—Garcia, Voltaggio, Clark, Runge, Rennert, Gregg. T—3:07. A—62,032.

the runs made in each inning and the final score. Under the line score there is a listing of errors (E), double plays (DP), runners left on base (LOB), two-base hits (2B), three-base hits (3B), home runs (HR), stolen bases (SB), sacrifices (S) and sacrifice flies (SF). This is followed by a listing of the pitchers that gives: innings pitched (IP), hits allowed (H), runs (R), earned runs (ER), bases on balls (BB) and strikeouts (SO). The winning and losing pitchers are indicated by W or L next to their names, along with their won-lost records. A save is indicated by "S," followed by the appropriate number for that pitcher for the season. The bottom line lists batters hit by a pitch (HBP), wild pitches (WP), the umpires, the time it took to play the game (T) and the attendance (A). The first box score, devised by Henry Chadwick, appeared in the New York *Clipper* in 1853.

BRETT, GEORGE. It was a hot, muggy August night in 1980 in Kansas City, where the summer heat can be oppressive. But instead of worrying about the thermometer, the Royals' fans were on their feet cheering madly as George Brett stood triumphantly on second base after hitting a double.

Finally, Brett took off his cap and waved it to the fans, acknowledging their cheers for his fourth hit of the game against Toronto. The hit had thrust him past the magic .400 mark, a batting average that no major leaguer has maintained through season's end in the past 50 years.

For the next six weeks the Kansas City star carried on an exciting drive in an attempt to end up at .400. The Royals were light-years ahead of the other teams in the American League Western Division, and only Brett's quest for .400 kept the interest of fans through the stretch of season commonly called the dog days.

George Brett: the man who has come closest to hitting .400 in the past 50 years.

becoming the first player to win batting titles in three different decades.

Born on May 15, 1953, in Glendale, West Virginia, Brett grew up with dreams of becoming a major leaguer. These were heightened when he sat in the stands during the 1967 World Series and watched his brother Ken, 19 at the time, become the youngest pitcher in Series history. "That clinched it for me," Brett said. "After that, all I could think about was being a ball-player."

And that is exactly what happened. An artist at bat, a master of the craft of hitting a baseball, he became the textbook definition of a successful batter—patient, selective, smart and talented.

BROCK, LOU. Of all the one-sided trades in baseball history, the one that sent Lou Brock to the Cardinals from the Cubs in

Brett fell short, finishing at .390, with 24 home runs and 118 runs batted in for his magic season. Five more hits—less than one hit per month over the course of the season—would have produced the .400 season. But a thumb injury in September hurt his swing and kept him from making it.

His .400 challenge in 1980 touched off a hugely productive decade for Brett. He batted over .300 five more times during the 1980s, including .335 in 1985, when he won his first Gold Glove and also slugged a career-high 30 home runs. He was the MVP of the playoffs that year and hit .370 as the Royals won the World Series. He ended the decade with a .310 career batting average and less than 500 hits away from 3,000 for his career. He started the 1990s off by hitting a league-leading .329,

Stealing was Lou Brock's trademark. On September 10, 1974, he stole his record-breaking 105th base of the season. Philadelphia's Larry Bowa tries to put the tag on him.

1964 takes the cake. The Cubs received three players who wound up making no real contributions, while Brock went on to reach the 3,000-hit mark and become baseball's all-time stolen-base king.

In 1974 Brock, a native of El Dorado, Arkansas, broke Maury Wills's single-season base-stealing mark with 118, an amazing feat for a man of 35. His career total of 938 topped Ty Cobb's old mark of 892, and he led the National League in stolen bases eight times.

Brock retired in 1979 with 3,023 hits to go with the stolen-base records, as well as a .391 batting average in three World Series, credentials that earned him election to the Hall of Fame. He was at his best in the 1967 World Series, when he batted .414 and stole seven bases, helping St. Louis to the world championship.

Only 5 feet 5 inches tall, Freddie Patek made the most of the bunt during his 14-year career.

BRUSHBACK.   *See* Duster.

BULLPEN.   An area adjacent to the playing field, often alongside the foul lines, where relief pitchers and other substitutes warm up. The word "bullpen," which is also prison slang for a place of temporary confinement, is of uncertain origin in baseball. Some think it can be traced to the Bull Durham tobacco signs that were posted on the fences of many ballparks in 1909. Featured on the sign was a picture of a gigantic bull, and in many parks relief pitchers warmed up directly in front of it. As far back as 1877, though, bullpen was the name used for a roped-off section of the outfield where the overflow crowd stood. The term was used in Civil War days to describe the stockade, or prison.

BUNT.   A ball that is hit not with a full swing of the bat but rather with a push of the bat. Ideally, a bunt is placed somewhere in the infield where neither the pitcher nor any of the infielders can reach it. The maneuver is perfected, usually, by fast runners, who can use their speed to turn a well-placed bunt into a hit. Among those more skilled at the art of bunting for a base hit were Jackie Robinson and Maury Wills of the Dodgers, Phil Rizzuto of the Yankees and Freddie Patek of the Royals and Angels.

Vince Coleman (Cardinals, Mets) and Brett Butler (Braves, Indians, Giants, Dodgers) are among the best bunters of recent times. (*See* Drag bunt, Sacrifice.)

BUSH.   Any league below the majors, but especially a league of very low classification. Bush is also the ballplayers' scornful adjective for any person, thing or action not meeting with their approval, whether

Playing in the bushes means playing in minor-league parks like this one in Dubuque, Iowa, where Illinois Central trains rumble past the outfield fence.

it has anything to do with baseball or not. A player whose conduct or ability is considered not befitting major-league status is called bush, bush-league or a busher. Playing in the minor leagues is also called playing in the bushes.

BUTCHER. A player who is a very poor fielder. He is also said to have a bad glove or bad hands. Such a player was Dick Stuart, a hard hitter for the Pittsburgh Pirates, Boston Red Sox and Philadelphia Phillies, but one who never dazzled with his defensive work at first base. A Boston sportswriter dubbed him Dr. Strangeglove. Another who had a reputation for being a poor fielder, perhaps without justification, was Chuck Hiller, a second baseman with

the San Francisco Giants and New York Mets. His nicknames were Iron Hands, No Hands and Dr. No.

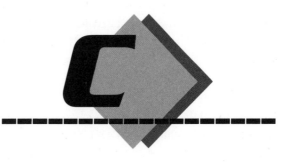

CACTUS LEAGUE. Name given to the teams that have their spring-training camps in Arizona, where the cactus plant flourishes. (*See also* Grapefruit League.)

CALIFORNIA ANGELS. The situation seemed impossible. Nolan Ryan needed 16 strikeouts in his final game of the 1973 season to break Sandy Koufax's record for strikeouts in a season (382). Ryan was tired; he had already been in 40 games and pitched 315 innings. Could he find enough strength to strike out 16 Minnesota Twins?

Ryan started well, striking out the side in the first inning. Gradually he closed in on the record, but he still needed one more strikeout as the game entered the 11th inning. With two out, Rich Reese came up. Fastball, strike one. Another fastball, strike two. Finally Ryan fired his hardest pitch of the night, and Reese went down swinging. Ryan had struck out his 383rd batter.

Ryan's achievements were among the few highlights for the team that had begun life in 1961, when the American League voted to expand to 10 teams and awarded one of two new franchises to a Los Angeles group headed by movie cowboy Gene Autry.

The Angels stunned the baseball world when they finished third in the league their second year and a zany, much-traveled minor leaguer named Bo Belinsky pitched a no-hitter against the Baltimore Orioles.

The Angels started out in little Wrigley Field, Los Angeles, and then for the next four years shared Dodger Stadium in Chavez Ravine with their National League counterparts. In 1966 they moved to nearby Anaheim and into their own ballpark, Anaheim Stadium. They changed their name from the Los Angeles Angels to the Cali-

fornia Angels. Everyone agreed that it was a more stately name. But it wasn't until 1979 that the Angels, with Rod Carew, MVP Don Baylor, Dan Ford and Bobby Grich, achieved their first divisional title.

They won divisional titles again in 1982 and 1986, and in 1986 were within one out of reaching the World Series before Dave Henderson sparked the Boston Red Sox to a dramatic victory. The Red Sox went from there to win the last two games of the playoff series and deprive California of its first World Series appearance.

CALLED GAME. A game in which, for any reason, the umpire-in-chief ends play. The most common reason is rain, but games have been called because of snow, fog and wind. If a game is called before the team that is trailing has been to bat five times, it is replayed from the beginning. If a game is called after the team that is trailing has been to bat five times, it is an official game and goes into the records as a shortened game.

CAMPANELLA, ROY. The Los Angeles Coliseum's lights were turned off, and all at once the huge ballpark was plunged into darkness at a Dodger-Yankee exhibition game in 1959. Then the fans, 93,103 of them, lit matches and lighters, as Roy Campanella, one of baseball's immortals, was wheeled to home plate. It was one of the most emotional moments in sports history.

The Dodgers and Yankees, longtime World Series rivals, were playing an exhibition game that night to honor Campanella, a Hall of Fame catcher whose career had been cut short when he was paralyzed in an automobile accident in the winter of 1958. Campy played 10 seasons with the Dodgers in Brooklyn and appeared in five

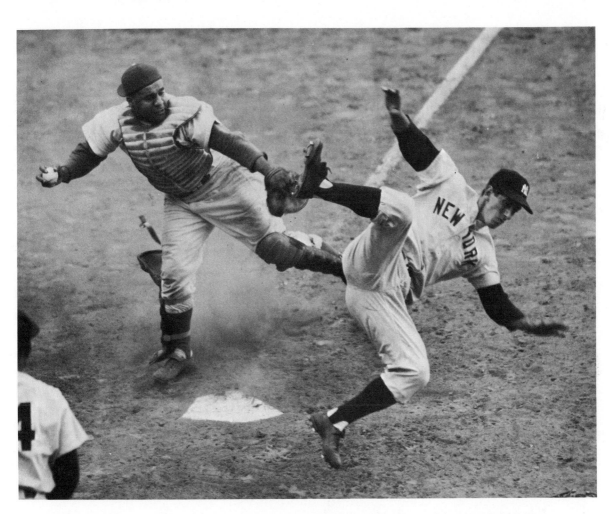

The Dodgers' Roy Campanella nails the Yankees' Billy Martin at the plate in the 1953 World Series.

World Series, all of them against the Yankees. He was one of the sturdiest, most dependable catchers of his era.

Born in Philadelphia on November 19, 1921, Campy played his early baseball in the Negro leagues, where he honed his skills. He was an accomplished catcher when he came to the Dodgers in 1948, one year after Jackie Robinson had been the first black player to perform in the major leagues.

For the next decade Campanella was a feared slugger. He won MVP awards in 1951, 1953 and 1955; led the National League with 142 RBIs in 1953; and was a defensive giant behind the plate and a genius at handling pitchers.

CAN OF CORN. A high fly within easy reach of a fielder.

CAREW ROD. Rod Carew stepped off third base, measuring his strides, watching the pitcher, studying every move the man on the mound made. Slowly but surely Carew lengthened his lead, growing a bit bolder with each delivery. Finally he was off, dashing down the line, streaking for home plate. As the batter fell away, Carew came in flying, sliding across the plate with another Minnesota run.

The year was 1969, and Carew was on his way to the first of his seven American League batting championships. He batted

Rod Carew won seven American League batting crowns between 1969 and 1978. In 1991 he was elected to the Hall of Fame.

After his first batting title in 1969, Carew won the crown six times in seven years (1972–78). His best season was 1977, when he batted .388 and won the American League's Most Valuable Player Award.

In 1979 he became a California Angel and continued his productive career, batting over .300 his first five years with the team. He retired after the 1985 season, with 3,053 hits, a .328 batting average and 353 stolen bases.

Carew was born on October 1, 1945, on a train traveling between Gatun and Panama City in the Panama Canal Zone. His family moved to New York City when Rod was a teenager, and Twins scout Herb Stein discovered him. He came to the majors as a second baseman and switched to first in 1975, making the transfer as smoothly as he hit baseballs.

.332 that season, and as deadly as he was at the plate he proved almost as destructive on the bases, especially when he was on third base. Carew had 19 stolen bases that season, not that unusual. But seven of those steals were suicidal dashes down the third-base line, which meant runs for Minnesota and a line in the record book for Carew. No American League player has stolen home as frequently in one season as did Carew that season.

But Carew made his mark in baseball as a hitter, not a base stealer. Blessed with a classic stroke, Carew was a line-drive hitter who sprayed the ball all over the diamond. "I could always hit a baseball," he once said. "When I'm hitting, there's nobody in the world who can get me out."

American League pitchers reluctantly agreed. During the 1970s Carew batted .343.

CARLTON, STEVE. The cheers began slowly but built quickly into a wall of sound. The fans in St. Louis's Busch Stadium were saluting a unique accomplishment by a visiting player. Steve Carlton of the Philadelphia Phillies had just struck out Tony Scott—the 2,833rd batter Carlton had sent back to the dugout, dragging his bat behind him. No left-hander in the history of baseball had ever struck out as many hitters.

On the mound Carlton did nothing to acknowledge the moment. There was no wave of the cap to the crowd, no sign of emotion, not even a smile. Carlton merely went to work on the next Cardinal batter, biting the corners of the plate with his curve, slipping his slider past, exploding his fastball. July 6, 1980, was just another day at the office for the efficient southpaw who was so private a person that he avoided interviews.

When he pitched the deciding victory in Philadelphia's 1980 World Series triumph over Kansas City, Carlton sipped his celebration champagne in the trainer's room, avoiding the traditional clubhouse turmoil.

Carlton, who was born in Miami on December 22, 1944, began his big-league career with the Cardinals in 1965. By the time he threw his final pitch in 1988, he had won 329 games (ninth-best in major-league history), had captured a record four Cy Young Awards and had struck out 4,136 batters.

CASEY. The well-known nickname of the late Charles Dillon Stengel, famed manager of the Brooklyn Dodgers, Boston Braves, New York Yankees and New York

All the world knew Charles Dillon Stengel simply as Casey, the most colorful manager of them all.

Steve Carlton talked only with his arm.

Mets. He holds the record of having won 10 American League pennants and seven world championships in 12 years, and was the only manager to win five championships in a row (1949 to 1953, with the Yankees). Along with Babe Ruth, Casey was regarded as baseball's greatest ambassador, and he had spent more than 50 years in the game by the time he retired from the Mets in 1965 after his seventy-fifth birthday. His nickname stems from the fact that he came from Kansas City (KC), Missouri.

CASEY AT THE BAT. The foremost ballad of baseball, written in 1888 by Ernest L. Thayer and made popular by De Wolf Hopper.

It dealt with a batter named Casey and the Mudville nine. And it ended this way:

*Oh, somewhere in this favored land
    the sun is shining bright,
The band is playing somewhere,
    and somewhere hearts are light;
And somewhere men are laughing,
    and little children shout;
But there is no joy in Mudville
    —mighty Casey has struck out.*

CASTOFF. A discarded player, often one who makes a major comeback with another team. Among outstanding examples of castoffs are Dixie Walker, Lew Burdette, John Mayberry and Dave Stewart.

Walker could not succeed with the Yankees, White Sox or Tigers, but he was picked up by the Brooklyn Dodgers, for whom he played nine seasons, and he won the National League batting title in 1944 with a .357 average. He finished with a lifetime batting average of .306. He became such a great favorite with Brooklyn fans that he got to be known as the Peepul's Cherce (or, People's Choice).

Burdette was a minor leaguer in the Yankee farm system when they traded him to the Braves, who then played in Boston. Burdette went on to win 179 games in 11 seasons with the Braves, and in the 1957 World Series he beat the Yankees three times, including two shutouts.

Mayberry was traded by the Houston Astros to the Kansas City Royals when he was just 21 years old, and he became a star in the American League. In his first four seasons he drove in 100 or more runs three times.

Stewart, a hard-throwing right-hander, started his career with the Los Angeles Dodgers in 1978. He was traded twice—to the Rangers and to the Phillies—and then released before the Oakland Athletics signed him to a free-agent contract in 1986. Stewart repaid the A's for their faith by winning 20 or more games in 1987, 1988, 1989 and 1990. He was the World Series MVP in 1989, when he led Oakland to the championship.

CATCH. When a fielder gets firm possession in his hand or glove of a ball in flight and holds it. If a fielder has made the catch and drops the ball while in the act of throwing, the ball is considered to have been caught. In establishing that a catch was made, a fielder must hold the ball long enough to prove that he has complete control of it and that his release of the ball is voluntary and intentional.

CATCHER. The fielder who squats behind the plate to receive the pitch. Included among the catcher's special equipment are a mask made of metal, shin guards and a padded chest protector. Until 1966 the catcher was allowed to wear a glove of unlimited size, shape or weight—the only restriction being that it be made of leather. However, some players took advantage of this rule, using oversized gloves—usually for the purpose of catching the unpredictable knuckleball—so the rule was changed, and the size of the catcher's glove was restricted to no more than 38 inches all the way around and no more than 15½ inches from top to bottom.

The catcher gives signals to the pitcher, telling him what pitch to throw. But the pitcher can disagree, by shaking his head, and then the catcher will ask for another pitch. (*See also* Signals.)

CATCHER'S BALK. A rare call in which the catcher is cited by the umpire for leaving the catcher's box while the pitcher is in the process of delivering a pitch (on an intentional walk, for example). All runners advance one base.

Carlton Fisk of the White Sox: a picture-book catcher, both offensively and defensively.

CENTER FIELD. The outfield territory beyond second base and between that usually covered by the right and left fielders. The outfielder who covers center field is called the center fielder. He is usually the fastest and best of the three outfielders. Among the outstanding center fielders have been Tris Speaker of the Boston Red Sox and the Cleveland Indians, Terry Moore of the St. Louis Cardinals, Joe DiMaggio of the New York Yankees, Duke Snider of the Brooklyn Dodgers, Willie Mays of the New York and the San Francisco Giants, Mickey Mantle of the Yankees, Paul Blair of the Baltimore Orioles, Eric Davis of the Cincinnati Reds and Andy Van Slyke of the Pittsburgh Pirates.

CHANCE. Any opportunity to field a ball with the possibility of making or helping to make a putout. Usually, the first baseman accepts the most chances, since most infield outs end with him. The record for the most chances accepted in a season was set by a first baseman, John Donahue of the Chicago White Sox, who had 1,998 chances in 1907; the record for most chances in a nine-inning game is 22, shared by many first basemen.

CATCHER'S BOX. Where the catcher crouches until the pitcher delivers the ball. He may stay anywhere in the area, which is 8 feet long and 43 inches wide, as long as he does not interfere with the batter.

CATCHER'S INTERFERENCE. Interference by the catcher with the batter. The batter goes to first base and is not charged with a time at bat, and the catcher is charged with an error. If a base runner attempts to steal at the time the catcher interferes with the batter, the runner is awarded the stolen base (even if he was tagged out), and the batter is still awarded first base.

CHANGE OF PACE. Also called change-up, change, letup or pulling the string. A slowball usually thrown after a fastball, with the same motion as the fastball, in order to catch the batter off stride. A slow curveball can also be used as a change of pace after a fast curveball. The forkball, palmball and slip pitch are all examples of pitches used as changes of pace.

CHARITY HOP. The last, long hop taken by some groundballs, making them easy to field.

CHICAGO CUBS. No other franchise can look back on a history as checkered with early triumphs—and later failures—as that of the Chicago Cubs.

From the time Al Spalding pitched and managed the White Stockings (they became the Cubs in 1900) to a pennant in the first National League race in 1876 through the next 70 years, Chicago won 16 league titles, the third-highest total among National League teams. But since 1945 no pennant flag has flown above the ivy-covered walls of Wrigley Field.

Many of the most celebrated Cubs were part of the team's early successes. Three-time batting champ Cap Anson managed

five winners in the 1880s. First baseman Frank Chance led the team to the best regular-season record in major-league history (116-36) in 1906 and to World Series victories the next two seasons. Chance is most often remembered as the player who, along with Joe Tinker and Johnny Evers, formed the Cub double-play combination that was immortalized in verse as Tinker-to-Evers-to-Chance.

Rogers Hornsby, who batted .380 in 1929; Hack Wilson, who in 1930 had a league-record 56 homers and 190 runs batted in; and Gabby Hartnett, whose dramatic final-week homer sparked the Cubs to the 1938 pennant, were Cub legends. After they departed, the team fell on hard times.

The Cubs got their fans excited again in 1969, when future Hall of Famers Ernie Banks and Billy Williams helped Chicago open a commanding lead in the National League East. But just when it appeared that the Cubs' drought was over, the New York Mets won 34 of their last 44 games to capture the division title.

The Cubs surprised the baseball world in 1984, when they won the Eastern Division title and then took a two-games-to-none lead in the best-of-five playoffs against the San Diego Padres. But the Cubs' good fortune ended there, as the Padres fought back to win the series with three straight victories on the West Coast.

Not even the addition of lights to ancient Wrigley Field in 1988 could change the Cubs' luck. They won the Eastern Division championship again in 1989 but were beaten by the San Francisco Giants in the playoffs.

In recent years the most celebrated Cub has been second baseman Ryne Sandberg, a peerless fielder and power hitter. He had his finest season in 1990, when he led the NL in home runs (40), total bases (344) and runs (116) and was second in slugging percentage (.559).

Mr. Cub: Ernie Banks.

CHICAGO WHITE SOX. There have been glorious moments in the history of the Chicago White Sox. In 1906 they won the American League pennant and went on to win the World Series against their hated

Shortstop Luis Aparicio, who made his mark as a stolen-base leader and exceptional fielder with the White Sox, retires the Indians' Vada Pinson to start a game-ending double play in 1970.

crosstown rivals, the Cubs. In 1917 they won another world championship, beating the New York Giants in six games, despite their nickname of the Hitless Wonders (they had a team batting average of .228).

But the focus of any story written about the White Sox will always be how they became known as the Black Sox after purposely losing the 1919 World Series to the underdog Cincinnati Reds.

It was an exceptional White Sox team that won the American League pennant in 1919. It had two 20-game winners in Eddie Cicotte and Lefty Williams and a magnificent hitter in Shoeless Joe Jackson. But something went wrong. The Reds battered Cicotte, 9–1, in the first game. One team had to win five out of nine games, and the Reds clinched the Series, five games to three.

Rumors spread quickly that the Series had been fixed, and in 1920 American League president Ban Johnson revealed the full details of an alleged conspiracy among eight Chicago players and gamblers. Although the eight players, including Jackson, Cicotte and Williams, were never found guilty in the courts, Baseball Commissioner Kenesaw Mountain Landis banned them from baseball for life.

It took years for the White Sox to recover. It wasn't until 1936 that they got out of the second division. And it wasn't until 40 years later, in 1959, that the White Sox made it back to the World Series, losing to the Los Angeles Dodgers in six games.

That 1959 team had some fine players, including American League MVP Nellie Fox at second base, major-league stolen-base king Luis Aparicio at short and a pitching staff that included Hall of Famer Early Wynn.

More recently the White Sox have shown signs of their past glory only once—in 1983, when behind the pitching of 20-

game winners LaMarr Hoyt and Richard Dotson and the hitting of Carlton Fisk, Greg Luzinski and Ron Kittle, they won their first American League Western Division title. Their path to the World Series, though, was blocked by the Baltimore Orioles, who defeated them in the playoffs.

CHOKE. To grip a bat several inches up from the end. It is done deliberately for better bat control and to lessen the chance of striking out, or to bunt the ball.

Choke also means to fail in a crucial situation, or to let your emotions get the better of you. So, under pressure, a player may choke, choke up, get the apple, get the lump, get the olive, get tight.

CINCINNATI REDS. In a sense baseball started in Cincinnati, which became the home of the sport's first all-professional team in 1869. The Red Stockings, who won 130 games over two seasons before suffering their first loss, and became the Redlegs, or Reds, in 1876, were involved in a series of baseball firsts.

Cincinnati, whose home opener traditionally starts each National League season, was the first franchise to play a night

The Big Red Machine of 1975: Front row *(left to right):* Pete Rose, Joe Morgan, Ted Kluszewski, coach; Alex Grammas, coach; Sparky Anderson, manager; George Scherger, coach; Larry Shepard, coach; Fred Norman, Doug Flynn, Merv Rettenmund. In front: Tim McGinn, batboy.

Middle row: Bernie Stowe, equipment manager; Paul Campbell, traveling secretary; Johnny Bench, Bill Plummer, Clay Kirby, George Foster, Jack Billingham, Tom Carroll, Pat Darcy, Rawly Eastwick, Tony Perez, Pedro Borbon, Larry Starr, trainer.

Back row: Dan Driessen, Darrel Chaney, Ken Griffey, Gary Nolan, Dave Concepcion, Ed Armbrister, Clay Carroll, Will McEnaney, Terry Crowley, Cesar Geronimo, Don Gullett.

game (May 24, 1935, against Philadelphia at Crosley Field), to have a Ladies' Day, to option a player, to travel by air and to play a televised game (August 26, 1939, in Brooklyn).

With pitchers Bucky Walters and Paul Derringer leading the way, Cincinnati won back-to-back pennants in 1939 and 1940. After being swept by the Yankees in the 1939 World Series, the Reds bounced back to beat the Tigers in seven games the following year. That was actually the Reds' second World Series victory; their first—in 1919 over the Chicago "Black Sox"—was tarnished by the gambling scandal that blackened the game.

Southpaw Johnny Vander Meer left his mark in 1938, when he pitched two no-hit games in a row.

The Reds rode the bats of Frank Robinson and Vada Pinson to a 1961 pennant, but after dropping that Series to the Yankees, the club was forced to rebuild. When it did, the result was the Big Red Machine, which dominated baseball in the 1970s under the direction of Sparky Anderson.

Fueled by such great hitters as Joe Morgan, Pete Rose, Ken Griffey, Johnny Bench and Tony Perez, the Reds won pennants in 1970 and 1972 and world championships in 1975 and 1976. The 1975 seven-game struggle against the Red Sox is remembered as perhaps the greatest Series in history.

The Reds rebuilt through much of the 1980s, and their farm system produced young stars like pitcher Tom Browning, who hurled a perfect game against the Dodgers in 1988, and outfielder Eric Davis.

Cincinnati became the focal point of baseball news in 1989, when Rose, the local hero who had been the manager since 1984, was suspended from baseball for life for alleged involvement with gambling. In 1990 Rose was sent to prison for income-tax evasion.

But Cincinnati fans also had reason to cheer in 1990, when the Reds stunned the baseball world by sweeping the heavily favored defending champion Oakland A's in the World Series. Jose Rijo, whose pitching won two games and brought him MVP honors; Billy Hatcher, with a record seven straight hits; and Chris Sabo, with two consecutive homers in Game 3, powered the new Red Machine in the Series.

CIRCUIT. A home run (a circuit clout) or a league (senior circuit for National League, junior circuit for American League).

CIRCUS CATCH. A spectacular catch of a fly ball, usually by an outfielder.

CLEAN-UP BATTER. The fourth position in the batting order, so called because it is usually manned by a slugger who regularly drives in any runners who are on base—thereby cleaning the bases. It used to be customary for a manager to bat his best hitter in the clean-up position, but in recent years the trend has been to bat the best hitter third because of the possibility that the third batter will get more times at bat than the clean-up hitter.

CLEMENS, ROGER. The man they call the Rocket in Boston was really launching them at Fenway Park on the night of April 29, 1986. Overmatched by fastball after fastball, 18 Seattle hitters had struck out through eight innings. Now the 23-year-old Roger Clemens had a chance to make major-league history.

The Red Sox right-hander wasted little time. He simply blew away Spike Owen, the first hitter in the ninth, on a 1–2 fastball, to tie the major-league mark with his

Roger Clemens's smoking fastball has made him one of the most awesome pitchers in the game.

19th K. When Clemens got Phil Bradley to watch a 2–2 heater, the record was his.

That remarkable 20-strikeout, no-walk game was the perfect centerpiece for a 24-4 season that featured 14 consecutive wins, a league-leading 2.48 ERA and 238 Ks. Clemens became the only pitcher to win MVP, Cy Young and All-Star Game MVP honors in the same year.

Born August 4, 1962, in Dayton, Ohio, Clemens grew to a muscular 6 feet 4 inches and 220 pounds, with a fastball as imposing as his physique.

After winning his second straight Cy Young Award with a 20-9 mark in 1987, Clemens set a club mark with 291 strikeouts in 1988.

He posted his third 20-victory season in 1990, when he went 21-6 and led the league with a 1.93 ERA while pitching the Red Sox to the Eastern Division title. But everything came apart in the playoffs, when the Athletics swept Boston, and Clemens was thrown out of the finale for using obscene language to plate umpire Terry Cooney.

After seven seasons with the Red Sox, Clemens stands as the franchise's all-time strikeout king with 1,424, having surpassed Cy Young's mark in 1990.

CLEMENTE, ROBERTO. It was New Year's Eve, 1972, a time for celebration. But a party was the last thing on Roberto Clemente's mind. He was thinking, instead, of a rescue mission to take food and supplies to the victims of an earthquake in Managua, Nicaragua.

Clemente, a Pittsburgh Pirate superstar, helped load a rescue plane and took off in it from his native Puerto Rico. But the plane crashed at sea and Clemente was killed.

It was a devastating loss, especially for the fans who had finally come to appreciate Clemente's vast skills during Pittsburgh's 1971 World Series victory over Baltimore. The Pirate right fielder was brilliant in those seven games, batting .414 and fielding, running and throwing magnificently.

Clemente won four batting championships in 18 National League seasons and

Roberto Clemente won his third National League batting title in 1965 with a .329 average. League president Warren Giles presents the plaque and the silver bat to him.

compiled a lifetime average of .317. When he got his 3,000th hit in 1972, the last one of his life, he became only the eleventh player in history to achieve that level.

Within three months of his death Roberto Clemente, who was born on August 18, 1934, was elected to the Hall of Fame.

CLEVELAND INDIANS. The crowd of 56,715 at Cleveland's Municipal Stadium was lured mainly by the presence of Frank Robinson, the first black manager in the major leagues. Robinson's first move that cold April day of 1975 was to insert himself in the batting order as the designated hitter.

And Robinson the hitter made Robinson the manager look good when he blasted a home run in the first inning to send the Indians to a 5–3 victory over the Yankees.

It was not the first time the two teams had been linked in history. Between 1947 and 1958 the Yankees won 10 pennants; the team that kept them from making it 12 straight was the Indians. In 1948 the Indians won a one-game playoff over the Boston Red Sox for the pennant, then polished off another Boston entry, the Braves, in the World Series. And after chasing the Yanks without success for the next five

A mainstay of the Indians for nearly 20 years, Bob Feller greets the press after pitching the second of his three no-hitters—this one a 1–0 victory over the Yankees on April 30, 1946.

years, the Indians had an unbelievable season in 1954, winning 111 games and the pennant. Pitchers Bob Lemon, Early Wynn, Mike Garcia, Art Houtteman and Bob Feller combined to post 93 victories; Al Rosen, Larry Doby and Bobby Avila were the hitting stars. It was the third and last pennant in Cleveland history.

In the franchise's early days the Indians had their share of great players, starting with Cy Young, who won 268 of his 511 victories for them. Then came Napoleon Lajoie, who was so outstanding that the team was called the Naps while he was on it. The legendary Tris Speaker joined the team in 1916 and managed it to its first pennant four years later.

CLOSER. Term used for the ace reliever who is called on to protect a lead in the late innings. (*See also* Relief pitcher, Fireman.)

Max Patkin's antics have always drawn a crowd . . . and a laugh.

CLOWN. A player with a sense of humor or an entertainer who is part of a baseball sideshow before games, between games of a doubleheader and so on. He is there to help amuse the fans.

The most famous baseball clown, Al Schacht, a pitcher with the Washington Senators between 1919 and 1921, had limited skill but great humor and became a successful New York restaurant owner. Schacht's antics at major- and minor-league ballparks brought him the title Clown Prince of Baseball.

Another successful baseball clown is Max Patkin, who works mainly in the minor leagues. Like Schacht, Patkin is a former pitcher, but one who never made the major leagues.

San Diego's KGB Chicken became a favorite of the fans in the late 1970s and later took his act to ballparks around the nation.

CLUTCH. A player who constantly comes through in a tough spot is known as a clutch hitter or pitcher, or a money player. Such a player was Tommy Henrich of the New York Yankees. During the late 1940s Henrich was such a successful clutch hitter that he was dubbed Old Reliable. Another was Hank Aaron of the Milwaukee (later Atlanta) Braves and the Milwaukee Brewers. He was called Money in the Bank or Mr. Chips by his teammates because he usually delivered in important situations. Among the all-time clutch hitters have been Tony Perez, Reggie Jackson and Pete Rose. Current outstanding clutch hitters are Will Clark, Kevin Mitchell, Dave Parker, Don Mattingly and Tony Gwynn.

COACH. One of the manager's assistants, almost always a former player. Coaches serve as hitting, pitching and fielding instructors. When a team is at bat, one coach is stationed near first base and one near third base to direct the base runners. The third-base coach also flashes signs to the batter telling him what the manager wants him to do—for example, bunt, execute the hit-and-run or take a pitch.

COBB, TY. The runner arrived in a cloud of dust, spikes high, barreling into the bag as the fielder stepped gingerly out of the way. Credit Ty Cobb with another stolen base.

Slashing spikes and a remarkable bat made Ty Cobb a legend on the diamond. He's sliding into third in a game in 1909, a year in which he hit .377, scored 116 runs and stole 76 bases.

Cobb was the most successful base runner of his day and the very best hitter in the history of baseball. He stole 96 bases in one season (1915) and 892 over his career, and both records stood for decades as the measure of running ability. Cobb worked hard on the baseball diamond, playing the game with a vengeance and running the bases with daring.

It's obvious that you can't steal first base, and Cobb didn't have to. Three thousand hits is considered the measure of a first-quality hitter. Cobb, however, was the first and for many decades the only player in the history of the game to get more than 4,000 hits. He finished his career with an awesome total of 4,191 hits in 24 seasons with the Detroit Tigers and Philadelphia Athletics. His hit total stood as the all-time record until Pete Rose passed him late in the 1985 season.

Cobb batted a remarkable .367 for his career and soared over .400 three times, with a high point of .420 in 1911, when he had 248 hits in 591 at-bats. That was one of nine batting titles in a row. He won 12 batting championships overall.

Cobb, who was born on December 18, 1886, in Narrows, Georgia, received the most votes in the first Hall of Fame election in 1936. He died on July 17, 1961.

COLLAR. Going through an entire game without getting a hit. If a player fails to hit, he is said to have gotten the collar.

COMMISSIONER. Baseball's top-ranking administrator. The first commissioner was appointed in 1921 following disputes among major-league owners, capped by the revelation that several members of the Chicago White Sox had conspired with gamblers to purposely lose the 1919 World Series to the Cincinnati Reds.

Baseball's first commissioner, Judge Kenesaw Mountain Landis, at Game 2 of the 1933 World Series. He ruled with an iron hand.

In an attempt to restore public confidence in the game, baseball appointed the respected Judge Kenesaw Mountain Landis as commissioner. He served from 1921 until his death in 1944 and was succeeded by Albert B. (Happy) Chandler, former governor of Kentucky. Chandler reigned until 1950, when the owners voted him out of office and gave the job to National League president Ford C. Frick, who retired after the 1965 season.

As Frick's successor the baseball owners selected William D. Eckert, a retired lieutenant-general of the U.S. Air Force. Eckert took up his duties beginning with the 1966 season. In 1969 he was fired, and Bowie Kuhn, former counsel to the National League, became baseball's fifth commissioner. An owners' revolt to oust Kuhn in 1975 failed, and, instead, he was elected to a new seven-year term.

Kuhn served through the 1984 season and then was replaced by Peter Ueberroth, who had been president and chief executive officer of the Los Angeles Olympic Organizing Committee. Ueberroth retired after four seasons and was replaced by A. Bartlett Giamatti, president of the National League.

Sadly, Giamatti lasted only a few months on the job before he died of a heart attack on September 1, 1989. In his short term as commissioner, Giamatti handed down the decision to suspend Cincinnati Reds manager Pete Rose for alleged involvement with gambling.

Upon Giamatti's death, his aide, Fay Vincent, was elected to succeed him and guide baseball into the 1990s.

The commissioner's major duties include settling grievances of players, clubs or leagues in organized baseball, including the minor leagues; investigating and punishing acts that he believes may hurt baseball; and running the World Series. In addition to the commissioner, each league has its own president—Dr. Bobby Brown in the American League and Bill White in the National League are the current presidents—whose functions are to act in the manner of a commissioner within their leagues.

CONTRACT. All major-league and minor-league teams hire players on a contract basis. In the past, players were usually signed for one year at a time, with winter negotiations generating daily publicity. Now star players are usually signed to multiyear contracts, as clubs seek to keep their best players from the free-agent market. Most multiyear deals are for at least three seasons, and some players have even signed lifetime contracts that include postplaying career broadcasting or front-office jobs.

COUNT. The number of balls and strikes on a batter. The highest count is three and two—three balls and two strikes—which is known as a full count.

CURVE. One of the two standard pitches of baseball, the other being the fastball. The orthodox curveball is thrown with a decided snap and twist of the wrist. A right-hander's curve breaks from right to left as he faces the plate; a left-hander's curve breaks from left to right.

The sinker or drop is a curve that breaks down as well as out. Most curveballs sink, some more sharply than others. A slider is a fast curve with a small break, sometimes called a nickel curve. It is probably the most widely used breaking pitch, since it gets its effectiveness from breaking late, is easier to control and causes less strain on the pitcher's arm. By the time a curve-

Bert Blyleven, a master of the curve.

ball breaks, the hitter may be swinging in the wrong place or he may let it go only to see it slip into the strike zone. A curveball is also known as a jug (for jug handle), rainbow, dipsy-do, hook and snake. Among the more talented curveball pitchers have been Sal Maglie, Johnny Sain, Camilo Pascual, Mike Flanagan and Bert Blyleven.

The curveball was first used in 1867 by W. A. Cummings. There have been many claims by scientists that a curveball is nothing more than an optical illusion. To dispute such claims, pitcher Freddie Fitzsimmons of the Brooklyn Dodgers staged a demonstration that silenced the doubters for good. On December 1, 1941, he set up three posts in a straight line between himself and home plate, 60 feet 6 inches away. He released the ball to the right of the first post and made it go to the left of the second post and to the right of the third post.

Whitlow Wyatt, also a Dodger pitcher of that time, offered to perform a more spectacular demonstration. Anyone who did not believe that a curveball curves could stand behind a tree, Wyatt proposed, "and I'll whomp him to death with an optical illusion." There were no takers.

CUTDOWN DATE. That time of year when a team must cut its roster to the maximum number of players allowed, by trading players, selling them or sending them to the minor leagues. The maximum number of players a team is allowed is 25, and the cutdown date is opening day.

CUTOFF. The interception of a thrown ball, usually from the outfield, for the purpose of trapping a runner off base or attempting to keep a runner or runners from advancing. If performed properly, it is one of the most exciting and important plays in the game. Its importance was obvious in the final game of the 1962 World Series.

The Yankees led the Giants, 1–0, with two out in the last of the ninth, a man on first and Willie Mays at bat. Mays hit a line drive down the right-field line, a ball that would normally score a man from first. But Roger Maris raced over, picked up the ball on the run and threw quickly to the cutoff, second baseman Bobby Richardson, who had gone into short right field for the throw. Richardson turned and threw quickly, strongly and accurately to home plate, preventing the tying run from scoring. The next batter lined out, and the Yankees won the game and the World Series, largely because Maris and Richardson had performed the cutoff play to perfection.

CYCLE. When a batter hits a single, double, triple and home run, not necessarily in that order but all in the same game, it is called hitting for the cycle. It is so rare a feat that a couple of years may go by without it happening in the major leagues.

CY YOUNG AWARD.   *See* Young, Cy.

DEAD BALL.   A ball legally out of play that results in the temporary suspension of play. Examples are a fair ball that hits a base runner, or a foul ball.

DEAD-BALL ERA. In baseball's early years, pitchers dominated the game, with power hitters settling for many fewer home runs than are common in today's game. That period, when the leading home-run hitters seldom managed even a dozen long balls in a season, is known as the dead-ball era. Later, the baseball became livelier, and home runs became more commonplace.

DEAN, JAY AND PAUL. See Dizzy and Daffy.

DEKED. Short for "decoyed," usually used by an infielder to fool a runner into thinking that he is about to catch the ball—or, conversely, that he is *not* about to catch the ball.

DESIGNATED HITTER. A rule adopted by the American League in 1973 that allows each team to appoint a hitter to substitute for the pitcher when his team is at bat. The designated hitter, or DH, does not play in the field but takes a regular turn at bat in place of the pitcher, in any spot in the batting order the manager chooses.

The DH is used throughout the minor leagues. It is used in alternate years in the All-Star Game and in all World Series games hosted by American League clubs.

Alan Trammell, a Tiger stalwart at shortstop since 1978, was World Series MVP in 1984, when he helped lead Detroit over the San Diego Padres.

DETROIT TIGERS. Manager Sparky Anderson was so high on the potential of the Detroit Tigers in the spring of 1984 that he compared them favorably with Cincinnati's Big Red Machine, which he had managed to two consecutive world championships in the 1970s.

The Tigers did everything to back Anderson's assessment. With Kirk Gibson, Lance Parrish, Alan Trammell and Lou Whitaker on the offense and a super pitching staff of Jack Morris, Willie Hernandez, Dan Petry, Milt Wilcox and Aurelio Lopez, the Tigers won 35 of their first 40 games and coasted to the American League Eastern Division crown.

Then they swept the Kansas City Royals in the playoffs and defeated the San Diego Padres in the World Series in five games.

Trammell took MVP honors, and Morris won two games. Hernandez was the Cy Young Award winner and the American League's MVP.

It was the Tigers' first title since the pitching tandem of Denny McLain and Mickey Lolich had mastered the St. Louis Cardinals in 1968.

Detroit's achievement in 1984 marked the third world championship for a franchise that has featured some of the greatest hitters of all time. From Ty Cobb to Al Kaline to Norm Cash, the Tigers have boasted 22 American League batting champions, led by Cobb, who won the title 12 times.

Cobb led Detroit to three pennants in a row, from 1907 to 1909. The team didn't win another one until 1934, when the hitting of Charlie Gehringer and Hank Greenberg sparked the Tigers to the first of two straight flags. The team won the World Series in 1935, under player-manager Mickey Cochrane, and three years later the mighty Greenberg slammed 58 home runs. Greenberg was still on the team in 1945 when Detroit won its second world championship and southpaw Hal Newhouser led the majors with 25 victories and an ERA of 1.81.

In 1990 the Tigers unveiled a new slugger in first baseman Cecil Fielder. Never a powerhouse in his four seasons with the Toronto Blue Jays, Fielder found the range in Japan in 1989, and came back as a fearsome Tiger in 1990, hitting 51 homers and also leading the league in RBIs (132), slugging percentage (.592) and total bases (339).

DEUCE. Players' name for the curveball. The term is a carry-over from sandlot days, when the catcher's signals to the pitcher were simply one finger for the fastball, two for the curve.

DIAMOND. Originally the infield, which is shaped like a diamond, but now used to refer to the entire field.

DIMAGGIO, JOE. The streak began innocently enough on May 15, 1941, with one hit, a single, in four at-bats. Joe DiMaggio of the Yankees could never have known that at that moment he had begun a unique voyage through the baseball record book.

Day after day DiMaggio continued to punish pitchers with anything from one to four hits per game. On June 29 he broke George Sisler's American League record of hitting safely in 41 straight games. Three days later, on July 2, Wee Willie Keeler's 44-game major-league record tumbled.

The end finally came in Cleveland on July 17, when two brilliant plays by Cleveland third baseman Ken Keltner stopped DiMaggio. After 56 games, the hitting streak was over. It is a record that has never been broken.

Born on November 25, 1914, in Martinez, California, DiMaggio became an American folk hero. He played the outfield with style and grace and was one of the finest hitters of his time.

Known as the Yankee Clipper, DiMaggio won two batting championships and two MVP trophies. When he retired after the 1951 season, he had a career batting average of .325, with 361 home runs and a ticket to baseball's Hall of Fame.

DIZZY AND DAFFY. Nicknames of the famous Dean brothers of the 1930s, Jay Hanna (Dizzy) Dean and Paul Dee (Daffy) Dean, who came out of Arkansas with little education and captivated the public with their pranks on and off the field. Dizzy, the older, more successful and zanier of the two, became a successful broad-

The classic Joe DiMaggio swing produced a record hitting streak of 56 games in 1941.

Dizzy Dean *(left)* **and Daffy Dean pitched the St. Louis Cardinals to the world championship in 1934.**

caster and telecaster whose trademark was telling stories in his country jargon and singing country songs on the air.

Once, the mother of a young boy scolded Dizzy for his horrible grammar on the air, which, she said, was a bad example for her son. "You don't even know the king's English," the woman said.

"Old Diz knows the king's English," Dean protested, "and not only that, I also know the queen is English."

Despite their reputation as characters, the Dean brothers were among the best pitchers of their day. Dizzy won 20 or more games in four straight years for the

St. Louis Cardinals, was the last National League pitcher to win 30 games (30-7 in 1934) and achieved 150 victories before his career was shortened by a foot injury. Brother Paul twice won 19 games for the Cardinals. In 1934 the brothers won 49 games between them, pitching the Cardinals to the pennant, then won all four games as the Cardinals defeated the Detroit Tigers in the World Series.

DOUBLE. A two-base hit. Also called a two-bagger. Tris Speaker, whose career spanned 22 years and four American

League teams, hit a record 793 doubles. Pete Rose is second on the list with the National League record of 746 doubles.

DOUBLEHEADER. Two games for the price of one. Also known as a bargain bill or a twin bill. Doubleheaders have been a feature of the baseball schedule since 1882, although because of economics and the need to charge a separate admission for every game, they are almost never scheduled anymore. Today's doubleheaders are almost always the result of making up rained-out games and are usually played starting in the evening instead of early in the afternoon. Once, Sunday was almost an automatic doubleheader date, with Monday an off-day for the players. (*See also* Twi-night.)

DOUBLE PLAY. The act of getting two men out on a single play, in a continuous sequence. It is also known as a twin killing and, among players, as getting two. The Philadelphia Athletics made a record 217 double plays during the 1949 season, and three clubs have turned as many as seven double plays in one game. While it is desirable to make many double plays, it is not always a sign of strength, because for a team to make a large number of double plays, there must be an unusual number of opposition players on base during the course of the season.

The most famous of all double-play combinations was the one known as Tinker-to-Evers-to-Chance. Joe Tinker (shortstop), Johnny Evers (second baseman) and Frank Chance (first baseman) played together for the Chicago Cubs from 1902 to 1912 and helped the Cubs win three straight pennants, in 1906, 1907 and 1908. Although this double-play combination was not the greatest of all time, it was the most feared of its day and inspired Franklin P. Adams of the New York *Evening Mail* to immortalize them with this poem:

These are the saddest of possible words:
   "Tinker to Evers to Chance."
Trio of bear Cubs and fleeter than birds,
   "Tinker to Evers to Chance."
Ruthlessly pricking our gonfalon bubble,
   Making a Giant hit into a double—
Words that are heavy with nothing
            but trouble:
   "Tinker to Evers to Chance."

DOUBLE STEAL. Two base runners successfully stealing bases on the same play.

DOWN BROADWAY. A pitch thrown through the middle of the strike zone; a fat pitch.

DRAFT. The selection of players by major-league clubs. There are two types of drafts. The first is the amateur draft in which clubs choose eligible high school and college players. The other draft permits a team to select players from other clubs' minor-league teams when those players have spent six years in the minors without a promotion to the majors.

DRAG BUNT. A bunt pulled down the first-base line by a left-handed hitter. A bunt in the same direction by a right-handed hitter is a push bunt. A bunt toward the third-base line by either type of batter is dropped or dumped, while "laying one down" is an expression that applies to bunting in general. A drag bunt is the favorite device of many fast runners because it is a virtual certainty that they will make first base safely if the bunt is well placed. Among the more effective drag bunters have been Mickey Mantle of the Yankees, Maury Wills of the Dodgers, Rod Carew of the Twins and Angels and Brett Butler, now of the Dodgers.

DUGOUT. The area with a long bench for the manager, coaches, players, substitutes and other team members not in the game. It gets its name from the fact that most dugouts are dug into the ground, so part of the dugout is below the playing field.

DUSTER. A pitch thrown close to the batter's head, to keep the batter from digging in at the plate. Unlike the beanball, a duster does not usually hit a batter, but accidents can happen, and some dusters become beanballs, intentionally or not. Also

called a brushback pitch. When a player has been dusted or brushed back so that he has to fall to the ground to avoid being hit, he says he was decked or flipped. If hit, he has been beaned (in the head) or plugged (elsewhere).

EARNED RUN. A run for which the pitcher is held accountable—as opposed to an unearned run, which scores as the direct or indirect result of an error, a passed ball, interference or obstruction.

EARNED RUN AVERAGE. A method of evaluating the efficiency of a pitcher, determined by dividing the total number of earned runs by the total number of innings pitched, then multiplying by nine. This gives the pitcher's earned run average, or ERA, for a nine-inning game—that is, the number of earned runs he has allowed for every nine innings. Anything under three earned runs per game is considered very good. The lowest ERA on record for 300 innings or more is 1.09 by Walter Johnson of the Washington Senators in 1913. More recently, Bob Gibson of the St. Louis Cardinals had an ERA of 1.12 in 1968.

EMERY BALL. A ball that has been illegally roughed up by rubbing a piece of sandpaper over its surface, causing it, when thrown, to rise, fall or break away sud-

Kansas City's George Brett ducks out of the way of a duster thrown by Philadelphia's Dickie Noles in the 1980 World Series.

denly and unexpectedly. This was a common practice in the 1920s, but it was declared illegal.

ERROR. A fielding mistake charged for each bobble or wild throw that prolongs the time of a batter at bat or the stay of a runner on base, or that permits a runner to advance or a batter to reach base safely. Kicking one or booting one is the players' usual parlance for making an error. Errors have become less frequent through the years as players' skills—and their gloves—have improved.

EXHIBITION GAME. A baseball game that has no bearing on the official records of either the players or the teams, such as spring-training games and barnstorming games. Teams play a full schedule of 20 to 30 exhibition games in spring training in order to (1) help pay spring-training expenses by charging admission, (2) get advance publicity and (3) enable the manager to evaluate the strengths and weaknesses of both his team and the opposition. An exhibition game is played each year at the Baseball Hall of Fame in Cooperstown, New York, as part of the ceremonies during which new members are inducted into the Hall of Fame. In recent years exhibition games have also been scheduled during the season, usually for the benefit of charity.

EXTRA-BASE HIT. A hit good for more than one base—that is, a two-base hit (double), three-base hit (triple) or four-base hit (home run). Also called a long hit.

Babe Ruth holds the record for having made 119 extra-base hits in one season (44 doubles, 16 triples and 59 home runs in 1921).

Four players since 1900 have had five extra-base hits in one game: Joe Adcock of the Milwaukee Braves, who hit four home runs and one double on July 31, 1954; Lou Boudreau, who hit four doubles and one home run for Cleveland on July 14, 1946; Willie Stargell, who hit two home runs and three doubles for Pittsburgh on August 1, 1970; and Steve Garvey, who did the same for Los Angeles on August 28, 1977.

EXTRA INNINGS. When a game is tied after nine innings, play continues until one team has scored more runs than the other in a completed inning, or until the team batting last takes the lead. On May 1, 1920, the Boston Braves and the Brooklyn Dodgers struggled through a 1–1, 26-inning game, the longest ever played in the major leagues. Both starting pitchers, Joe Oeschger and Leon Cadore, lasted the whole game.

The longest game in terms of time took place between the Chicago White Sox and Milwaukee Brewers on May 8 and 9, 1984. The game went 25 innings—the first 18 of which were played on the night of May 8. With the teams tied at 6–6, the game was called on account of the American League curfew (which states that no inning can begin after 1 A.M.) and resumed the following evening. The White Sox pushed across a run to win it in the 25th, thus ending the eight-hour, six-minute marathon.

The longest game played in one day was the second game of a doubleheader between the San Francisco Giants and New York Mets on May 31, 1964. That game, which went 23 innings, lasted 7 hours and 23 minutes.

The longest scoreless game in history took place between the Houston Astros and the Mets on April 16, 1968, at the Astrodome. The Astros won on an unearned run in the 24th inning.

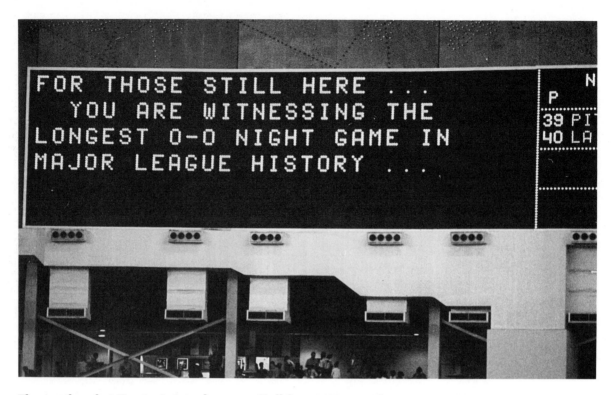

FOR THOSE STILL HERE . . .
YOU ARE WITNESSING THE
LONGEST 0-0 NIGHT GAME IN
MAJOR LEAGUE HISTORY . . .

N
P
39 PIT
40 LA

The scoreboard at Houston's Astrodome says it all for a 1968 game that went 24 innings.

EYE IN THE SKY. Describes the coach who sits in the press box or upper deck and positions his team's players through use of a walkie-talkie to the dugout.

FAIR BALL. A legally batted ball that is hit in fair territory—that is, within the foul lines.

FAN. To strike out swinging; to fan the breeze. The term also means a rooter or a supporter of a team or of baseball in general, and is a short form of the word "fanatic."

FARM SYSTEM. Branch Rickey introduced "chain-store" baseball when he was running the St. Louis Cardinals in the 1920s. Big-league players had been optioned to the minors as far back as 1887, but Rickey was the first to build a network of farm teams controlled by the parent club through either ownership or exclusive agreements. Other teams borrowed the idea after it began producing pennants for the Cardinals.

There is, of course, more to a farm system than the acquisition of minor-league teams. The secret of success is to keep the farm teams stocked with good players and to know which players to advance and which to sell, and when. (*See also* Minor leagues.)

FASTBALL. Also fireball, high hard one. The speediest pitch that a pitcher can throw. The most frequently used pitch in the game.

FELLER, BOB. Bob Feller started his first game as a major-league pitcher when he was just 17 years old. He struck out 15 batters that day for the Cleveland Indians and began a career that would see him pitch three no-hitters and win 266 games, all with the Indians, from 1936 to 1956. His fastball, which was clocked at 100 mph, certified him as one of the hardest throwers in baseball history. How appropriate that "Bob Feller" immediately follows the entry for "fastball." They were always linked.

Feller's fastball was first in evidence when he pitched against the side of the family barn in Van Meter, Iowa, where he was born on November 3, 1918. In 1946 he struck out 348 batters, a major-league record that stood for 20 years until it was broken by Sandy Koufax. By then, "Rapid

The camera catches a Bob Feller fastball.

Robert" Feller was in the Hall of Fame, elected in 1962.

FENCE. Outfield fences have two major effects on the game. Their height and dis-

Distance of Outfield Fences (in feet)

NATIONAL LEAGUE				AMERICAN LEAGUE			
Ballpark	*Left*	*Center*	*Right*	*Ballpark*	*Left*	*Center*	*Right*
Atlanta	330'	402'	330'	Baltimore	309'	405'	309'
Chicago	355'	400'	353'	Boston	315'	420'	302'
Cincinnati	330'	404'	330'	California	333'	404'	333'
Houston	330'	400'	300'	Chicago	347'	409'	347'
Los Angeles	330'	400'	330'	Cleveland	320'	400'	320'
Montreal	325'	404'	325'	Detroit	340'	440'	325'
New York	338'	410'	338'	Kansas City	330'	410'	330'
Philadelphia	330'	408'	330'	Milwaukee	315'	402'	315'
Pittsburgh	335'	400'	335'	Minnesota	343'	408'	327'
St. Louis	330'	414'	330'	New York	318'	408'	314'
San Diego	330'	405'	330'	Oakland	330'	400'	330'
San Francisco	335'	400'	335'	Seattle	316'	410'	316'
				Texas	330'	400'	330'
				Toronto	330'	400'	330'

tance from home plate help control the number of home runs, and they also affect fielding, since outfielders must learn how far and at what angle a ball is likely to bounce off them. Most major-league parks were built before distance hitting, or fence busting, came into fashion, and for many years the fences were beyond the range of the hitters. However, in order to increase the number of home runs, stands have been built to shorten the outfields of some parks, while inner fences have been strung across the outfields of others. The table on page 55 shows distances to the left-field, center-field (farthest point) and right-field fences in each park.

FIELD. To handle a batted or thrown ball while on the defense. Also, the area on which opponents do battle.

FIELDER'S CHOICE. The act of a fielder who catches a ground ball and throws it to some base other than first, attempting to retire a runner who is already on base rather than the batter. The assumption is that the fielder could have retired the batter but chose to make a play on the runner instead. Whether the fielder completes the play successfully or not, the play is scored a fielder's choice and the batter is charged with an official time at bat and no hit.

FINE. A fee charged to a player by his manager, owner, league president or the commissioner for any action believed harmful to his team, league or all of baseball, or for breaking any rule set down by his team, league or the baseball commissioner's office.

In 1925 the largest fine ever levied on a player (up to that point) was slapped on Babe Ruth. His manager, Miller Huggins,

had had his fill of the Babe's consistent violation of training regulations, so he fined Ruth $5,000. There is a story that when Joe McCarthy followed Huggins as Yankee manager, he got Babe's $5,000 back, in an effort to win the big guy over.

Babe also suffered the second largest fine, this one from Commissioner Landis in 1921. The Babe hit 59 home runs that year, and after the season he lined up an exhibition tour, which was against league rules. When Landis found out about it, he fined Babe his entire check from the 1921 World Series ($3,362.26) and suspended him until May 20, 1922, so that Ruth also lost a month's pay.

In 1965 pitcher Juan Marichal of the San Francisco Giants hit Johnny Roseboro, catcher for the Los Angeles Dodgers, on the head with a baseball bat. Marichal was suspended nine days in the midst of a close pennant race and was fined $1,750.

In 1980 Bill Madlock, third baseman for the Pittsburgh Pirates, was hit with the largest fine in National League history when he slapped umpire Jerry Crawford across the face with his glove. He had to pay $5,000 and was suspended for 15 days.

In 1989 the celebrated Pete Rose, manager of the Cincinnati Reds, drew the ultimate from Commissioner Bart Giamatti. He wasn't fined but, much worse than that, he was banned from baseball for life for allegedly betting on baseball games.

FIRST BALL. A pregame ceremony usually associated with the opening day of the season and the president of the United States. It all began in 1910, when President William Howard Taft attended the season's starter between the Washington Senators and the Philadelphia Athletics. As an added touch Taft tossed out the first ball from his box seat and began what has become a ritual practiced by most presi-

President William Howard Taft threw out the *first* first ball in 1910.

dents since then. Over the years the throwing out of the first ball has preceded other important games, such as the playoffs and the World Series, and assorted dignitaries are usually chosen for the tossing.

FIRST BASE. The base to which the batter runs first. It is a 15-inch-square bag that is located diagonally to the right of, and 90 feet from, home plate. The defensive player whose responsibility it is to cover the area around first base is the first baseman.

FLY BALL. A batted ball that goes high in the air.

FLY-OUT. A ball hit fairly that is caught by a fielder—usually, but not always, an outfielder—before it touches the ground.

FOOT IN THE BUCKET. A batting stance in which the front foot is positioned toward the foul line (toward the old water bucket in the dugout) instead of pointing toward the plate. Often such a stance is a sign of timidity, the foot being planted that way to give the batter a head start in getting out of the way of a close pitch. But the foot-in-the-bucket stance has been used by a number of outstanding hitters, among them Al Simmons, who had a lifetime batting average of .334 for 20 big-league seasons, Roy Campanella and Arky Vaughan.

FORCED OUT. A fielder retiring a base runner by touching the base to which the runner is forced to advance. A force play can happen only when there is a runner on first base, or runners on first and second or runners on first, second and third, and a batted ball hits the ground, either in the infield or the outfield. In each case, the runner already on base is forced out if he doesn't reach the next base ahead of the ball.

FORFEIT. Any one of several rules violations, most of them concerned with the refusal of a team or player to continue playing, may cause the umpire to declare the game forfeited. The forfeit score is 9–0 in favor of the offended team.

FORKBALL. A ball that is pitched by being held at the top with the index and middle fingers wide apart (like a fork) and at the bottom by the thumb. In its delivery it breaks like a knuckleball. The leading user of the forkball was Elroy Face, who pitched it to win 18 games and lose only one for the Pittsburgh Pirates in 1959.

FOUL BALL. Any legally batted ball that lands in foul territory, whether it is a fly ball or a ground ball, a ball barely tipped by the batter or one hit out of the park. A foul ball is a strike unless it is caught on the fly by a fielder, in which case the batter is out. If a ball is tipped by the batter, it is a strike; if there are already two strikes on the batter and the catcher catches the foul tip, the batter is out, and the pitcher is credited with a strikeout. A foul ball is not an automatic third strike if the batter already has two strikes on him. However, if the batter has two strikes and he tries to bunt, and it goes foul, he is automatically out.

FOXX, JIMMIE. He was a barrel-chested son of a farmer, and he slugged home runs with the strength of a mule. Jimmie Foxx was known as Double X, and from 1925 to 1945 he drove 534 homers, most of them for the Philadelphia Athletics and the Boston Red Sox.

Foxx, born on October 22, 1907, in Sudlersville, Maryland, hit 58 homers in 1932, was voted the American League's Most Valuable Player three times (1932, '33, '38) and ended with a .325 lifetime batting average.

His biggest year came in 1933, when he won the Triple Crown — 48 homers, 169 runs batted in and a .364 batting average—the league leader in all three categories.

Double X, chiefly a first baseman, also caught, played third and the outfield and even pitched in 10 games. He was elected to the Hall of Fame in 1951 and died in 1967.

FRANCHISE. The right granted by a governing body to run a business in a certain place. In baseball, the commissioner grants a person or persons the right to operate a team in a particular city.

FREE AGENT. Any player who is not under contract to a team and is, therefore, free to sign a contract with any team. He may be a young player who has never been under contract or an older one who, after six years in the majors, has fulfilled his obligation to another team—such as Mark Langston, who ended the 1989 season with the Montreal Expos and then signed a five-year deal with the California Angels for $16 million.

Free agency has sent baseball salaries skyrocketing as teams compete for players' services. Back in the 1960s, superstars like Willie Mays and Mickey Mantle earned $100,000. By the end of the 1980s, most teams had at least one player earning ten times that amount, or $1 million a year. There were some players over the $3 million mark. (*See* Major League Baseball Players Association.)

FUNGO. A ball hit to the infield or outfield during fielding practice. Fungoes are hit with a specially constructed thin, light bat, called a fungo stick. The fungo hitter tosses the ball a few feet in the air and swings, directing fly balls at the outfielders or ground balls at the infielders. The practice is run by a coach, who usually takes pride in his precision with a fungo stick. A dying art, however, is the trick of fungoing a high pop-up straight overhead for the catcher. The word "fungible" means one thing that can be substituted for another, and it is thought that in baseball the thin fungo stick got its name because it replaces the conventional bat.

GAME. A game of baseball consists of nine full innings, each team having nine turns at bat, except when the home team is ahead after 8½ innings, at which point the game ends automatically. A game is also considered finished if play is halted (by rain, snow and so on) after the team that is trailing has been to bat at least five times.

GASHOUSE GANG. A nickname given to the St. Louis Cardinals of the 1930s because they were a collection of rowdy, fiery, daring players who included player-manager Frankie Frisch, Pepper Martin, Ducky Medwick, Leo Durocher and Dizzy Dean. Frank Graham, then with the New York *Sun*, suggested to Durocher that the Cardinals were so good that they could win in any league, including the powerful American League. "They wouldn't let us play in the American League," Durocher corrected. "They'd say we were just a lot of gashouse players." Graham picked up the expression and started calling the Cardinals the Gashouse Gang, and the name stuck.

GEHRIG, LOU. On June 2, 1925, New York Yankee first baseman Wally Pipp asked for the day off, complaining of a headache. Manager Miller Huggins chose a rookie, 22-year-old Lou Gehrig, to take Pipp's place. For the next 2,130 games—a

It was a tearful time for all at Yankee Stadium on Lou Gehrig Day, July 4, 1939, when the ailing Gehrig told his teammates and the 62,000 fans, "Today, I consider myself the luckiest man on the face of the earth."

major-league record that may never be broken—Gehrig was never out of the Yankee lineup.

Born in New York on June 19, 1903, the Iron Horse played most of his career in the shadow of the more colorful Babe Ruth, but he was a mighty hitter in his own right. He played briefly at Columbia University before launching a professional career that would see him lead the league in homers three times (sharing it once with Ruth), drive in 150 or more runs seven times, hit four home runs in one game and set a major-league record that still stands for most home runs with the bases full: 23.

Larrupin' Lou was the American League's Most Valuable Player in 1927 and 1936, belted 493 home runs and had a lifetime batting average of .340.

He didn't leave the Yankee lineup until May 2, 1939, when a crippling illness—amyotrophic lateral sclerosis (now also known as Lou Gehrig's disease)—forced his retirement. He died in 1941, two years after he was voted into the Hall of Fame.

GIBSON, BOB. The pitching match-up was perfect for a World Series setting. For Detroit, 31-game-winner Denny McLain, the first pitcher since 1931 to win more than 30. For St. Louis, Bob Gibson, enjoying a dream year that included a 1.12

earned run average, the lowest in National League history for a 300-inning season.

This was the opening game of the 1968 World Series between the Tigers and the Cardinals, each with a powerhouse pitcher. But it was no match. McLain was gone by the sixth inning. Gibson, meanwhile, mowed down the Tigers, setting a Series record with 17 strikeouts on the way to a 4–0 victory.

Gibson was at his absolute best in World Series competition. He won seventh-game Series assignments in 1964 and 1967. In nine World Series starts, he finished eight games, compiled a 7-2 record with a 1.89 ERA and recorded 92 strikeouts in 81 innings.

Gibby was a very basic pitcher, armed with an explosive fastball that challenged hitters. More often than not, he won that challenge.

Born on November 19, 1935, in Omaha,

Bob Gibson was supreme in the World Series, particularly in 1967, when he was 3–0 with an ERA of 1.00.

Gibson was a four-sport star at Creighton University and played basketball with the Harlem Globetrotters for one year before turning to baseball. He pitched 17 seasons for the Cardinals, finishing with 251 victories and 3,117 strikeouts, 11th on the all-time list. Those accomplishments earned his election to the Hall of Fame in 1981.

GIBSON, JOSH. "He can do anything. He hits the ball a mile. And he catches so easy he might as well be in a rocking chair. Throws like a rifle. Too bad this Gibson is a colored fellow."

These were the words of Walter Johnson, the great Washington Senator pitcher who was speaking at a time long before blacks were permitted to play in the major leagues.

Josh Gibson was known as the black Babe Ruth by those who saw him strike fear in the hearts of Negro league pitchers. Had he played "organized baseball," he would have been recognized universally as one of the all-time great sluggers.

Born on December 21, 1911, in Buena Vista, Georgia, Gibson hit 75 homers for the Homestead Grays in 1931. The next year he joined the Pittsburgh Crawfords, and in 1934 he hit 69 homers, the most memorable of which occurred at Yankee Stadium.

He was batting against Slim Jones of the Philadelphia Stars in the second game of a four-team doubleheader when he hit a ball over the triple deck next to the bullpen in left field. Nobody in major-league baseball—not even Babe Ruth—has ever hit a fair ball out of Yankee Stadium. But Gibson did it.

He rejoined the Homestead Grays in 1937 and led them to nine straight Negro league pennants. Although statistics are incomplete, the best estimates are that Gibson finished with 950 career homers and a 17-season batting average of more than .350.

Catcher Josh Gibson was one of the greatest sluggers of all time.

Sadly, Gibson died of a brain tumor on January 20, 1947, without getting a chance to show his greatness in the majors. Those privileged to see him exhibit his power from 1930 through 1946 know justice was served in 1972 when he was inducted into the Hall of Fame.

GLOVE. Originally intended for protection of the hand, the glove became a field-

In the 1970 World Series against Cincinnati, Baltimore's third baseman Brooks Robinson showed what makes a glove man.

the season the Mets' right-hander, respectfully called "Doc" by his teammates and opponents, dominated the game as few pitchers ever have.

Combining a searing fastball, a sharp curve, extraordinary poise and remarkable control, Doctor K became the first pitcher since Sandy Koufax to lead the majors in wins (at 24-4), ERA (1.53) and strikeouts (268). He also set the National League pace in innings pitched (276.2) and complete games (16). He posted eight shutouts and became the youngest player ever to receive the Cy Young Award.

Born on November 16, 1964, in Tampa, Florida, Gooden exploded onto the major-league scene in 1984 after one year in the minors. He set a major-league rookie record for strikeouts with a major-league-leading 276, won 17 games and was NL Rookie of

ing aid as well. The early gloves were form-fitting. As late as 1920 George Sisler's first-baseman's mitt was scarcely larger than his hand. Today's gloves, particularly first-basemen's trapper models, are enormous, wide-webbed affairs that have led to a general improvement in fielding.

GLOVE MAN. An outstanding fielder, also called a leather man. Perhaps the best glove man of the 1980s was Ozzie Smith of the St. Louis Cardinals. The term is usually, but not necessarily, applied to infielders. Brooks Robinson of the Baltimore Orioles, Billy Cox of the Brooklyn Dodgers and Marty Marion of the Cardinals have all been considered great glove men.

GOODEN, DWIGHT. Though not 21 years old, and in only his second major-league season, Dwight Gooden achieved the status of a legend in 1985. That was

Doc Gooden set a blistering pace for the Mets as a rookie in 1984.

the Year in leading the Mets out of the cellar to a second-place finish.

In 1986 he helped pitch the Mets to a world championship with a 17-6 mark and a 2.84 ERA. However, the following March, he tested positive for cocaine use and missed the first two months of the 1987 season in rehabilitation. He still managed to go 15-7 that year, and followed that with an 18-9 mark for the NL East champs of 1988.

On June 19, 1989, he defeated Montreal at Shea Stadium, 5–3, to become the third youngest pitcher in history to reach the 100-win plateau. Only Bob Feller and Noodles Hahn reached the milestone sooner.

Though a muscle tear in his right shoulder shelved him for most of the second half of the 1989 season, Gooden finished 9-4 with a 2.89 ERA. In 1990 he posted a 19-7 mark, and his 223 strikeouts were second only to teammate David Cone's 233 in the National League.

GOPHER BALL. A pitch hit for a home run. The term was first used when Lefty Gomez pitched for the New York Yankees. Writers joked about his gopher ball, which would "go fer the stands" or "go fer four bases." The one-year record for gophers allowed is held by Bert Blyleven, who gave up 50 while pitching for the Minnesota Twins in 1986. The career record is held by Robin Roberts, who watched his pitches leave the park 505 times.

GRAND SLAM. Home run with the bases full, sometimes called a jackpot. Lou Gehrig hit 23 career grand slams, the major-league record. Willie McCovey, who played for the San Francisco Giants and San Diego Padres, holds the National League record with 18. The record for grand slams in a season is six, set by the Yankees' Don Mattingly in 1987.

GRANDSTAND PLAY. A comparatively easy fielding play made to look more difficult by a player who wants to attract the spectators' attention.

GRAPEFRUIT LEAGUE. General term for spring training, technically referring to exhibition games played in Florida and differing from the Cactus League in Arizona. In theory, the idea of spring training is to get the athletes into playing condition, aided by a warm climate, but it has equal if not greater value as an extended publicity stunt that keeps baseball in the head-

Willie McCovey's 18 grand slams are a National League record.

lines for two months before the season opens. Even southern minor-league teams pitch camp away from home on the theory that distance lends magic to their doings.

The Chicago White Stockings started the custom when they trained in New Orleans in 1870. By the 1890s the practice had become general, although the teams were still treated like outcasts. Connie Mack, remembering a trip to Jacksonville, Florida, with the Washington Senators in 1888, said, "The hotel clerk made the strict stipulation that the ballplayers would not mingle with the other guests or eat in the same dining room."

Eventually the clubs were welcomed as a tourist attraction. Thanks to a Florida booster named Al Lang, who first invited teams to his area in 1914, the Tampa Bay region has long been the center of big-league training activity. As a tribute to Al Lang, the field in St. Petersburg on which the St. Louis Cardinals play their spring-training games is called Al Lang Field. (*See also* Cactus League.)

GREEN MONSTER. Term used to describe the left-field wall at Boston's Fenway Park. The wall, which is 315 feet from home plate, is 37 feet high, with a 23-foot-high screen on top of it. Carl Yastrzemski learned to play the caroms off the wall so well that often he would hold batters to a single on balls that were hit off the Green Monster.

GROUNDER. Also ground ball, roller, bouncer, hopper, grass cutter. A batted ball that rolls or bounces on the ground to an infielder, or through the infield for a hit.

GROUND OUT. To hit a ground ball to an infielder and be thrown out at first base.

GROUND RULES. Special rules covering conditions in a given park. Most ground rules have to do with whether or not a batted ball or thrown ball is in play if it strikes certain obstacles on the sidelines or on the walls.

A funny incident concerning ground rules happened during the 1965 World Series. A guest at the first game was Vice-President Hubert Humphrey, who sat next to the Minnesota Twins' dugout. It became part of the ground rules for the game that the ball still would be in play if it hit the Secret Service man sitting on the field guarding the vice-president.

GWYNN, TONY. Celebrated in San Diego as a beacon of excellence and consistency through so many bleak Padre seasons, Tony Gwynn remains a superstar whom the working man can admire.

Tony Gwynn won National League batting crowns in 1984, 1987, 1988 and 1989.

No one works harder at improving his hitting and fielding techniques than Gwynn. In fact, this four-time National League batting champion can usually be found studying videotapes of himself at the plate, searching for bad habits. He doesn't have many.

Born on May 9, 1960, in Los Angeles, Gwynn attended San Diego State and spurned a chance to play pro basketball with the San Diego Clippers. He signed with the Padres in 1981. In seven full seasons with the Padres through 1990, this left-handed-hitting outfielder has never hit less than .309.

His league-leading .370 average in 1987 was the highest in the NL since Stan Musial batted .376 in 1948. Gwynn won a furious, down-to-the-wire duel with the Giants' Will Clark for another batting title in 1989, when he hit .336 and exceeded 200 hits for the fourth time in his career. He also became the first NL player to win three in a row since Musial did it from 1950 to 1952.

Shifted from right field to center, Gwynn has made himself into one of the best defensive outfielders in baseball. That surprises nobody familiar with this seven-time All-Star's burning desire to be the complete player.

GEORGE HERMAN (BABE) RUTH
BOSTON—NEW YORK, A.L.; BOSTON, N.L.
1915 – 1935
GREATEST DRAWING CARD IN HISTORY OF BASEBALL. HOLDER OF MANY HOME RUN AND OTHER BATTING RECORDS. GATHERED 714 HOME RUNS IN ADDITION TO FIFTEEN IN WORLD SERIES.

Babe Ruth's plaque hangs with those of other immortals in the Baseball Hall of Fame in Cooperstown, New York.

HALF SWING. The action of a batter trying to stop his swing, but failing to do so. Even a half swing counts as a whole strike.

HALL OF FAME. Baseball maintains a Hall of Fame honoring outstanding players, managers, umpires and others connected with the game. Proposed by Ford Frick in 1935 soon after he became National League president, the Hall of Fame was begun in 1936 with the election of Ty Cobb, Walter Johnson, Christy Mathewson, Babe Ruth and Honus Wagner. There are now more than 200 members.

The method of selection has varied from time to time, but under present regulations, members are chosen each year from two categories by two independent groups. To qualify for the Hall of Fame, a player must have been retired at least five years. Members of the Baseball Writers Association of America vote on players who have been out of the game for at least five but not more than 20 years. The Committee on Baseball Veterans (mostly writers and ex-baseball officials) votes on players of the more distant past and on others who have distinguished themselves, such as umpires, managers, sportswriters and league and team officials.

Each year a baseball game between two major-league teams is played when new members are inducted into the Hall of Fame. The actual Hall of Fame, containing bronze plaques honoring those elected, is a room in the Baseball Museum in Cooperstown, New York, a site chosen in the now disputed belief that baseball was invented there by Abner Doubleday. Iron-ically, Doubleday is not in the Hall of Fame.

In addition to the plaques of the members, there are other mementos in the Hall of Fame that help make it a favorite tourist attraction. Among them are the bench Connie Mack sat on in the Philadelphia Athletic dugout for many years; a ball used in 1866; Stan Musial's spikes; the baseball with which Cy Young won his 500th game; the lockers of Honus Wagner, Babe Ruth, Lou Gehrig and Joe DiMaggio; the sliding pads used by Ty Cobb when he stole 96 bases in 1915; Don Mattingly's bat from the game in 1987 when he connected for a record sixth grand slam; the ball that Hank Aaron hit for his 714th home run on April 4, 1974, to tie Babe Ruth; and Nolan Ryan's uniform from the game in 1990 when he pitched his sixth no-hitter.

Besides the players, managers and um-pires elected to the Hall of Fame, others honored include Morgan Bulkeley, first president of the National League; Henry Chadwick, an early baseball writer credited with inventing the box score; commission-ers Kenesaw Mountain Landis and Ford Frick; and Alexander Cartwright, whom many historians recognize as the true founder of baseball rather than Doubleday.

HENDERSON, RICKEY. His hands hanging by his sides, his eyes narrow slits focused on the mound, his leg muscles taut and set to send him hurtling toward second, Rickey Henderson is the picture of the master base-stealer, the ultimate nightmare for every pitcher.

Henderson, born on Christmas Day, 1958, in Chicago, could have played any sport with his unique blend of strength and speed. Through 1990 this remarkable left fielder for the Oakland A's (1979–84, 1989–90) and New York Yankees (1985–89) has led the American League in steals 10 times. His 936 steals in 12 seasons left him in need of only three more to pass all-time king Lou Brock's total of 938. In 1982 Henderson thrilled the baseball world by stealing 130 bases in a season to break Brock's all-time single-season mark of 118.

Stolen bases are just part of Henderson's value. He has unusual power for a leadoff

Rickey Henderson, the American League's MVP in 1990, is off and running for another stolen base.

man (28 homers in 1986), and his .293 career average combined with the patience to draw a walk have enabled this nine-time All-Star to score 100-plus runs in a season nine times, including 146 as a Yankee in 1985.

After returning to Oakland in a midseason trade in 1989, Henderson sparked the Athletics in the fall. He was the MVP of the AL playoffs against Toronto, and he was a prime force behind the World Series sweep of the Giants. In 1990 he hit a career-high .325, second only to George Brett's .329, and was voted the AL's MVP.

HERNANDEZ, KEITH. His true impact goes beyond a knack for collecting clutch hits and turning brilliant plays at first base. His enormous pride, his unique intensity and his ability to lead were the vital intangibles Keith Hernandez contributed to world-championship teams in two cities.

Born on October 20, 1953, in San Francisco and tutored by his dad, John, a former minor-league first baseman, Keith began his pro career with much to prove. After being thrown off his high school team for disciplinary reasons, he was passed over until the 40th round of the 1971 draft.

Before long, however, he distinguished himself in St. Louis with his disciplined approach to hitting and remarkable fielding instincts.

Hernandez introduced aggressiveness to the art of playing first base, fearlessly charging bunts and ranging far from the bag to field grounders. He won a record 12 straight Gold Gloves, beginning in 1977, before injuries ended his streak in 1989.

Keith's greatest offensive season came in 1979, when he shared National League MVP honors with the Pirates' Willie Stargell, hitting .344 with a career-high 105 RBIs and 116 runs scored. He batted .299 and had 94 RBIs on the way to the

First with the Cardinals, then with the Mets, Keith Hernandez fielded and hit with the best.

Cards' winning a world championship in 1982. A year later he was traded to the New York Mets, and then came the low point in his career when he was called as a witness at baseball's drug trials in Pittsburgh and admitted having used drugs. But Met fans cheered him for his candor, and he helped their young team win the world championship in 1986.

Nicknamed "Mex" in recognition of his Spanish bloodline, he played briefly with the Indians in 1990 and has a career mark of .296. Whatever his average, the bottom line with Hernandez has always been the same: he's a winner.

HERSHISER, OREL. This slender right-hander with the choirboy smile who is

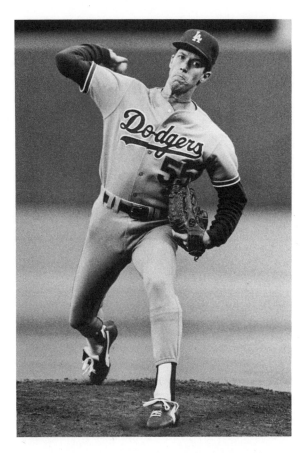

Orel Hershiser's pitching brought him a Cy Young Award, and the Dodgers a world championship.

pitched 10 shutout innings to push his personal scoreless streak to 59 innings, shattering the major-league record held by Don Drysdale. He closed the season with five straight shutouts and a league-leading total of eight.

Nicknamed "Bulldog" by manager Tommy Lasorda because of his competitive nature, Hershiser posted a 19-3 record with a 2.03 ERA in 1985. However, his excellence through his first six full seasons in Los Angeles was rarely reflected in his record. Frequently victimized by poor defense and meager run support, Hershiser had only 98 career victories to go with an impressive 2.69 career ERA through 1989. Then disaster struck. Hershiser hurt his shoulder early in 1990, was operated on and missed the entire season.

HIT. A hit, safety, safe blow, bingle or base knock is a batted ball on which the

known for singing hymns on the mound saw his prayers answered in 1988, when he led the crippled, underdog Los Angeles Dodgers to a world championship.

Hershiser was named MVP of the National League Championship Series after he shut out the New York Mets in Game 7 to cap a two-win, one-save performance. For an encore, he beat the Oakland A's twice in the World Series, collected three hits in one game and was again named MVP.

Even before the postseason, he put his stamp on the 1988 season. Hershiser, born on September 16, 1958, in Buffalo, New York, finished with a 23-8 record and a 2.26 ERA en route to the Cy Young Award. His greatest achievement that year came in San Diego on September 28, when he

Until Pete Rose surpassed him, nobody had come close to the 4,191 career hits by Ty Cobb.

Pete Rose swings for No. 4,192. His record-breaking hit came against San Diego's Eric Show on September 11, 1985, at Cincinnati's Riverfront Stadium. Catcher Bruce Bochy and umpire Lee Weyer watch.

the stands, but the scorer may well have been right in deciding that the batter would have beaten it out even if the ball had been fielded cleanly.

Pete Rose is baseball's all-time hit producer, having smacked out 4,256 in his 24-year National League career. Ty Cobb holds the American League record with 4,191 hits. George Sisler made the most hits in one season, 257 for the St. Louis Browns in 1920—three more than Lefty O'Doul made for the Philadelphia Phillies in 1929 and Bill Terry for the New York Giants a year later. O'Doul and Terry share the National League record.

Many players have had six hits in one game, but Rennie Stennett of Pittsburgh had seven hits in a nine-inning game in 1975, and John Burnett of the Cleveland Indians had nine hits in an 18-inning game in 1932.

The standard of excellence is 200 hits in a season, and Pete Rose did it 10 times, a record. He is one of only 16 players to make more than 3,000 hits in a career.

The team record for hits in a season is 1,783 by the Philadelphia Phillies in 1930. The New York Giants made 31 hits in a game in 1901, and the Boston Red Sox made 14 hits in one inning in 1953.

batter reaches base without benefit of an error, fielder's choice, interference or the retirement of a preceding runner. A one-base hit is a single, a two-base hit is a double, a three-base hit is a triple and a four-base hit is a home run.

The official scorer decides whether or not a hit has been made. Most hits are obvious and some are automatic, such as when a batted ball strikes an umpire or a runner before touching a fielder, but there are close decisions in almost every game.

To the casual fan, many a hit looks like an error. But the scorer must allow for such things as freak hops or drives that are smashed too hard for the fielder to handle smoothly. Often, when a slow ground ball is bobbled, it will still be scored as a hit. Usually this brings a hoot from

HIT-AND-RUN. A prearranged play in which the runner on first starts for second as the ball is pitched and the batter swings. Ideally, the batter pokes a hit through the spot left empty by the infielder who is drawn away to cover second. It is rare for the hit-and-run to be executed successfully, although it used to be practiced with particular success by Maury Wills and Jim Gilliam of the Los Angeles Dodgers. The hit-and-run can still be an effective weapon in avoiding double plays even if the batter does not achieve the desired result. The run-and-hit differs slightly from the hit-

and-run in that the batter is not committed to hit the ball in the run-and-hit unless the pitch is to his liking.

HIT BATTER or HIT BY PITCH.   A batter hit by a pitched ball is entitled to first base, a rule that goes back to 1884, when a Cincinnati pitcher named Will White made a fetish of hitting batters in order to keep them at a respectable distance from the plate.

HITCH.   A flaw in a batter's swing, considered undesirable because it goes against the theory that a batter must have a smooth swing to be effective. Many hitters have been successful even with a hitch.

HOLDOUT.   A player who delays signing his contract to bargain for more money. The most celebrated baseball holdout was Edd Roush, the old Cincinnati Red and New York Giant outfielder. In 1929 Roush hit .324 for the Giants in the last year of a three-year contract calling for $21,500 a year. Roush expected a raise, but when the Giants sent him his 1930 contract, it called for a cut. Roush and the Giants entered into a bitter dispute, with neither backing down. As a result, Roush sat out the entire 1930 season.

In 1919 Zack Wheat, a Brooklyn Dodger outfielder, was unhappy with his contract. A war of nerves resulted between Wheat and Dodger owner Charley Ebbets. It was settled when Abe Yaeger, sports editor of the Brooklyn *Eagle,* sent the following wire to Wheat from the Dodgers' spring-training headquarters: "Report immediately." It was signed "Charley Ebbets." When Wheat reported, he had a good laugh with Ebbets over the joke. He then signed his contract.

Babe Ruth frequently held out. He once insisted on a raise over his previous year's salary of $50,000. Colonel Jake Ruppert, the Yankee owner, thought $50,000 was plenty. The Babe settled for $50,001.

Thanks to Babe's insistence on value for value, ballplayers' salaries in general were raised. In 1965 Willie Mays of the San Francisco Giants signed for the then highest salary of all time, $105,000, joining Joe DiMaggio, Stan Musial, Ted Williams and Mickey Mantle in the $100,000-a-year bracket. Since then salaries have soared to the extent that some players are earning more than $3 million a year.

HOME RUN.   A four-base hit, also known as a homer; round-tripper; four-bagger; four-ply swat, blow or wallop; circuit blow or circuit clout. The ball is usually driven

Babe Ruth hit 60 home runs in 1927, and a total of 714 in his career.

Home-Run Leaders

NATIONAL LEAGUE

Year	Player, Club	HRs	Year	Player, Club	HRs
1900	Herman Long, Boston Beaneaters	12	1944	Bill Nicholson, Chicago Cubs	33
1901	Sam Crawford, Cincinnati Reds	16	1945	Tommy Holmes, Boston Braves	28
1902	Tom Leach, Pittsburgh Pirates	6	1946	Ralph Kiner, Pittsburgh Pirates	23
1903	Jim Sheckard, Brooklyn Dodgers	9	1947	Ralph Kiner, Pittsburgh Pirates	51
1904	Harry Lumley, Brooklyn Dodgers	9		Johnny Mize, New York Giants	51
1905	Fred Odwell, Cincinnati Reds	9	1948	Ralph Kiner, Pittsburgh Pirates	40
1906	Tim Jordan, Brooklyn Dodgers	12		Johnny Mize, New York Giants	40
1907	Dave Brain, Boston Doves	10	1949	Ralph Kiner, Pittsburgh Pirates	54
1908	Tim Jordan, Brooklyn Dodgers	12	1950	Ralph Kiner, Pittsburgh Pirates	47
1909	Jim Murray, New York Giants	7	1951	Ralph Kiner, Pittsburgh Pirates	42
1910	Fred Beck, Boston Doves	10	1952	Ralph Kiner, Pittsburgh Pirates	37
	Frank Schulte, Chicago Cubs	10		Hank Sauer, Chicago Cubs	37
1911	Frank Schulte, Chicago Cubs	21	1953	Eddie Mathews, Milwaukee Braves	47
1912	Heinie Zimmerman, Chicago Cubs	14	1954	Ted Kluszewski, Cincinnati Reds	49
1913	Gavvy Cravath, Philadelphia Phillies	19	1955	Willie Mays, New York Giants	51
1914	Gavvy Cravath, Philadelphia Phillies	19	1956	Duke Snider, Brooklyn Dodgers	43
1915	Gavvy Cravath, Philadelphia Phillies	24	1957	Hank Aaron, Milwaukee Braves	44
1916	Dave Robertson, New York Giants	12	1958	Ernie Banks, Chicago Cubs	47
	Cy Williams, Chicago Cubs	12	1959	Eddie Mathews, Milwaukee Braves	46
1917	Gavvy Cravath, Philadelphia Phillies	12	1960	Ernie Banks, Chicago Cubs	41
	Dave Robertson, New York Giants	12	1961	Orlando Cepeda, San Francisco Giants	46
1918	Gavvy Cravath, Philadelphia Phillies	8	1962	Willie Mays, San Francisco Giants	49
1919	Gavvy Cravath, Philadelphia Phillies	12	1963	Hank Aaron, Milwaukee Braves	44
1920	Cy Williams, Philadelphia Phillies	15		Willie McCovey, San Francisco Giants	44
1921	George Kelly, New York Giants	23	1964	Willie Mays, San Francisco Giants	47
1922	Rogers Hornsby, St. Louis Cardinals	39	1965	Willie Mays, San Francisco Giants	52
1923	Cy Williams, Philadelphia Phillies	41	1966	Hank Aaron, Atlanta Braves	44
1924	Jack Fournier, Brooklyn Dodgers	27	1967	Hank Aaron, Atlanta Braves	39
1925	Rogers Hornsby, St. Louis Cardinals	39	1968	Willie McCovey, San Francisco Giants	36
1926	Hack Wilson, Chicago Cubs	21	1969	Willie McCovey, San Francisco Giants	45
1927	Cy Williams, Philadelphia Phillies	30	1970	Johnny Bench, Cincinnati Reds	45
	Hack Wilson, Chicago Cubs	30	1971	Willie Stargell, Pittsburgh Pirates	48
1928	Jim Bottomley, St. Louis Cardinals	31	1972	Johnny Bench, Cincinnati Reds	40
	Hack Wilson, Chicago Cubs	31	1973	Willie Stargell, Pittsburgh Pirates	44
1929	Chuck Klein, Philadelphia Phillies	43	1974	Mike Schmidt, Philadelphia Phillies	36
1930	Hack Wilson, Chicago Cubs	56	1975	Mike Schmidt, Philadelphia Phillies	38
1931	Chuck Klein, Philadelphia Phillies	31	1976	Mike Schmidt, Philadelphia Phillies	38
1932	Chuck Klein, Philadelphia Phillies	38	1977	George Foster, Cincinnati Reds	52
	Mel Ott, New York Giants	38	1978	George Foster, Cincinnati Reds	40
1933	Chuck Klein, Philadelphia Phillies	43	1979	Dave Kingman, Chicago Cubs	48
1934	Rip Collins, St. Louis Cardinals	35	1980	Mike Schmidt, Philadelphia Phillies	48
	Mel Ott, New York Giants	35	1981	Mike Schmidt, Philadelphia Phillies	31
1935	Wally Berger, Boston Braves	34	1982	Dave Kingman, New York Mets	37
1936	Mel Ott, New York Giants	33	1983	Mike Schmidt, Philadelphia Phillies	40
1937	Joe Medwick, St. Louis Cardinals	31	1984	Dale Murphy, Atlanta Braves	36
	Mel Ott, New York Giants	31		Mike Schmidt, Philadelphia Phillies	36
1938	Mel Ott, New York Giants	36	1985	Dale Murphy, Atlanta Braves	37
1939	Johnny Mize, St. Louis Cardinals	28	1986	Mike Schmidt, Philadelphia Phillies	37
1940	Johnny Mize, St. Louis Cardinals	43	1987	Andre Dawson, Chicago Cubs	49
1941	Dolph Camilli, Brooklyn Dodgers	34	1988	Darryl Strawberry, New York Mets	39
1942	Mel Ott, New York Giants	30	1989	Kevin Mitchell, San Francisco Giants	47
1943	Bill Nicholson, Chicago Cubs	29	1990	Ryne Sandberg, Chicago Cubs	40

Home-Run Leaders

AMERICAN LEAGUE

Year	Player, Club	HRs	Year	Player, Club	HRs
1901	Napoleon Lajoie, Philadelphia Athletics	13	1949	Ted Williams, Boston Red Sox	43
1902	Ralph Seybold, Philadelphia Athletics	16	1950	Al Rosen, Cleveland Indians	37
1903	John Freeman, Boston Red Sox	13	1951	Gus Zernial, Philadelphia Athletics	33
1904	Harry Davis, Philadelphia Athletics	10	1952	Larry Doby, Cleveland Indians	32
1905	Harry Davis, Philadelphia Athletics	8	1953	Al Rosen, Cleveland Indians	43
1906	Harry Davis, Philadelphia Athletics	12	1954	Larry Doby, Cleveland Indians	32
1907	Harry Davis, Philadelphia Athletics	8	1955	Mickey Mantle, New York Yankees	37
1908	Sam Crawford, Detroit Tigers	7	1956	Mickey Mantle, New York Yankees	52
1909	Ty Cobb, Detroit Tigers	9	1957	Roy Sievers, Washington Senators	42
1910	Jake Stahl, Boston Red Sox	10	1958	Mickey Mantle, New York Yankees	42
1911	Home Run Baker, Philadelphia Athletics	9	1959	Rocky Colavito, Cleveland Indians	42
1912	Home Run Baker, Philadelphia Athletics	10		Harmon Killebrew, Washington Senators	42
1913	Home Run Baker, Philadelphia Athletics	12			
1914	Home Run Baker, Philadelphia Athletics	8	1960	Mickey Mantle, New York Yankees	40
	Sam Crawford, Detroit Tigers	8	1961	Roger Maris, New York Yankees	61
1915	Bob Roth, Cleveland Indians	7	1962	Harmon Killebrew, Minnesota Twins	48
1916	Wally Pipp, New York Yankees	12	1963	Harmon Killebrew, Minnesota Twins	45
1917	Wally Pipp, New York Yankees	9	1964	Harmon Killebrew, Minnesota Twins	49
1918	Babe Ruth, Boston Red Sox	11	1965	Tony Conigliaro, Boston Red Sox	32
	Clarence Walker, Philadelphia Athletics	11	1966	Frank Robinson, Baltimore Orioles	49
1919	Babe Ruth, Boston Red Sox	29	1967	Carl Yastrzemski, Boston Red Sox	44
1920	Babe Ruth, New York Yankees	54		Harmon Killebrew, Minnesota Twins	44
1921	Babe Ruth, New York Yankees	59	1968	Frank Howard, Washington Senators	44
1922	Ken Williams, St. Louis Browns	39	1969	Harmon Killebrew, Minnesota Twins	49
1923	Babe Ruth, New York Yankees	43	1970	Frank Howard, Washington Senators	44
1924	Babe Ruth, New York Yankees	46	1971	Bill Melton, Chicago White Sox	33
1925	Bob Meusel, New York Yankees	33	1972	Dick Allen, Chicago White Sox	37
1926	Babe Ruth, New York Yankees	47	1973	Reggie Jackson, Oakland A's	32
1927	Babe Ruth, New York Yankees	60	1974	Dick Allen, Chicago White Sox	32
1928	Babe Ruth, New York Yankees	54	1975	George Scott, Milwaukee Brewers	36
1929	Babe Ruth, New York Yankees	46		Reggie Jackson, Oakland A's	36
1930	Babe Ruth, New York Yankees	49	1976	Graig Nettles, New York Yankees	32
1931	Babe Ruth, New York Yankees	46	1977	Jim Rice, Boston Red Sox	39
	Lou Gehrig, New York Yankees	46	1978	Jim Rice, Boston Red Sox	46
1932	Jimmie Foxx, Philadelphia Athletics	58	1979	Gorman Thomas, Milwaukee Brewers	45
1933	Jimmie Foxx, Philadelphia Athletics	48	1980	Ben Oglivie, Milwaukee Brewers	41
1934	Lou Gehrig, New York Yankees	49		Reggie Jackson, New York Yankees	41
1935	Hank Greenberg, Detroit Tigers	36	1981	Eddie Murray, Baltimore Orioles	22
	Jimmie Foxx, Philadelphia Athletics	36		Tony Armas, Oakland A's	22
1936	Lou Gehrig, New York Yankees	49		Dwight Evans, Boston Red Sox	22
1937	Joe DiMaggio, New York Yankees	49		Bobby Grich, California Angels	22
1938	Hank Greenberg, Detroit Tigers	46	1982	Reggie Jackson, California Angels	39
1939	Jimmie Foxx, Boston Red Sox	35		Gorman Thomas, Milwaukee Brewers	39
1940	Hank Greenberg, Detroit Tigers	41	1983	Jim Rice, Boston Red Sox	39
1941	Ted Williams, Boston Red Sox	37	1984	Tony Armas, Boston Red Sox	43
1942	Ted Williams, Boston Red Sox	36	1985	Darrell Evans, Detroit Tigers	40
1943	Rudy York, Detroit Tigers	34	1986	Jesse Barfield, Toronto Blue Jays	40
1944	Nick Etten, New York Yankees	22	1987	Mark McGwire, Oakland A's	49
1945	Vern Stephens, St. Louis Browns	24	1988	Jose Canseco, Oakland A's	42
1946	Hank Greenberg, Detroit Tigers	44	1989	Fred McGriff, Toronto Blue Jays	36
1947	Ted Williams, Boston Red Sox	32	1990	Cecil Fielder, Detroit Tigers	51
1948	Joe DiMaggio, New York Yankees	39			

Roger Maris's 61 homers in 1961 sparked a controversy.

out of the playing field, but a ball hit within the park that allows the batter to circle the bases also counts as a home run. When a batter hits one out of the park, it's an automatic home run, but he must touch all the bases on his way back to home plate. If nobody is on base, it counts for one run. If one man is on base, it counts for two runs. And so on.

Babe Ruth set the big-league standard of 60 home runs in one season (1927) and 714 for a career, records that lasted for years and were believed unbreakable.

But in 1961 Roger Maris of the New York Yankees hit 61 home runs and set up a storm of controversy. First, it was said that Maris hit his home runs during the era of the lively ball (when the ball was thought to be made of different materials that would make it travel farther). Second, it was pointed out that he hit his home runs during a 162-game schedule, while Ruth had hit his during a 154-game schedule (Maris had 59 home runs after 154 games). Commissioner Ford Frick decreed that Maris's record would stand, but with an asterisk noting the 162-game schedule, and that there would be *two* records—Ruth's for 154 games and Maris's for 162 games.

Ruth's career mark of 714 home runs lasted until April 8, 1974, when Hank Aaron hit number 715 for the Atlanta Braves against Al Downing and the Los Angeles Dodgers. Again, defenders of Ruth as the game's greatest slugger came forward to point out that Babe's 714 home runs came in 8,399 at-bats, while Aaron had been to bat more than 11,000 times.

Ballplayers have other expressions for a home run. They say a batter hit one "downtown" or "went for the pump." Homers are also known as "dingers" or "taters" and, in a tribute to hotel telephone systems, "Dial Eight"—for long distance. Casey Stengel liked to say that a batter "hit one over a building."

HOME TEAM. The team on whose grounds the game is played. By tradition the home team bats last, which is considered to be an advantage.

HOOK. Another name for a curveball. Also used to describe what a manager does to a pitcher in trouble: he comes out and gives him the hook.

HOP. A sudden rise taken by a pitch, usually a fastball. Also, the bounce of the ball. A grounder takes a bad hop when the infielder doesn't catch it, or a good one when he does.

HORNSBY, ROGERS. There's plenty of room for argument over who is baseball's greatest player ever, but there's little doubt that from 1920 to 1925 the game's greatest hitter was Rogers Hornsby, the St. Louis Cardinal second baseman.

Hornsby, born on April 27, 1896, in Winters, Texas, won six National League batting titles over that six-year period, hitting .370, .397, .401, .384, .424 and .403. He also won the batting title in 1928 when he hit .387 with the Boston Braves.

The Rajah (a play on "Roger") played for five teams—the Cardinals, Giants, Cubs, Braves and Browns—and managed five, including the 1926 National League champion St. Louis Cardinals, whom he led as player-manager to the world championship. His .358 lifetime average is second only to Ty Cobb's, and he hit 301 homers. Elected to the Hall of Fame in 1942, Hornsby died in 1963.

HOT CORNER. Third base, so called because of the hot shots hit at the third baseman. Third base is also called the far turn or far corner.

HOT DOG. Not only the kind you put mustard on, but also a player who, the opposition believes, is showing off for the fans or the television camera. A leading hot dog was Reggie Jackson, and going back a few years there was none like Vic Power, a Fancy Dan first baseman who had the then unusual habit of catching every ball with one hand. Because Power was a Spanish-speaking native of Puerto Rico, hot dog was translated into *perro caliente* for his and his followers' benefit.

HOT-STOVE LEAGUE. Fan-to-fan baseball conversation, discussion or argument during the winter, so called because of the custom of a group of men sitting around a potbellied stove in the local general store to talk baseball.

HOUSTON ASTROS. It was the afternoon of September 25, 1986, and the Houston Astros were within one win of clinching their second National League Western Division title. The Astros felt good about their chances because on the mound for them was Mike Scott, a hard-throwing right-hander who was on his way to winning the Cy Young Award. But while the Astros expected to win, they couldn't have dreamed of winning in this fashion: Scott hurled a no-hitter to clinch the title.

The Astros went on to lose an exciting six-game playoff series to the New York Mets, but in the process they won the hearts of the fans in the Lone Star State. It had been a long struggle.

When Houston joined the league in 1962, the owners were determined the team would be called the Houston Colt .45s—guns, not horses. But everyone called them the Houston Colts—horses, not guns. And in their early years a lot of people called them patsies. The team, like all new teams, didn't win too often.

In 1964 they became the Astros when they moved to baseball's first indoor stadium, the plush Astrodome. By the late 1960s the emergence of stars like Rusty Staub, Larry Dierker and Don Wilson made the Astros respectable. In 1967 the Astros had their first homegrown power hitter in Jimmy Wynn, the Toy Cannon, who blasted 37 homers and knocked in 107 runs that season.

It wasn't until 1979, though, that the Astros started repaying their opponents for all those early-day defeats. Pitcher J. R. Richard, reliever Joe Sambito, outfielders Cesar Cedeno and Jose Cruz and infielder Enos Cabell kept the team in contention right to the wire.

When the team added free-agent right-hander Nolan Ryan in 1980, all the pieces were in place. The Astros won the Western Division title that year but lost to the Philadelphia Phillies in five games in the playoffs.

Game 3 of the 1980 National League Championship Series between Houston and Philadelphia was the first postseason game ever played in the Astrodome.

HUBBELL, CARL. Carl Hubbell had been a starting pitcher for the New York Giants since 1928, pitching a no-hitter in 1929 against the Pirates and an incredible 18-inning, complete-game shutout against the Cardinals in 1933. But he had never had to face the kind of lineup that he was up against as he took the mound to start the 1934 All-Star Game for the National League.

The lineup was awesome, with Babe Ruth, Lou Gehrig, Jimmie Foxx, Al Simmons and Joe Cronin, all future Hall of Famers. But the Carthage, Missouri, native was up to the task, striking out all five in a row in one of baseball's greatest pitching exhibitions ever.

Hubbell, who was known as King Carl and also as the Meal Ticket, wound up with 253 career wins, all with the Giants, including five consecutive seasons of 20 or more victories. His career ERA was 2.97. He was elected to the Hall of Fame in 1947.

INFIELD. The territory that includes the four bases and the area encompassed by them, although there is no strict ruling on where the infield ends and the outfield begins. Sometimes called the diamond even though the infield is actually shaped like a square. The infield is also the all-inclusive term for the four infielders—the first baseman, second baseman, third baseman and shortstop.

INFIELDER. One who plays a defensive position in the infield. The first baseman, second baseman, third baseman and shortstop are generally thought of as a team's infielders, although, technically, the pitcher and catcher are also members of the infield.

INFIELD FLY. A fair fly ball (not a line drive or bunt) that can be caught by an infielder with ordinary effort, when first and second bases or first, second and third bases are occupied before there are two outs. The umpire simply says, "Infield fly," and the batter is automatically out whether the ball is caught or not. This is for the protection of the runners, who otherwise could easily be caught in a double, or even triple, play.

INFIELD HIT. A base hit, usually a grounder, that is not hit beyond the infield. Often called a bleeder or scratch hit.

INNING. That part of a game within which the teams alternate on offense and defense and in which there are three putouts for each team. Each team's time at bat is a half-inning, and a regulation game consists of nine full innings, or 8½ innings if the home team is ahead after the visiting team has been at bat nine times. A game will go longer if the score is tied after nine innings.

INTENTIONAL WALK. Deliberate, strategic base on balls. The pitcher throws so wide that the batter has little chance of reaching the pitch. Unpopular with fans, the intentional walk is standard practice in certain situations, most commonly in the late innings of a close game. If second base is occupied and first is not, a dangerous batter may be walked in the hope of setting up a double play or a force play.

An intentional walk is usually a sign of respect for the batter. In 1969 Willie McCovey of the San Francisco Giants received 45 intentional walks. The record for intentional walks in one game is 5, set by the Chicago Cubs' Andre Dawson in 1990. Henry Aaron holds the record for intentional walks in a career with 293.

INTERFERENCE.   The act of obstructing a play. Interference may be caused by the offense (getting in the way of a fielder attempting to make a play), defense (preventing a batter from swinging at a pitched ball), umpire (hindering a catcher's throw or being hit with a batted ball) or spectator (reaching out of the stands to touch a live ball). On any interference the ball is dead, and all runners must return to the last base that was, in the judgment of the umpire, legally touched at the time of interference, unless otherwise provided by the rules.

IN THE HOLE.   A batter is said to be in the hole when he is behind by two strikes in the count. The term also refers to the territory to the shortstop's right or second baseman's left, or any other unguarded territory. If the shortstop or second baseman goes into the hole to field a ground ball and then throws the man out, it's an exceptionally good play.

IRON MAN.   A player who rarely leaves a game, playing despite minor injuries.

Although this pioneer version of Iron Mike occasionally needed some oil, it was one pitcher whose arm never tired—and who never posed a problem in contract negotiations.

Some examples are Iron Man Joe McGinnity, a New York Giant pitcher soon after the turn of the century who often pitched two games in one day, and first baseman Lou Gehrig of the New York Yankees, who played in a record 2,130 games in a row. First baseman Steve Garvey holds the National League Iron Man record, having played in 1,207 games in a row when he was with the Los Angeles Dodgers and San Diego Padres.

In 1990 Cal Ripken of the Baltimore Orioles moved into the second spot on the consecutive-games-played list, passing Everett Scott's total of 1,307. It was the eighth season in the streak for Ripken, who finished the year with 1,311.

IRON MIKE. Automatic pitching device. Such machines have been experimented with since 1896, but they did not come into practical use until Branch Rickey, as president of the Brooklyn Dodgers, used them for batting practice in training camps after World War II. Now Iron Mike has been perfected to such a point that he can deliver just about every kind of pitch except a spitball. He is the coolest pitcher of them all, he does not need three days' rest between starts and he never complains about a sore arm or breaks training.

JACKSON, REGGIE. Reggie Jackson cocked his bat, waiting for the pitch like a coiled snake sizing up its prey. This was the 1977 World Series, and Jackson was turning it into a one-man show. He had already hit four home runs, two of them on consecutive first-pitch swings in the sixth game. Now he was at the plate again and Yankee Stadium was a sea of sound as more than 55,000 fans roared in anticipation.

Sure enough, Jackson swung at the first pitch again, and this time he sent a towering drive into an unoccupied area of the bleachers, his third straight homer and his fifth of the Series, writing his name in the record books—with an exclamation point next to it. The only other man to hit three homers in a single World Series game was the legendary Babe Ruth, who did it against the St. Louis Cardinals in 1926 and again in 1928. But no one—not even Ruth—had ever hit five homers in a single Series.

The power show earned Jackson the 1977 Series MVP award and capped a soap opera season for the slugger, who had signed a $2.9 million free-agent contract with the Yankees in November 1976. Jackson quarreled with manager Billy Martin and some teammates who resented his style. But there could be no quarrel about Jackson's performance on the field.

He retired after the 1987 season with a total of 563 home runs, sixth on the all-time list, and with the reputation as one of the all-time greatest clutch players. He was a member of five world championship teams—three with the Oakland A's and two with the Yankees—and his postseason feats earned him the nickname Mr. October.

Jackson was born on May 18, 1946, in Wyncote, Pennsylvania, and was a four-sport star in high school before moving on to Arizona State. In two years there he broke all of the school's home-run records. Then Jackson signed a bonus contract with Charlie Finley's Oakland A's, starting a

Power hitter Reggie Jackson made for an ongoing soap opera at Yankee Stadium—and for some dramatic home runs, especially in the 1977 World Series.

major-league career that had its peaks and valleys but was never dull.

JAMMED.   A batter says he was jammed when he's been pitched close (the intention being to restrict his swing, not hit him).

JOCKEY.   A player who rides the opposition with taunts. He is often called a

bench jockey because he heckles chiefly from the dugout. It is an art and a vital part of the tradition of the game. The taunts are designed to disturb, upset and break the concentration of a rival player, and they are usually given and taken in good spirit, but occasionally they cause ill feelings. It is legend that in the 1932 World Series the Chicago Cubs so annoyed Babe Ruth with their bench jockeying that in the fifth inning of the third game Ruth deliberately took two strikes from pitcher

Charlie Root, then pointed to the most distant part of Wrigley Field and hit the next pitch right where he had pointed.

Miller, the junk man, is that he had three speeds—slow, slower and slowest.

JOHNSON, WALTER. When Walter Johnson was 14, in 1901, he moved with his family from Humboldt, Kansas, to California, where his father hoped to strike it rich in the oil fields.

No oil came the Johnsons' way, but their son did start playing baseball for oil company teams, where he was discovered by a traveling salesman scouting for the Washington Senators. Things were never the same for the Johnsons.

From 1907 to 1927 Johnson was the Senators' top pitcher. He won 20 or more games a total of 12 times, including an American League–high 36 in 1913. In 21 seasons the Big Train (so called because the speed of his fastball was said to match that of a roaring locomotive) won 416 games, second only to Cy Young. Johnson is seventh on the all-time strikeout list with 3,508. In 1936 he joined Babe Ruth, Honus Wagner, Ty Cobb and Christy Mathewson as the original members of the Hall of Fame. He died in 1946.

JUNK MAN. Term applied, not necessarily with disparagement, to a pitcher who relies on off-speed pitches and tricks instead of a fastball. It was first applied to Ed Lopat of the Yankees and then to Stu Miller of the Baltimore Orioles.

Garry Schumacher, public relations director of the San Francisco Giants, once described Miller's fastball as the Wells Fargo pitch—"It comes to you in easy stages."

Dusty Rhodes of the Giants said of Miller: "He's the only pitcher I ever saw who changes speeds on his changeup."

The most famous remark concerning Stu

KALINE, AL. One of the few major-league players who never played in the minor leagues, Al Kaline was the youngest player ever to win the American League batting title. In 1955, before his 21st birthday, he hit .340 for the Detroit Tigers.

Al Kaline was Mr. Tiger.

Kaline, born in Baltimore on December 19, 1934, missed hitting 400 homers by just one, but reached the coveted 3,000-hit mark before retiring in 1974 after 22 seasons. He was one of baseball's best right fielders, with great speed and an excellent arm.

In 1980 Kaline became only the 10th man in baseball history to win election to the Hall of Fame his first time on the ballot. He has been a broadcaster since retiring.

Bo Jackson leaves his football at home when he goes to bat for Kansas City.

KANSAS CITY ROYALS. The situation certainly looked grim for the Kansas City Royals. They had just given up three runs in the ninth inning to blow a 1–0 lead and fall behind, three games to one, against the Toronto Blue Jays in the 1985 American League playoffs.

But the next day left-hander Danny Jackson shut out the Blue Jays, 2–0. And George Brett's home run put the Royals ahead in a 5–3 victory in Game 6, evening the series. In Game 7, Jim Sundberg's two-run triple propelled the Royals to a 6–2 victory, making them the first team in playoff history to overcome a 3–1 deficit.

Kansas City dropped the first two games to the St. Louis Cardinals in the World Series. No team had ever lost the first two games at home and gone on to win. Then they fell behind three games to one. But the Royals took the final three games to give Kansas City its first world championship.

An expansion team in 1969, the Royals experienced tough times in their first two seasons, losing a total of 190 games. But the development of players like Brett, outfielder Amos Otis and second baseman Frank White made the Royals contenders in the late 1970s. The team won three Western Division titles, only to be eliminated by the Yankees each time. Finally, in 1980, the Royals beat the Yankees in the playoffs before losing to the Philadelphia Phillies in the World Series.

The Royals entered the 1990s with Brett winning his third batting title (1976, 1980 and 1990), Bret Saberhagen coming off a Cy Young Award-winning season (1989, 23-6) and power-hitting outfielder (and Los

Angeles Raider football star) Bo Jackson providing additional excitement.

KEYSTONE. Second base, so called because it is often the scene of the most important action in the infield. The shortstop and second baseman make up the keystone combination.

KILLEBREW, HARMON. Wide-shouldered and strong as a lumberjack, Harmon Killebrew had the facility for clouting baseballs tremendous distances.

A native of Payette, Idaho, where he was born on June 29, 1936, Killebrew was signed by the Washington Senators in 1954, launching a 22-year career in which he would hit 573 home runs, the most ever produced by a right-handed batter in the American League.

Mighty Harmon Killebrew walloped 573 home runs, including 49 in 1964.

On six occasions he either led the league or tied for the league lead in homers, eight times he belted 40 or more and nine times he had more than 100 RBIs.

Initially signed as a second baseman, Harmon played first, third and the outfield for the Senators (who became the Minnesota Twins in 1961), and was a designated hitter for the Kansas City Royals.

He played in 11 All-Star Games and was the American League's Most Valuable Player in 1969. He was inducted into the Hall of Fame in 1984.

KNOTHOLE GANG. In baseball's earliest days, youngsters who couldn't afford a ticket would watch a game by peeping through knotholes in the wooden fences. After World War II some major-league teams, in a promotional effort, organized knothole gangs made up of kids who got in free or received cut-rate tickets.

KNUCKLEBALL. A pitch thrown by gripping the ball with the fingernails, fingertips or knuckles and thrown with little effort. It is used as an off-speed pitch and is usually acted on by air currents or wind, which makes the ball react in a strange manner. The pitcher rarely knows how the ball will break, so it is a difficult ball to catch or to hit. It is also difficult to throw effectively.

The leading pitcher of the knuckleball, butterfly or flutterball was Hoyt Wilhelm, who pitched for nine major-league teams in a 21-year career that produced 143 wins and 227 saves. Other outstanding knuckleball pitchers have been Dutch Leonard, Wilbur Wood and Phil Niekro. But the knuckleball seems to be falling out of fashion. During the 1990 season only two pitchers, Charlie Hough and Tom Candiotti, were throwing it regularly.

his finger limited him to 14–7 the next year, but he led the league with a 2.54 earned run average. Then came 25 victories, 306 strikeouts and a 1.88 ERA in 1963, when he also pitched two of Los Angeles' four World Series victories over the New York Yankees. He followed that with seasons of 19–5, 26–8 and 27–9 as he often bordered on the unhittable.

There were a then record four no-hitters, including a perfect game; five ERA titles in a row; four strikeout crowns, including a record 382 (since broken by Nolan Ryan) in 1965, and three Cy Young awards.

Hampered by an arthritic elbow, Koufax, who was born December 30, 1935, in Brooklyn, New York, retired at age 30, cutting short a brilliant career that sent him to the Hall of Fame in 1971, the youngest man to win that honor.

Phil Niekro grips the knuckleball, a pitch that baffles and bewilders.

KOUFAX, SANDY. The bus ride was one of dozens that teams take in spring training, crisscrossing Florida to play exhibition games. But it was the most significant ride of Sandy Koufax's life.

Koufax was a talented but erratic left-hander for the Los Angeles Dodgers and had struggled through six mostly average seasons. He was depressed and talked over his trouble with reserve catcher Norm Sherry. The solution they hit on was for the pitcher to ease up on the mound, stop trying to overpower every hitter, and to mix curves and changeups with his explosive fastball.

The formula worked immediately, and from 1961 to 1966 Koufax established one of the most remarkable pitching records in baseball history. He led the National League with 269 strikeouts and posted an 18–13 record in 1961. A circulation problem in

LAUGHER. Ballplayers' description of a game in which they have such a commanding lead that they can stop worrying. In their first four years the New York Mets had one laugher—when they had a 19–1 lead over the Cubs with two out in the ninth inning. After that game the sports department of a Connecticut newspaper received a call from a fan:

"Is it true the Mets scored nineteen runs today?" asked the fan.

"Yes," said the newspaperman, "it's true."

"Did they win?" asked the fan.

Sandy Koufax wraps up a perfect game against the Cubs on September 9, 1965. The Dodgers won, 1–0.

LAY ONE DOWN. To bunt.

LEAD-OFF MAN. The first batter in the lineup or in any inning. The lead-off man in the lineup is a very important player because he comes to bat more often than anyone else on the team. Because of that, a lead-off man should be an exceptional judge of a pitch and therefore get many bases on balls, or he should be an exceptional hitter with excellent speed.

LEFT FIELD. The outfield territory beyond third base and extending down that line in fair territory, bordered by the area covered by the center fielder. The outfielder who covers left field is the left fielder.

LEFT-HANDER. Left-handers are known as southpaws or portsiders and, traditionally and affectionately, as eccentrics. This applies only to left-handed throwers, particularly pitchers. There is nothing crazy about left-handed batters. In fact, being able to hit left-handed is something to be desired, even cultivated.

Left-handed hitters have two advantages. First, swinging from the first-base side, they get a head start toward the base and have a better chance of beating out ground balls or double-play relays. Second, the average batter is more effective against a pitcher who throws from his opposite side, giving left-handed swingers another edge, since most pitchers are right-handed.

Many batters, naturally right-handed but bothered by right-handed curveballs, turn left-handed in their youth. This accounts for the fact that while fewer than a fifth of the players who reach the majors are left-handed throwers (and most of these are pitchers), almost a third are left-handed batters.

LINE DRIVE. A hard-hit ball that travels a straight, relatively low course and carries as far as the infielders or farther before bouncing or being caught. Also called a blue dart, screamer, rope or clothesline. A player who hits a line drive is said to have hung out the clothes.

LINEUP. *See* Batting order.

Chris Drury of Trumbull, Connecticut, celebrates after pitching his team to the Little League championship in 1989.

LITTLE LEAGUE. In 1939 in the city of Williamsport, Pennsylvania, Carl E. Stotz started the first Little League, made up of three teams of neighborhood boys. Its purpose was to provide summer activity. The following year there were four teams in the league, and soon the idea of a Little League began to spread and grow by leaps and bounds.

By 1990 the Little League included 2.5 million boys and girls on 150,000 teams in 39 countries. Girls have been playing Little League hardball against boys since 1974. The greatest number, however, are competing in the Little League's softball program. Little League has also instituted a Little League Challenge Division for disabled children.

Each season culminates with the Little League World Series in Williamsport, which is official Little League headquarters. Little League has its own rules and regulations, the most basic of which is that no youngster is eligible to compete if he or she will be 13 years old before August 1 of that year.

Since 1967 the Little League World Series has been dominated by teams from Asia, particularly Taiwan. When Trumbull, Connecticut, won the 1989 Series, it marked only the fourth time in 22 years that a United States team had taken home the championship trophy.

LIVELY BALL. *See Ball.*

LOCKOUT. In baseball or any other business a lockout occurs when the employer bars the doors to employees, usually in the hope of getting the employees to agree to the terms of a new contract. Baseball had its first lockout in 1976, and it was ended by Commissioner Bowie Kuhn in mid-March despite the lack of an agreement. In 1990 there was a 32-day lockout at spring training that was resolved when the owners and the players' union settled on a new contract. (See Strike and Major League Baseball Players Association.)

LONG BALL. A ball that is batted deep to the outfield or out of the playing area. A long-ball hitter is a home-run hitter.

LONG MAN. A relief pitcher who comes in early in the game and is expected to pitch five or six innings.

LONG STRIKE. Television commentators' vernacular for a batted ball that travels a long distance but is foul. Also called a loud foul.

LOS ANGELES DODGERS. It was October 6, 1963, and the Dodgers were on the verge of getting revenge. They had

When the Brooklyn Dodgers moved to Los Angeles, their new audience included stars from Hollywood. Actor Walter Matthau *(center),* who coached the Bad News Bears in the movie of that name, and comedian Jerry Lewis *(right)* share a laugh with first baseman Steve Garvey.

taken the first three games of the World Series from their arch-rivals, the Yankees, and were leading the fourth game, 2–1, in the ninth inning.

Seven times previously the Dodgers had won the National League pennant and played the Yankees in the Series; six of those seven times the Dodgers had failed to win the championship. Their only success against the Yankees had come way back in 1955, when the team was based in Ebbets Field in Brooklyn. But in the 1963 Series, Hector Lopez's ground ball became an easy third out for Maury Wills, and the Dodgers had their revenge, a sweep of the hated Yankees. The championship in Los Angeles was celebrated in Brooklyn, too.

The Dodgers' early days in Brooklyn were filled with comedy and failure, although the team did win pennants in 1900, 1916, 1920 and 1941. Crazy things happened in Brooklyn: Casey Stengel, as a

They were the Boys of Summer, Brooklyn's Dodgers in the 1950s: *(left to right)* Duke Snider, Gil Hodges, Jackie Robinson, Pee Wee Reese and Roy Campanella.

Pirate playing at Ebbets Field, tipped his hat and a bird flew out; pitcher Billy Loes lost a ground ball in the sun; the Dodgers blew a 13½-game lead in August.

But the team became a powerhouse in the 1950s under Branch Rickey, who in 1946 had signed Jackie Robinson, the first black in major-league baseball. With such stars as Robinson, Pee Wee Reese, Gil Hodges, Duke Snider, Roy Campanella, Carl Furillo, Don Newcombe and Preacher Roe, the Dodgers won six pennants between 1947 and 1956.

Although their address changed to Los Angeles in 1958, their taste for winning remained the same—they won the 1959

world championship. After winning three pennants in a four-year span, from 1963 to 1966 (with Sandy Koufax and Don Drysdale the stars), the Dodgers hit a drought until 1974, when they started a streak of three pennants in five years. The Dodgers of the 1970s (Steve Garvey, Ron Cey, Don Sutton) carried on a tradition that had its roots on another shore. It was a tradition of winning.

The Dodgers maintained that tradition in the 1980s. They lost the first two games of the 1981 World Series against the Yankees before battling back to sweep the next four games and take the world championship with a team led by Cy Young Award winner Fernando Valenzuela and first baseman Steve Garvey.

Then, in 1988, they won the Western Division title but were underdogs against the New York Mets in the playoffs. That meant little to the Dodgers, who defeated the Mets in seven games and then, sparked by a dramatic ninth-inning home run by Kirk Gibson in Game 1, went on to stun the Oakland Athletics and win the World Series in five games.

Gibson was the National League MVP and Orel Hershiser, winner of two games in the World Series, took the Cy Young Award and was MVP of both the playoffs and the Series.

LOSING PITCHER. The pitcher charged by the official scorer as being the loser of the game. Often referred to simply as the loser. A pitcher is called the loser if he leaves the game with his team trailing and if his team never ties the score.

LOWER HALF. The last half of an inning.

MAGIC NUMBER. Near the end of the season, newspapers begin printing the magic number—that is, the number of games the leading team must win or how many games any other team must lose for the leader to clinch the division title. Get-

ting smaller as the victories and defeats add up, the magic number dramatizes the approaching end of the race.

To determine a magic number, start with two teams: Team A has won the most games so far and Team B is any other team. Add the number of games that Team B has won to the number of games it still has to play. From that amount subtract the number of games that Team A has won. Add 1 to that number and you have the magic number, the number that will eliminate Team B.

For example, assume the Minnesota Twins have won 93 and lost 59. The Chicago White Sox have won 89 and lost 63. The schedule consists of 162 games, leaving both teams with 10 games to play. Add the number of White Sox victories (89) to their games remaining (10). Subtract the number of Minnesota victories (93), then add 1. The result is 7, the magic number. Thus, as long as the Twins win seven more games, or the White Sox lose seven more games—or any combination of Twin victories and White Sox defeats totaling seven—the Twins will beat out the White Sox in the division race.

Stated more simply, the idea is to see how many victories the trailing team would have if it won all its remaining games, and how many victories the leading team would need to top that. In this example the White Sox could win 99 games at most. The Twins, having won 93, would need 7 victories to top 99.

MAJOR LEAGUE BASEBALL PLAYERS ASSOCIATION. The union (also called MLBPA) of big-league ballplayers. On their behalf it has won several important rulings, including the ending of the reserve clause, which bound a player to the team that owned his contract and prevented him from having a say in any trade. This

1973 landmark case, involving pitchers Andy Messersmith and Dave McNally, ushered in the era of the millionaire free agent.

The MLBPA also won the right to salary arbitration. All players with three years' experience have the right to seek arbitration from an impartial person when the player and his team can't agree on salary. In addition, 17 percent of the players with two to three years' service are eligible for arbitration.

Strikes called by the union in 1972, 1980, 1981 and 1985, and the owners' lockout in 1990, resulted in the players achieving many of the gains that had been sought by the union. Any player with six years of major-league experience can now file for free agency, and any club can bid for him. Under the 1990 contract the minimum salary is $100,000. (*See also* Free agent, Lockout and Strike.)

MAJOR LEAGUES. The term applies to the American and National leagues combined. Often called the big leagues or simply the bigs or the majors.

MANAGER. The field director of a team, usually not a player, although there have been player-managers, particularly in the minor leagues. The manager makes all the important decisions, from picking the starting lineup to deciding strategy—bunt? steal? pinch-hit? replace the pitcher? He also keeps in close touch with the head of the team's farm system so that a player doing well in the minors can be tapped to fill in as needed. Players traditionally call the manager Skipper or Skip to his face and the Old Man or worse behind his back. In print the manager may be the pilot, boss, boss man or the fearless, peerless or cheerless leader.

MANTLE, MICKEY. Mickey Mantle brought the bat forward. The crunch of the ball against it had that true, deep sound that told everyone who heard it to watch this one.

It was April 17, 1953, and Mantle was starting his third season with the New York Yankees. Chuck Stobbs was Washington's pitcher, and Mantle connected against him in old Griffith Stadium. The ball soared high and far, but it was no ordinary home run. An enterprising Yankee employee whipped out a tape measure, tracked the ball down and dutifully reported that Mantle's shot had traveled 565 feet. It was baseball's first tape-measure homer, and it was not Mantle's last.

One of the game's most feared power hitters during the 1950s and 1960s, Mantle threatened to hit the ball out of the park every time he came to bat.

Mantle was born on October 20, 1931, in Spavinaw, Oklahoma, and was not yet 20 years old when he started in right field, next to the immortal Joe DiMaggio, in the 1951 World Series. A year later he took DiMaggio's place as the Yankee center fielder.

A three-time MVP, Mantle won the Triple Crown in 1956 when he batted .353, with 52 homers and 130 RBIs—the best in his league in all three categories. He finished his career with 536 homers, 1,509 RBIs and a ticket to the Hall of Fame.

MARIS, ROGER. He later remembered the day in a way that nobody else could. It was October 1, 1961, and the pressure on Roger Maris was unbearable. The New York Yankee outfielder swung at a pitch thrown by Tracy Stallard of the Boston Red Sox. It landed in the right-field seats at Yankee Stadium, and it landed Maris in the record book. It was the home run (No. 61) that broke Babe Ruth's mark for

Mickey Mantle homers to win Game 3 of the 1964 World Series against the Cardinals, one of a record 18 home runs he hit in the 12 World Series that he played in between 1951 and 1964.

a single season, which had stood since 1927. (*See* Home run.)

Maris's 12-year career in the majors took him from Cleveland and Kansas City to New York before he finished with St. Louis. But for the baseball world, the only year that mattered was the one in which he chased and passed the Babe.

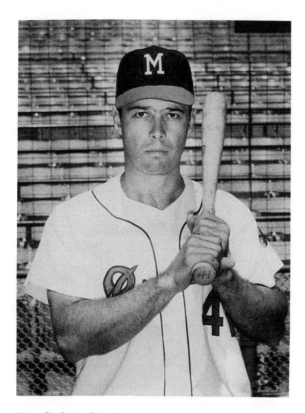

A total of 512 home runs propelled Eddie Mathews into the Hall of Fame.

MATHEWS, EDDIE. They played baseball, not polo, at New York's Polo Grounds, home of the New York Giants. And on September 27, 1952, Eddie Mathews came to town with the Boston Braves for a game against the Giants.

He was 21 years old, a rookie third baseman. Once, twice, three times he hit a home run that afternoon, the first rookie ever to do so.

The home run would be a trademark throughout Mathews's 17-year career. He hit 30 or more nine years in a row and wound up with a career total of 512, tied with Ernie Banks for 12th on the all-time list.

Mathews, born on October 13, 1931, in Texarkana, Texas, was an All-Star 12 times and played on two Milwaukee Braves pennant-winning teams. He was the only player ever to play for one team in three different home cities—the Boston, Milwaukee and Atlanta Braves. He finished with the 1968 world champion Detroit Tigers and made it to the Hall of Fame in 1978, after a brief stint as the Braves' manager.

MATHEWSON, CHRISTY. Winning 30 games in a season is an accomplishment only a handful of major-league pitchers have achieved even once in their careers. Yet in the 17 seasons Christy Mathewson hurled for the New York Giants, the right-hander known as Big Six (because he was six feet tall) topped the magic 30 mark four times, including 1908, when he won a modern National League record 37 games.

Born on August 12, 1880, in Factoryville, Pennsylvania, Mathewson began his major-league career with the New York Giants in 1900. By the time he retired in 1916, he'd won 373 games and had 12 seasons in a row of winning 20 games or more.

He also helped change baseball's image. At the turn of the century, baseball players were largely viewed as crude, uneducated men, unfit to be seen in the company of proper folks. Mathewson was different. He came from a fashionable family and had been president of his class at Bucknell University. He gave the profession of baseball a touch of class.

Mathewson entered the army at the age of 38 in 1918, and in World War I inhaled poisonous gas, which led to his death in 1925. Eleven years later he joined Ty Cobb, Babe Ruth, Honus Wagner and Walter Johnson in the first group elected to the Hall of Fame.

MATTINGLY, DON. It was July 18, 1987, and the Yankees were in Arlington, Texas. In the fourth inning, as Don Mattingly stepped into the box against the Rangers'

At bat or in the field, Don Mattingly has made his mark as one of the all-time Yankee greats.

hit .324, with 35 homers and 145 RBIs. In 1986, he set Yankee marks for hits with 238 and doubles with 53.

In 1987, in addition to equaling Long's record, he set a major-league record with six grand slams. A six-time All-Star, he has driven in 100-plus runs five times and has also been outstanding defensively, winning five straight Gold Gloves from 1985 to 1989.

Through a forgettable period in Yanks history, Mattingly has endured as a symbol of determination, dedication and dignity.

MAYS, WILLIE. The center fielder took off with the crack of the bat, turning his back on home plate and running straight toward the bleachers—the deepest part of an oval-shaped ballpark called the Polo Grounds. This was the opening game of the 1954 World Series, and Willie Mays, playing center field for the New York Giants against the Cleveland Indians, was about to write a memorable chapter of Series history.

With the score tied at 2–2 in the seventh inning, Vic Wertz walloped a huge drive to the deepest part of the park. There seemed no way for Mays to run it down, but somehow the Giant center fielder did just that. He overtook the ball a few steps from the bleachers, catching it with his back to the plate, then wheeled and uncorked a brilliant throw to the infield that kept the two Cleveland runners from advancing. The catch, which triggered a four-game Giant sweep, is considered one of the most brilliant defensive plays in World Series history.

That kind of play was almost routine for Mays, who played center field with a dazzle rarely approached in baseball history. Yet Mays is remembered more for his bat than his glove, because in addition to all

Jose Guzman, history was there for the making.

With homers in his previous seven games, Mattingly needed one more to match Dale Long's major-league mark. And, when the lefty with the picture-perfect swing drove Guzman's pitch into the right-center bleachers, even Texas fans joined in a salute. Eight consecutive games with a homer was indeed a stunning achievement, but only one measure of Mattingly's greatness.

Born on April 20, 1961, in Evansville, Indiana, Mattingly was hailed as the Lou Gehrig of the 1980s for many reasons. This classy first baseman hit more than .300 for six straight seasons through 1989 (before being stymied by injuries in 1990). He won the American League batting crown with a .343 mark in 1984. In 1985, he was named the American League's MVP as he his defensive skills he was also one of the top sluggers of his era.

Mays walloped 660 home runs in 22 seasons, third on the all-time list behind Hank Aaron (755) and Babe Ruth (714). But Aaron and Ruth did not have the all-around baseball ability of Mays, who also had 338 stolen bases. Mays finished among the leaders in most offensive departments, ending his career with 1,903 runs batted in, 2,062 runs and 3,283 hits. He batted over .300 ten times, including seven years in a row, and he had eight straight seasons with at least 100 RBIs. He is one of an elite group of players who hit four home runs in one game. He was the National League's Most Valuable Player in 1954 and again in 1965.

Mays was born on May 6, 1931, in Westfield, Alabama, and was elected to the Hall of Fame in 1979, his first year of eligibility. When he was asked who was the best player he ever saw, Mays was honest. "I was," he said. He got no arguments about that.

MEAT HAND. The hand unprotected by a glove. If a player throws right-handed, that is his meat hand. His left is his glove hand. Meat hand has no connection with meathead, another expression heard around the ballpark.

Willie Mays was known as the Say Hey Kid when he performed all sorts of offensive and defensive heroics for the New York Giants.

MILWAUKEE BREWERS. The odds were against the Milwaukee Brewers as

Milwaukee's Robin Yount won the American League MVP award twice, in 1982 and 1989.

to have the Brewers on the ropes when they took a 3–2 lead into the seventh inning, but Cecil Cooper lined a clutch two-run double to give Milwaukee the lead.

Reliever Pete Ladd protected the lead in the final inning and, unbelievably, the Brewers had won the American League title. Though they lost the World Series to the St. Louis Cardinals, nothing could take away from what the Brewers had accomplished.

The Brewers franchise was born in Seattle in 1969. But plagued by poor attendance, the Seattle Pilots lasted only one year before moving to Milwaukee's County Stadium a few days before the 1970 season opener. Brewers fans supported the club through some lean days in the early 1970s, but then young players like Robin Yount, Paul Molitor and Jim Gantner all blossomed to make the Brewers perennial contenders.

they approached the 1982 American League playoffs. Manager Buck Rodgers's team had struggled all season to hold off the Baltimore Orioles and did not clinch the Eastern Division title until the final day of the season.

When their pitching aces, left-hander Mike Caldwell and righty Pete Vuckovich, lost the first two games of the best-of-five series against the California Angels, there seemed no way the Brewers could prolong their season. After all, no team in playoff history had ever dropped the first two games of a best-of-five series and come back to win.

But veteran Don Sutton beat California, 5–3, in Game 3 and then Moose Haas came back the next day to win, 9–5, and force a decisive fifth game. The Angels seemed

MINNESOTA TWINS. "There's no place like home" is one of the most famous lines from the movie *The Wizard of Oz*. It was also the Minnesota Twins' favorite saying after their improbable rise to the top of the baseball world in 1987. The Twins gave new meaning to the term "home-field advantage" when their ability to win consistently in the cozy Metrodome carried them to a World Series win over the St. Louis Cardinals.

During the regular season, the Twins were an awful 29–52 on the road but a very impressive 56–25 under the roof in Minneapolis. Their total of 85 wins, which

Minnesota's Tony Oliva was the American League batting champion in 1964, 1965 and 1971.

faith was rewarded when Kent Hrbek's grand slam sparked an 11–5 Twins' win in Game 6, and then Series MVP Frank Viola brought the championship to Minnesota with a 4–2 triumph in the finale. It was the Twins' first title since the franchise moved from Washington, where they were the Senators until 1961.

In 1924, under player-manager Bucky Harris (in his first season as manager), the Senators won their first American League title and the World Series, with 23-game winner Walter Johnson leading the way. The following year they won the pennant again but lost the World Series in seven

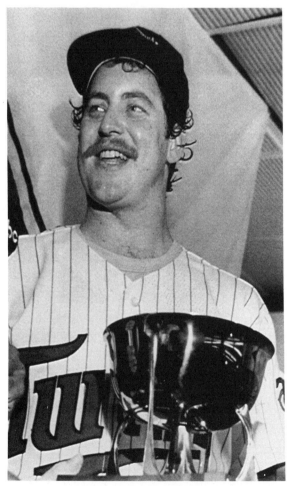

Frank Viola treasures the MVP trophy he won for pitching the Twins to the world championship over the Cardinals in 1987.

would have been good for fifth place in the American League East, was enough to win the West, two games ahead of the Kansas City Royals.

Once the playoffs started, the Twins' home-field edge took over. They defeated the heavily favored Detroit Tigers in the first two games at the Metrodome, and the Tigers never recovered, falling in five games. In the World Series the Twins again spurted to a two-game lead with wins at home, but the Cardinals came back to win three straight games at Busch Stadium.

Twin fans weren't worried, though, because they knew the last two games would be held at the noisy Metrodome. Their games to the Pittsburgh Pirates. Their last league title in Washington came in 1933 under another player-manager, Joe Cronin. The Senators lost the World Series that year to the New York Giants, four games to one.

The Twins won the pennant in 1965 but lost to the Los Angeles Dodgers in a seven-game World Series. They also won back-to-back American League West titles in 1969 and 1970 but lost the championship series to Baltimore both times.

MINOR LEAGUES. Leagues that are of less importance than the majors, yet still considered part of the overall structure of the sport. The minor leagues are the training ground for young players—the best players move up to the majors. There have been minor-league teams for almost as long as there have been major-league teams, but it wasn't until Branch Rickey thought up the idea in the 1920s that minor-league teams became part of the farm system of the majors.

Previously, minor-league teams had operated independently. They signed their own players and sold them to the highest bidder when they became in demand. Now, however, every minor-league team is either owned directly by a major-league team or has a working agreement with a major-league team, and more than 90 percent of the minor-league players are owned by the major leagues.

Minor-league teams are distributed among graded classifications: AAA leagues, AA leagues and rookie leagues. There was a time when there were also B, C and D leagues. In 1949 there were 59 minor leagues and a total of 448 teams; in 1990 there were only 18 leagues and 202 teams. The higher a league's classification, the greater the skills of the players in that league. (See *also* Farm system.)

MONTREAL EXPOS. The most memorable pitch in the Expos' history did not happen in an actual game. It was the ceremonial first toss by Montreal Mayor Jean Drapeau on the opening day of the 1969 season at New York's Shea Stadium. It

Seven-time All-Star Tim Raines won the National League batting title in 1986 with a .334 mark.

marked the end of his city's long wait for a major-league baseball franchise.

Though the Expos did win that first game, the franchise's early years were typical of a new team. Playing in tiny Jarry Park, the Expos didn't win many games. But it didn't take long for the club, named after the city's World's Fair—Expo '67—to win a devoted following. The Expos made a big splash just 10 days into their first season when Bill Stoneman pitched a no-hitter against the Philadelphia Phillies.

Montreal had its share of early heroes. Unquestionably, the most popular was Rusty Staub, a redheaded outfielder who captured the fans' imagination with his flair and his bat. Staub earned the affectionate nickname Le Grande Orange.

It wasn't until after the Expos' move into spacious, modernistic Olympic Stadium in 1977 that they became a real contender. Thanks to Steve Rogers, the team's best

pitcher, and young power hitters Gary Carter, Andre Dawson and Ellis Valentine, all products of their farm system, the Expos battled Pittsburgh until the 1979 season's final weekend.

In 1980, when Ron LeFlore stole 97 bases, Montreal again made it close before bowing to the Phillies on the next-to-last day of the season. In 1981 the Expos made it to the National League Championship Series, losing to Los Angeles in five games.

Stars like outfielders Tim Raines and Hubie Brooks and first baseman Andres Galarraga kept the Expos competitive through the late 1980s.

MOP-UP MAN. A pitcher used late in the game when the outcome of the game is no longer in doubt.

MORGAN, JOE. His career spanned five teams and 22 seasons, seven playoff series and four World Series. He won National League MVP honors in 1975 and 1976. He played 2,527 games at second base, won five Gold Gloves, stole 689 bases, slashed 2,517 hits, launched 268 homers and drove in 1,133 runs. Even playing alongside greats like Johnny Bench and Pete Rose, Joe Morgan was always the motor that propelled Cincinnati's fabled Big Red Machine.

Morgan, born on September 19, 1943, in Bonham, Texas, came to the Reds prior to the 1972 season after spending pieces of nine uneventful years with Houston. He blossomed almost immediately after the trade to Cincinnati, and the Reds won the NL pennant in his first year there.

However, this 5-foot 7-inch, 155-pound powerhouse didn't reach his peak until 1975 and 1976, when he led the Reds to back-to-back World Series triumphs. In 1975 he used his compact lefty stroke to hit .327, with 17 homers and 94 RBIs, and

Joe Morgan was a little guy who hit big, stole freely and achieved Gold Glove status as a Cincinnati second baseman on the way to the Hall of Fame.

he recorded 107 runs and 67 steals. The next season, his numbers were even better: .320, 27 homers, 111 RBIs, 113 runs and 60 steals. He batted .333 as the Reds swept the Yankees in the 1976 Series.

By the time he called it quits, after the 1984 season, Morgan was one of only three players in history to reach 250 homers, 2,500 hits and 250 steals. When he was elected to the Hall of Fame in his first year of eligibility in 1990, it marked the ultimate recognition for a little Joe who always played big.

MOUND. Also called the hill. The raised portion of the infield, 10 inches high at its highest point. The pitcher takes his position on the rectangular plate, known as the slab or rubber, set into the top of the mound.

MOVIES. Hollywood producers have been casting their stars in baseball movies from the earliest silent pictures (*Baseball Fan*, 1908) to today's made-for-TV films. Even former president Ronald Reagan once

Baseball Movies and Their Stars

Alibi Ike—Joe E. Brown
Angels in the Outfield—Paul Douglas, Keenan Wynn, Janet Leigh
Babe Comes Home—Babe Ruth, Anna Q. Nilsson
The Babe Ruth Story—William Bendix, Claire Trevor, Charles Bickford
The Bad News Bears—Walter Matthau, Tatum O'Neal
Bang the Drum Slowly—Robert DeNiro, Michael Moriarty
Baseball Madness—Gloria Swanson
The Big Leaguer—Edward G. Robinson, Jeff Richards, Vera-Ellen
The Bingo Long Traveling All-Stars and Motor Kings—Richard Pryor, James Earl Jones, Billy Dee Williams
Bull Durham—Kevin Costner, Susan Sarandon, Tim Robbins
Casey at the Bat—Wallace Beery, Sterling Holloway
Damn Yankees—Tab Hunter, Ray Walston, Gwen Verdon
Eight Men Out—Charlie Sheen, Christopher Lloyd, John Cusack, John Sayles
Elmer the Great—Joe E. Brown
Fear Strikes Out—Tony Perkins, Karl Malden, Norma Moore
Field of Dreams—Kevin Costner, Burt Lancaster, James Earl Jones
The Great American Pastime—Tom Ewell
It Happened in Flatbush—Lloyd Nolan
It Happens Every Spring—Ray Milland, Jean Peters, Paul Douglas
The Jackie Robinson Story—Jackie Robinson, Ruby Dee

The Kid from Left Field—Dan Dailey, Lloyd Bridges, Anne Bancroft
Kill the Umpire—William Bendix, Una Merkel
Ladies Day—Eddie Albert
Major League—Tom Berenger, Charlie Sheen, Corbin Bernsen
The Monty Stratton Story—James Stewart, June Allyson
The Natural—Robert Redford, Robert Duvall, Glenn Close
One in a Million—LeVar Burton, Madge Sinclair, Billy Martin
One Touch of Nature—John Bennett, John McGraw
Over the Fence—Harold Lloyd, Bebe Daniels
The Pinch Hitter—Charles Ray
The Pride of St. Louis—Dan Dailey, Joanne Dru
The Pride of the Yankees—Gary Cooper, Teresa Wright, Walter Brennan
Rhubarb—Ray Milland, Jan Sterling
Safe at Home!—Mickey Mantle, Roger Maris, Don Collier
Slide, Kelly, Slide—William Haines, Harry Carey, Sally O'Neil
Speedy—Harold Lloyd, Babe Ruth
Stepping Fast—Tom Mix
Take Me Out to the Ball Game—Frank Sinatra, Gene Kelly, Jules Munshin
Warming Up—Richard Dix, Jean Arthur
Whistling in Brooklyn—Red Skelton, Ann Rutherford
The Winning Team—Ronald Reagan, Doris Day, Frank Lovejoy

Jimmy Stewart and June Allyson starred in *The Monty Stratton Story.*

at a time when home runs were relatively rare.

MUSIAL, STAN. He was coiled in the batter's box like a human corkscrew. It seemed like an impossible position for a hitter to swing from, but Stan Musial managed.

He swung his bat like a magic wand with a precision that made him one of the most feared hitters of his time. He was so good that his last name didn't matter. He was simply Stan the Man.

Musial was born in Donora, Pennsylvania, on November 21, 1920, and began his career as a pitcher. But he was such a good hitter that his manager used him in the outfield when he wasn't pitching. One day, while playing the outfield, he fell on his arm. That was the end of his pitching

appeared in a baseball movie—as Hall of Famer Grover Cleveland Alexander (*The Winning Team*, 1952).

On page 99 is a list of baseball films for those days and nights when the games are rained out.

MURDERERS' ROW. Name given to the 1927 Yankees, considered to be the greatest hitting team ever assembled. There was no weak hitter on the team, which won 110 games. The Yankees were led by Babe Ruth's 60 home runs and Lou·Gehrig's 47,

Paul Winfield, in wheelchair, played Roy Campanella in *It's Good to Be Alive,* **a 1974 television special based on the life of the former Dodger catcher.**

Stan Musial was one of the best hitters in baseball history and the National League's Most Valuable Player in 1943, 1946 and 1948. He had a career batting average of .331.

career and the start of one of the greatest hitting careers in major-league history.

Musial came up with the St. Louis Cardinals in 1941 and, except for one year out for military service, remained with the club until 1963. He won seven batting championships, the last one in 1957, when he was 37 years old.

He was voted the NL's Most Valuable Player three times, and he hit .300 in 18 of his 22 full seasons. A veteran of 20 All-Star Games in a row, he holds the record for most homers (6) hit in All-Star Games.

He walloped 475 career homers among the 3,630 hits that make him fourth on the all-time list behind Pete Rose, Ty Cobb and Hank Aaron.

Left-handed Stan played outfield and first base. Naturally, he was an overwhelming choice for the Hall of Fame in 1969, his first year of eligibility.

MVP. Short for Most Valuable Player, chosen each year in both major leagues by a committee of baseball writers. The prac-

---

MVPs

NATIONAL LEAGUE

Year	Player, Club
1931	Frankie Frisch, St. Louis Cardinals
1932	Chuck Klein, Philadelphia Phillies
1933	Carl Hubbell, New York Giants
1934	Dizzy Dean, St. Louis Cardinals
1935	Gabby Hartnett, Chicago Cubs
1936	Carl Hubbell, New York Giants
1937	Joe Medwick, St. Louis Cardinals
1938	Ernie Lombardi, Cincinnati Reds
1939	Bucky Walters, Cincinnati Reds
1940	Frank McCormick, Cincinnati Reds
1941	Dolph Camilli, Brooklyn Dodgers
1942	Mort Cooper, St. Louis Cardinals
1943	Stan Musial, St. Louis Cardinals
1944	Marty Marion, St. Louis Cardinals
1945	Phil Cavaretta, Chicago Cubs
1946	Stan Musial, St. Louis Cardinals
1947	Bob Elliott, Boston Braves
1948	Stan Musial, St. Louis Cardinals
1949	Jackie Robinson, Brooklyn Dodgers
1950	Jim Konstanty, Philadelphia Phillies
1951	Roy Campanella, Brooklyn Dodgers
1952	Hank Sauer, Chicago Cubs
1953	Roy Campanella, Brooklyn Dodgers
1954	Willie Mays, New York Giants
1955	Roy Campanella, Brooklyn Dodgers
1956	Don Newcombe, Brooklyn Dodgers
1957	Hank Aaron, Milwaukee Braves
1958	Ernie Banks, Chicago Cubs
1959	Ernie Banks, Chicago Cubs
1960	Dick Groat, Pittsburgh Pirates
1961	Frank Robinson, Cincinnati Reds

Year	Player, Club
1962	Maury Wills, Los Angeles Dodgers
1963	Sandy Koufax, Los Angeles Dodgers
1964	Ken Boyer, St. Louis Cardinals
1965	Willie Mays, San Francisco Giants
1966	Roberto Clemente, Pittsburgh Pirates
1967	Orlando Cepeda, St. Louis Cardinals
1968	Bob Gibson, St. Louis Cardinals
1969	Willie McCovey, San Francisco Giants
1970	Johnny Bench, Cincinnati Reds
1971	Joe Torre, St. Louis Cardinals
1972	Johnny Bench, Cincinnati Reds
1973	Pete Rose, Cincinnati Reds
1974	Steve Garvey, Los Angeles Dodgers
1975	Joe Morgan, Cincinnati Reds
1976	Joe Morgan, Cincinnati Reds
1977	George Foster, Cincinnati Reds
1978	Dave Parker, Pittsburgh Pirates
1979	Keith Hernandez, St. Louis Cardinals
	Willie Stargell, Pittsburgh Pirates
1980	Mike Schmidt, Philadelphia Phillies
1981	Mike Schmidt, Philadelphia Phillies
1982	Dale Murphy, Atlanta Braves
1983	Dale Murphy, Atlanta Braves
1984	Ryne Sandberg, Chicago Cubs
1985	Willie McGee, St. Louis Cardinals
1986	Mike Schmidt, Philadelphia Phillies
1987	Andre Dawson, Chicago Cubs
1988	Kirk Gibson, Los Angeles Dodgers
1989	Kevin Mitchell, San Francisco Giants
1990	Barry Bonds, Pittsburgh Pirates

tice of honoring outstanding players began in 1911, when the manufacturers of Chalmers automobiles presented a car to the leading player in each league.

The Chalmers Award was eventually replaced by the league awards, sponsored by the two major leagues but with the provision in the American League that there

Hank Aaron *(right)* was the National League's Most Valuable Player in 1957. His teammate Warren Spahn won the Cy Young Award that year.

MVPs

AMERICAN LEAGUE

Year	Player, Club	Year	Player, Club
1931	Lefty Grove, Philadelphia Athletics	1961	Roger Maris, New York Yankees
1932	Jimmie Foxx, Philadelphia Athletics	1962	Mickey Mantle, New York Yankees
1933	Jimmie Foxx, Philadelphia Athletics	1963	Elston Howard, New York Yankees
1934	Mickey Cochrane, Detroit Tigers	1964	Brooks Robinson, Baltimore Orioles
1935	Hank Greenberg, Detroit Tigers	1965	Zoilo Versalles, Minnesota Twins
1936	Lou Gehrig, New York Yankees	1966	Frank Robinson, Baltimore Orioles
1937	Charley Gehringer, Detroit Tigers	1967	Carl Yastrzemski, Boston Red Sox
1938	Jimmie Foxx, Boston Red Sox	1968	Denny McLain, Detroit Tigers
1939	Joe DiMaggio, New York Yankees	1969	Harmon Killebrew, Minnesota Twins
1940	Hank Greenberg, Detroit Tigers	1970	Boog Powell, Baltimore Orioles
1941	Joe DiMaggio, New York Yankees	1971	Vida Blue, Oakland A's
1942	Joe Gordon, New York Yankees	1972	Dick Allen, Chicago White Sox
1943	Spud Chandler, New York Yankees	1973	Reggie Jackson, Oakland A's
1944	Hal Newhouser, Detroit Tigers	1974	Jeff Burroughs, Texas Rangers
1945	Hal Newhouser, Detroit Tigers	1975	Fred Lynn, Boston Red Sox
1946	Ted Williams, Boston Red Sox	1976	Thurman Munson, New York Yankees
1947	Joe DiMaggio, New York Yankees	1977	Rod Carew, Minnesota Twins
1948	Lou Boudreau, Cleveland Indians	1978	Jim Rice, Boston Red Sox
1949	Ted Williams, Boston Red Sox	1979	Don Baylor, California Angels
1950	Phil Rizzuto, New York Yankees	1980	George Brett, Kansas City Royals
1951	Yogi Berra, New York Yankees	1981	Rollie Fingers, Milwaukee Brewers
1952	Bobby Shantz, Philadelphia Athletics	1982	Robin Yount, Milwaukee Brewers
1953	Al Rosen, Cleveland Indians	1983	Cal Ripken, Baltimore Orioles
1954	Yogi Berra, New York Yankees	1984	Willie Hernandez, Detroit Tigers
1955	Yogi Berra, New York Yankees	1985	Don Mattingly, New York Yankees
1956	Mickey Mantle, New York Yankees	1986	Roger Clemens, Boston Red Sox
1957	Mickey Mantle, New York Yankees	1987	George Bell, Toronto Blue Jays
1958	Jackie Jensen, Boston Red Sox	1988	Jose Canseco, Oakland A's
1959	Nellie Fox, Chicago White Sox	1989	Robin Yount, Milwaukee Brewers
1960	Roger Maris, New York Yankees	1990	Rickey Henderson, Oakland A's

be no repeaters. Thus Babe Ruth, when he hit 60 homers in 1927, was not eligible because he had won it before. Lou Gehrig was named instead.

The league awards were abandoned after 1929, and the MVP award, sponsored by the Baseball Writers Association, has been voted annually since 1931. There is no rule against winning it more than once. In fact, several players have won it three times.

NATIONAL LEAGUE. The older of baseball's two major leagues (the other being the American League). Sometimes called the senior circuit. The National League began in 1876 and represented a rebellion against the establishment of the day, the National Association.

Early in the 1875 season, owners of the Chicago franchise, weary of constant failure, offered the team's presidency to William A. Hulbert, a successful business-man and rabid fan of the Chicago White Stockings. Hulbert asked for a few weeks to consider the offer.

When the champion Boston club visited Chicago, Hulbert met with A. G. Spalding, the league's outstanding pitcher. Hulbert begged Spalding to join him in Chicago. When Hulbert promised Spalding a huge contract for the 1876 season, Spalding agreed to come to Chicago the following year. What's more, Spalding helped Hulbert sign his teammates Ross Barnes, Cal McVey and Deacon Jim White, three of the outstanding players in the National Association.

The deal was not supposed to be announced until after the 1875 season, but it leaked out before the season ended, to the embarrassment of Spalding and his friends.

Now there were rumors that Spalding and the other club jumpers might be expelled from the National Association following the 1875 season, making it impossible for them to fulfill their contracts with Hulbert and the White Stockings. Spalding told Hulbert of his fears, and it gave Hulbert an idea. He decided to form a new league. He even had a name. Instead of the National Association of Base Ball Players, he would call his new league the National League of Professional Base Ball Clubs.

Hulbert had a formal constitution drawn up, and then he called officials of the St. Louis, Cincinnati and Louisville clubs to a secret meeting. He told them of his plan and got a strong vote of confidence. Now he had four teams in his new league, and the next step was to get some eastern teams represented. Hulbert invited the remaining National Association teams to a conference "on matters of interest to the game at large, with special reference to reformation of existing abuses." His summons was answered by all four eastern teams—Philadelphia, Boston, Hartford and New York.

Hulbert outlined the evils that were demoralizing the players and fans and charged that the National Association was either unable or unwilling to correct the abuses. He called for a new league and produced the constitution of his National League. He won complete support, and on April 22, 1876, the National League began play, with Boston defeating Philadelphia, 6–5, at Philadelphia, one of eight charter members in the National League.

The National League grew to twelve teams and flourished until 1899, when four teams were dropped. They promptly linked up with an outlaw league and formed the eight-team American League. In 1901, when the American League formally opened play as an eight-team league, teams in the National League included Pittsburgh, Philadelphia, Brooklyn, St. Louis, Boston, Chicago, New York and Cincinnati.

The National League stayed that way until 1953, when the Boston Braves asked for, and received, permission to move to Milwaukee.

In 1958 the Brooklyn Dodgers moved to Los Angeles and the New York Giants to San Francisco.

In 1962 the National League expanded to 10 teams—one franchise was awarded to New York and was named the Mets, the other went to Houston and was called the Colt .45s, later the Astros. Players for the two new teams were taken from a pool provided by the eight established teams, and the schedule was expanded from 154 games to 162.

In 1966 the Braves became the first club to move twice, shifting from Milwaukee to Atlanta after much legal action. Expansion came again in 1969, when Montreal and San Diego were admitted to the National League.

With the league expanded to 12 teams, division play was instituted. The Eastern

This mannequin represents a National League player in baseball's early days.

Division of the National League was made up of Chicago, Montreal, New York, Philadelphia, Pittsburgh and St. Louis. The Western Division included Atlanta, Cincinnati, Houston, Los Angeles, San Diego and San Francisco.

As in the American League, the winners of each division meet in a playoff series to determine which team will represent the National League in the World Series.

From 1969 to 1984, the playoffs were best-of-five. Both the American and National leagues expanded the playoffs to best-of-seven in 1985.

NEGRO LEAGUES. They traveled in dilapidated buses, stayed in fourth-rate hotels—when they could find one that would accept them—took their meals on the run and played as many as four games in a day and night in farm towns and in major-league stadiums.

Their teams were the Kansas City Monarchs, St. Louis Stars, Nashville Elite Giants, Homestead Grays, Pittsburgh Crawfords, Baltimore Black Sox, New York Black Yankees, Atlanta Black Crackers, Birmingham Black Barons, Chattanooga Black Lookouts, New York Cubans, Cuban Giants . . .

They played in such leagues as the Negro National League, Southern League, Eastern Colored League, Negro American League . . .

Their names were Cool Papa Bell, Buck Leonard, Josh Gibson, Smokey Joe Williams, John Henry Lloyd, Oscar Charleston, Rube Roster, Ray (Hooks) Dandridge, Martin Dihigo, Judy Johnson . . .

Many were superstars, but all were denied entry into the major leagues because of the color of their skin.

They played in the years before Jackie Robinson and the Brooklyn Dodgers shattered the color line in 1947. They were big leaguers in every sense except that theirs were known as the Negro leagues.

After Robinson, other distinguished Negro league graduates would make it to the majors, including the legendary Satchel Paige, Monte Irvin, Ernie Banks, Roy Campanella, Henry Aaron, Larry Doby, Minnie Minoso, Sam Jethroe, Dan Bankhead, Luke Easter and Henry Thompson.

It was a long time coming.

NEW YORK METS. The fly ball drifted lazily out toward left field, where Cleon Jones was waiting. Jones went down on one knee, cradled the ball and the miracle was complete. The New York Mets had won the World Series. It happened on October 16, 1969, and set off a wild celebration in the streets of New York.

Only seven years earlier, in the club's first season, the team was the laughing-stock of baseball. With a roster made up of over-the-hill players, the Mets lost 120 of 160 games and finished 60½ games out of first place. Casey Stengel, who had managed the Yankees to championship after championship, was the unfortunate one stuck with the chore of managing this motley crew.

But in 1964 things began to change. A new stadium, Shea, was built in Queens, and the team surpassed the Yankees as the area's favorite. The play on the field didn't improve much, but the farm system started sprouting good young players like Tug McGraw, Jerry Koosman and Tom Seaver.

On their way to the world championship in 1986: the Mets celebrate the winning of the National League East. *(Left to right):* Ron Darling, Dwight Gooden, Lee Mazzilli, Kevin Mitchell, Howard Johnson, Gary Carter and the batboy.

It was the pitching of Seaver and Koosman that drove the Mets in 1969. A 100-to-1 shot in spring training, the Mets stayed close to the Chicago Cubs through the summer and then passed them in early September to win the division by eight games. They then beat the Atlanta Braves in three straight playoff games to win their first pennant. After an opening-game loss in the World Series, the Mets won four straight from the Baltimore Orioles, capping the miracle year.

Darryl Strawberry, the Mets' all-time leader in home runs, with 252 in eight years (1983–1990), joined the Dodgers as a free agent in 1990.

The Mets remained a contender in the early seventies and won the pennant in 1973 behind Seaver, Koosman and Rusty Staub. But they lost the World Series to Oakland in seven games.

It wasn't until 1986 that the Mets, with such headline players as Keith Hernandez, Dwight Gooden, Gary Carter and Darryl Strawberry, experienced their next miracle. Trailing the Boston Red Sox in the World Series, three games to two, the Mets were behind in the sixth game by two runs in the bottom of the 10th inning, with none on, two out and two strikes on Carter. But the Mets rallied to win, 6–5, on singles by Carter, Kevin Mitchell and Ray Knight, a wild pitch and Mookie Wilson's grounder that Red Sox first baseman Bill Buckner let slip through his legs.

In the decisive seventh game the Mets trailed by three runs through five innings. After a three-run rally in the sixth, Knight's leadoff homer in the seventh sparked an 8–5 victory that gave the Mets their second world championship.

It was a Series in which Dwight Gooden lost twice and Knight, an unlikely hero, won MVP honors.

NEW YORK YANKEES. From Babe Ruth to Joe DiMaggio to Mickey Mantle to Reggie Jackson, the Yankees have stood for baseball excellence since 1921, when they won their first of a record 32 pennants.

Originally known as the Highlanders, the team changed its name in 1912 because "Yankees" fit better in newspaper headlines.

In 1920 owner Jacob Ruppert bought Ruth from the Red Sox for $100,000. Ruth became the greatest bargain in history, leading the Yanks to six pennants between 1921 and 1928. The Babe smashed 60 homers in 1927 and, with Lou Gehrig, formed the core of the famed, feared Murderers' Row.

After Ruth retired, DiMaggio became the best slugger on the team, starting in 1936. Nothing else changed, though: the Yanks kept winning. From 1936 through 1964 they captured 22 pennants and 16 world championships. DiMaggio played a key role in the early titles, then Mantle took over in 1951.

Highlights in the Yankees' fantastic success story include DiMaggio's 56-game hitting streak in 1941, five straight world championships from 1949 through 1953, Don Larsen's perfect game in the 1956 World Series and Roger Maris's 61 homers in 1961.

The Yankees hit upon hard times in the late 1960s and early 1970s, but new owner George Steinbrenner took over in 1973 and turned the team around. With the coming of the free agent, Steinbrenner opened his checkbook to buy players like Reggie Jackson, Catfish Hunter and Goose Gossage. They helped the Yanks win five division titles and two world championships from 1976 through 1981.

In the 1980s, when other owners started matching Steinbrenner dollar-for-dollar in the quest for free agents, the Yankees had to rely on their farm system more and more. But with the exception of first baseman Don Mattingly and outfielder Roberto Kelly, the Yankees did not produce enough everyday players to succeed on a consistent basis. The 1980s was the first decade since World War I in which the Yanks did not win a world championship.

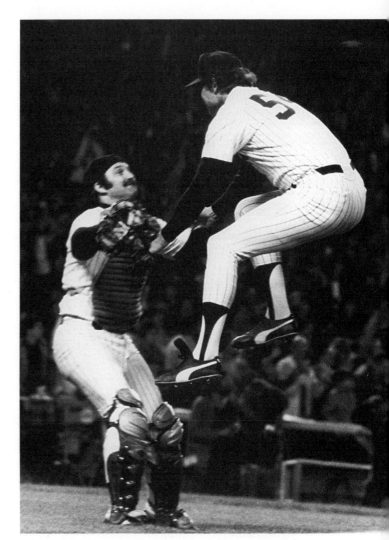

Relief pitcher Goose Gossage jumps for joy into the arms of Thurman Munson after the Yankees won the American League pennant for the third straight time, against the Royals, in 1978.

The Yankees have always had heroes, but they've also had notable managers, including Miller Huggins, Joe McCarthy, Casey Stengel and Billy Martin. Stengel, the most colorful and successful of all, guided the team to 10 pennants and seven world championships in 12 years. Martin was known as Battling Billy for the traits that led him into combat with players, umpires, fans and owners (especially the Yankees' George Steinbrenner, who was banned from the sport in 1990 because of conduct "not in the best interest of baseball"). He managed the Yankees five times, a major-league record for a single team, and won the AL pennant with them in 1976 and the World Series in 1977. He was killed in an auto accident in 1989.

NICKNAMES. Five players named Rhodes or Rhoades have appeared in the big leagues, and all but one were nicknamed Dusty. This illustrates two points about baseball nicknames: they're almost inevitable with certain last names (a Rhodes will be Dusty and a Watters will be Muddy), and they're not noted for their originality.

Some obvious physical characteristic or personality trait is the most common basis for a nickname. Examples include players named Red, Whitey or Lefty, as well as Dizzy Dean, Bugs Raymond, Sad Sam Jones, Slim Sallee, Fats Fothergill, Stubby Overmire, King Kong Keller, Moose Skowron, Ducky Medwick (for his waddling gait) and Hawk (for any large-nosed player) or Schnozz, as Ernie Lombardi was dubbed.

Harry Brecheen was the Cat because he looked like a cat in the way he sped off the mound to field, and Harvey Haddix was the Kitten because he looked like Harry Brecheen. Marty Marion was the Octopus because he seemed to be all arms as he fielded a ball at shortstop, and Emil Verban became the Antelope mostly because he was Marion's second-base partner with the St. Louis Cardinals.

Harold Reese became Pee Wee, not just because he was small but because he was once a marbles champion (a peewee is a small marble), and Jim Bouton was dubbed Bulldog because of his determination. Cap Peterson got his nickname because his real name was Charles Andrew Peterson and his initials were C.A.P.

Nervous habits lead to nicknames: Jittery Joe Berry, Fidgety Phil Collins, Shuf-fling Phil Douglas. One of the best of these, coined by columnist Jimmy Cannon, was Hot Potato Hamlin for Luke Hamlin, a pitcher who juggled the ball in the palm of his hand before winding up.

Babe, Rube, Kid and Doc are baseball nicknames of long standing. Bobo, made famous by Bobo Newsom, is now used less as a nickname than as an insult for any player who is thought of as the manager's pet ("He's the Old Man's bobo").

Many nicknames become famous although their origins are never discovered. Pumpsie Green, whose real name is Elijah, once said, "Someday I'll write a book and call it *How I Got the Nickname Pumpsie* and sell it for a dollar, and if everybody who ever asked me that question buys the book, I'll be a millionaire."

Nationalities have produced nicknames like Frenchy Bordagaray, Germany Schaefer, Lou (the Mad Russian) Novikoff and Shanty Hogan. Years ago almost any Native American player was known as Chief (Chief Bender, Chief Meyers, etc.). Almost half of the Spanish-speaking players used to wind up being called Chico: Chico Carrasquel, Chico Fernandez, Chico Salmon, Chico Cardenas and Chico Ruiz.

Charles Dillon Stengel became Casey because he came from Kansas City (KC), but most nicknames of that variety spring from quaint-sounding home towns: Wahoo Sam Crawford from Wahoo, Nebraska; Pea Ridge Day from a town of that name in Arkansas; and Vinegar Bend Mizell from the thriving metropolis of Vinegar Bend, Alabama.

Another popular source is a player's skill or his record, whether favorable or not. Denton Young threw so hard he became known as Cyclone, later shortened to Cy. Joe Wood, another fireballer, was to win fame as Smokey Joe Wood. Odell Hale was Bad News to the pitchers he clobbered. And then there was Home Run Baker, Sliding Billy Hamilton and Swish Nicholson (for his repeated practice swings, which fascinated the fans).

Not very flattering, although the recipients didn't seem to mind, were names like Boom Boom Beck, Line Drive Nelson and Losing Pitcher Mulcahy—pitchers who continually took their lumps. And Rocky for somebody with rocks in his head. Of course, if Rocky's given name happened to be Rocco, you could give him the benefit of the doubt.

There were certain annoying nicknames that were saved for the time and place when their use might have the most painful effect. John McGraw liked Muggsy about as much as he liked an extra-inning defeat, and a player who wanted the rest of the day off would only have to say to umpire Bill Klem, "Where was that last pitch, Catfish?" In a moment, he'd be in the shower.

But Klem is gone, and the name Catfish changed from insult to praise after it became the name by which the millionaire Yankee pitcher James Augustus Hunter was known.

It has been said that Catfish Hunter got his nickname when he was a boy of six. One day Jim was missing. His parents searched frantically for him for hours. When they finally found him that evening, he was at his favorite fishing hole, and he had hauled in a mess of catfish. From that day to this, he has been called Catfish—although the story may simply have been a figment of the imagination of Charles O. Finley, Hunter's colorful and controversial employer in Kansas City and Oakland.

NIGHT BALL. Baseball was first played under lights in 1880 at Nantasket Beach near Boston. However, it didn't come to the major leagues until 1935, when Larry MacPhail staged the first night game in Cincinnati.

Since then, every big-league club has installed lights and has been playing an increasing share of its schedule after dark. The Chicago Cubs were the last major-league team to succumb, installing lights at Wrigley Field in 1988.

At first, major-league clubs were limited to seven home night games a season, but the number kept growing until it has reached a point where afternoon games, except on a Saturday, Sunday or holiday, are rare in most big-league ballparks.

When, in 1971, the Baltimore Orioles and Pittsburgh Pirates played the first World Series game at night in Pittsburgh, baseball was firmly established as a nighttime spectacle.

NINE. A baseball team, so called because there are nine players on a side.

NO-HITTER. A no-hit game. A game in which the pitcher permits the opposing team no base hits for the entire game. No-hitters are rare enough to be a special event, but plentiful enough so as not to be freakish. As a typical 10-year period, take the years 1948 to 1957. In all, there were 17 no-hitters during those 10 years, or almost two per year. In 1951 there were four. In 1965 Sandy Koufax of the Los Angeles Dodgers became the first pitcher to pitch four no-hitters, a feat surpassed by Nolan Ryan of the Houston Astros in 1981. In 1990 no-hitters were almost commonplace—a total of nine of them were thrown, including a two-pitcher no-hitter (by Mark Langston and Mike Witt of the California Angels), a five-inning no-hitter (by Melido Perez of the Chicago White Sox) and a no-hitter loss (by Andy Hawkins of the New York Yankees).

Ryan is the unquestioned king of the no-hitter. Not only does the hard-throwing

The Yankees' Don Larsen delivers a third-strike pitch to the Dodgers' Dale Mitchell for the final out in the only perfect game in World Series history. It happened on October 8, 1956.

right-hander hold the career record for no-hitters, but in 1989, when there were no no-hitters, he took no-hit games into the eighth inning five times. He was finally rewarded a year later, when he pitched his sixth no-hitter, 17 years after hurling his first one.

A perfect game is a no-hitter in which not one batter reaches base safely, either by hit, walk or error. In a perfect game the pitcher faces the minimum of 27 opposing batters. Obviously, perfect games are rarer than no-hitters. There have been only 13 perfect games in major-league history, the

most recent occurring in 1988, when Cincinnati's Tom Browning threw one against the Los Angeles Dodgers.

The most famous perfect game was on October 8, 1956, and it was the only perfect game ever pitched in a World Series. Don Larsen, a mediocre pitcher who had won 30 and lost 40 in four big-league seasons, pitched it for the New York Yankees against the Brooklyn Dodgers in the fifth game. After the game, in the madhouse around Larsen's locker, a rookie reporter asked Don, "Is that the best game you ever pitched?"

OAKLAND ATHLETICS. Jose Canseco had always done things in a big way. From the day he broke into the Oakland lineup in September of 1985, Canseco was known for his fast cars and his tape-measure home runs. But not even Canseco could have prepared himself for what he did in Game 4 of the 1989 American League playoffs against the Toronto Blue Jays.

Canseco stepped to the plate in the third inning against left-hander Mike Flanagan. He took a strike and then got around on an inside fastball. The ball jumped off his bat and headed high and deep toward left field. Blue Jay outfielder Mookie Wilson took one look and realized he would need a plane to catch it. The ball landed halfway up the top deck of the Toronto Skydome, a drive that qualifies as one of the longest home runs ever hit.

Canseco's homer helped the A's eliminate the Blue Jays in five games. Oakland then went on to demolish the San Francisco Giants in four straight games (an earthquake halted play for 10 days between the second and third games) to win

The A's' Jose Canseco *(center)* is congratulated by Carney Lansford and Rickey Henderson after his three-run homer against the Giants in Game 3 of the 1989 World Series.

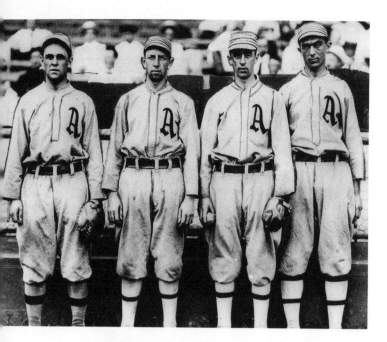

The Philadelphia A's' $100,000 infield of 1912: *(left to right)* Stuffy McInnis, Eddie Collins, Jack Barry and Frank (Home Run) Baker.

when the A's moved west to Kansas City, in 1955.

In the course of their stay in Missouri, a colorful, unconventional insurance executive named Charles O. Finley bought the team and changed its location as well as its destiny.

Finley shifted the A's to Oakland in 1968, and although he fired managers at will, he wound up running the most successful team of the early 1970s. With players like Catfish Hunter, Reggie Jackson, Sal Bando and Vida Blue, the A's strung together three world championships in 1972, 1973 and 1974.

the world championship. With Canseco, pitchers Dave Stewart and Dennis Eckersley, outfielder Rickey Henderson and first baseman Mark McGwire, Oakland ended the 1980s with unquestionably the strongest team in baseball. The results of the 1990 season helped confirm this—the A's won the AL West by 9 games and went on to capture their third consecutive pennant, although they were then swept in the World Series by the Cincinnati Reds.

The legacy of the A's began in 1901 when Connie Mack (short for Cornelius McGillicuddy) became manager of the Philadelphia team in the new American League. Mack, who also owned the team, was Mr. Baseball. He managed the team for 50 years, winning five world championships, the last in 1930, when he had such stars as Jimmie Foxx, Al Simmons, Mickey Cochrane, Lefty Grove and George Earnshaw.

Mack managed his last team in 1950 at the age of 88 and lived to see the sad day

ON DECK. The player waiting to follow the current batter is said to be on deck. According to the rules, he must wait in the on-deck circle, a chalk-marked area placed halfway between home plate and the dugout. The purpose of the on-deck circle is to speed up the game.

ONE O'CLOCK HITTER. This refers to a batter who is terrific during batting practice (which usually comes an hour or so before game time) but is a bust during a game. It used to be a two o'clock hitter when games were played at 3 P.M., and sometimes it is a seven o'clock hitter for night games, which generally start at 8 P.M.

The greatest two o'clock hitter of all time was Tommy Brown, a young wartime infielder for the Brooklyn Dodgers. Brown, who played his first major-league game when he was 16, used to keep complete records of his home runs during batting practice. Each year he would break Babe Ruth's home-run record by June at the latest—in batting practice. However, in 1953, his last year in the major leagues, he hit only two home runs in 65 games for the Chicago Cubs during working hours.

OUT. If you fail to reach first base, you're out. Each team gets three outs an inning. The game is never over until the last man is out. The umpire points his thumb upward to indicate an out.

OUTFIELD. All the area in fair territory beyond the infield and usually bounded by fences or stands. There is no strict dividing mark between the infield and the outfield. The players who cover the three outfield positions—left field, center field and right field—are called outfielders. One is called the left fielder, one the center fielder and one the right fielder, depending on the field he covers. An outfielder is called a gardener, fly chaser, member of the outer garden, outer pasture or picket patrol; and the entire outfield is often called the picket line.

OUT IN ORDER. A team is out in order, or a pitcher is said to have retired the side in order, if the first three batters in any inning are retired with none reaching base safely.

OUT MAN. An exceptionally weak hitter, sometimes called a lamb, flea hitter, ping hitter or weak sister. Traditionally the weakest hitter on a team bats eighth (in the National League) or ninth (in the American League, where the designated hitter is used). In the National League it is considered humiliating to bat after the pitcher, usually the poorest hitter on any team. But there are exceptions. It was no disgrace to bat after Don Drysdale of the Los Angeles Dodgers in 1965. An outstanding hitter for a pitcher, Drysdale's batting average that year—.300—was higher than that of any regular on the team, and of his 39 hits seven were home runs.

OWNERS. That curious band of monopolists who not only own the baseball teams but run the game, for all practical purposes. They are called the moguls, magnates and lords of baseball and, in most cases, they do call all the shots. It is the owners who make policy for the game and who approve or disapprove the shifting of a team from one city to another. The owners choose baseball's ranking authority, the commissioner. This sets up a situation in which an individual is expected to govern the very people who hired him.

It used to be that baseball teams were owned by individual citizens whose only interest was, and only income came from, the baseball team. That is no longer true. Baseball is now big business, and that is reflected in the ownership of the teams.

For instance, the St. Louis Cardinals are owned by the Busch family (makers of Budweiser beer), the Chicago Cubs are owned by the Chicago Tribune Company and the Detroit Tigers are owned by Tom Monaghan (makers of Domino's Pizza).

PAIGE, SATCHEL. "Don't look back. Someone might be gaining on you."

His words are just part of the legend of pitcher Leroy Robert (Satchel) Paige, baseball's ageless wonder. Prevented from playing in the major leagues until after Jackie Robinson became the first black player to sign with a major-league team, Paige came to the Cleveland Indians in

Satchel Paige made his mark with the Kansas City Monarchs in the Negro leagues long before he got a chance to play in the majors.

PALMER, JIM. The date was October 6, 1966, and on the mound in Dodger Stadium, Sandy Koufax was making his final start. A storybook finish would have called for at least a shutout by the Dodgers' Hall of Fame left-hander and, indeed, a shutout was pitched in that second game of the 1966 World Series. But it was pitched by a lanky 20-year-old Baltimore right-hander, Jim Palmer, who threw a four-hit shutout. He thus became the youngest pitcher in World Series history to record a shutout.

Palmer was born on October 15, 1945, in New York City, so he was still nine days away from his 21st birthday when he pitched the shutout. He had won 15 games

Jim Palmer had eight seasons in which he won 20 or more games.

1948, when, according to a Mobile, Alabama, birth certificate, he was 42 years old.

His major-league record, which includes three scoreless innings for the Kansas City Athletics in 1965 when he was 59, was 28-31, remarkable in view of the fact that he was well past his prime. In the Negro leagues he regularly recorded 40-victory seasons, and once he struck out 22 major leaguers in an exhibition game. His long overdue election to the Hall of Fame came in 1971.

that season, but a year later his arm went dead and his career seemed finished. "They told me I would never pitch again," he said.

Determined to work his way back, Palmer spent the next two years pitching in places like Elmira, Rochester and Miami. Slowly but surely the power returned to his right shoulder, and by 1969 he was back in Baltimore.

Palmer pitched a no-hitter against Oakland that season and compiled a 16-4 record. A year later he achieved the first of eight 20-victory seasons over nine years, stamping himself as one of baseball's top pitchers of the 1970s.

He retired after the 1984 season with 268 wins, a career winning percentage of .638 and an earned run average of 2.86. He was elected to the Hall of Fame in 1990.

PASSED BALL. The catcher's failure to control a pitched ball that should have been controlled with ordinary effort and that results in a base runner advancing. It is also charged as an error to the catcher if the batter reaches first base because of a dropped third strike. There can be no passed ball charged unless there is an advance by a base runner.

PAYOFF PITCH. The pitch that follows a three-ball, two-strike count on the batter. It is so called because, except for a foul ball, this pitch disposes of the batter, one way or another. A batter who has reached a count of three and two is said to have "run out the string."

PENNANT. The term most commonly used for a league championship. When it is said that the Yankees won the pennant, it means they won the league championship. Less important is the fact that the league champion also receives an actual flag, or pennant.

The raising of the championship flag at the beginning of each season is a traditional ceremony in the park of the previous year's league champion. It is a ceremony the Yankees have enjoyed more than any other team. Through 1990 the Yankees had won 33 pennants, almost twice as many as any other club. The pennant winners in the American and National leagues meet each fall in the World Series.

PEPPER. Traditional warm-up game played on the sidelines. One batter and one or more throwers take positions at rather close range, the batter rapping or peppering sharp ground balls to each of the throwers in turn.

PERRY, GAYLORD. His hand moved first across the letters of his uniform. Then he tugged at the bill of his cap. His fingers flicked across his mouth, and then he slid them down the side of his pants. Clearly, Gaylord Perry was moistening the baseball. Or was he? If so, when? and where?

Perry used the spitball as a psychological weapon for years. He openly confessed to occasionally using the illegal spitball, but umpires never caught him in the act. As long as batters thought he was throwing a doctored ball and were worried about trying to hit it, Perry figured he had the edge.

Perry, who was born on September 15, 1938, in Williamston, North Carolina, once admitted that he threw a spitball for the first time during a 23-inning marathon game between the San Francisco Giants and New York Mets in 1964—his first full season in coined by Garry Schumacher, who was public relations director of the New York and San Francisco Giants. He applied it to Clint Hartung, a player with the Giants just after World War II.

Hartung, nicknamed the Hondo Hurricane, because he hailed from Hondo, Texas, came to the Giants with such a reputation for versatility and great deeds that the manager's major concern was whether to make him a .400-hitting outfielder or a 30-game winning pitcher. Hartung lasted six years with the Giants, during which time he won 29 games and lost the same number, and had a lifetime batting average of only .238. Since then the term "phenom" has had a skeptical ring.

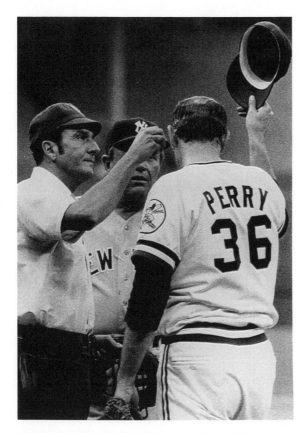

Yankee manager Ralph Houk watches while umpire Lou DiMuro checks the Indians' Gaylord Perry to see if he's using any "greasy kid stuff" when throwing the ball.

the majors. He finished his career in 1983 with the Kansas City Royals, his eighth major-league team. He wound up with 314 victories—14th on the all-time list—and 3,534 strikeouts, and in 1991 he was elected to the Hall of Fame.

PHANTOM INFIELD. A stunt drill, occasionally put on before exhibition games, in which a team goes through the motions of infield practice—fungo hitter and all—without a ball.

PHENOM. Modern lingo for a highly touted rookie, pronounced FEE-nom. Taken from the word "phenomenon," it was

PHILADELPHIA PHILLIES. Top of the ninth, two out, bases loaded, Phillies lead the Royals, 4–1, in the sixth game of the 1980 World Series.

Tug McGraw peers down from the mound at KC's Willie Wilson. Black-helmeted riot police and trained attack dogs ring Veterans Stadium, preparing to control the celebration of long-suffering Philadelphia fans. McGraw fires a fastball past Wilson for a third strike and leaps several feet off the ground.

The Phillies, sustained by the arm of Cy Young Award winner Steve Carlton, the bat of Series MVP Mike Schmidt and the heart of Pete Rose, had finally done it. They'd won their first world championship.

Tug McGraw expresses the joy of victory as the Phillies finish off the Royals in the sixth game of the 1980 World Series.

In 1915, behind pitcher Grover Cleveland Alexander, the Phillies won their first pennant, only to lose to the Boston Red Sox in the World Series. They didn't win another pennant until Eddie Sawyer's Whiz Kids (all of them under 30) rode a Dick Sisler homer to a final-day clinching of the 1950 flag. But despite a formidable pitching staff that included Robin Roberts and MVP Jim Konstanty, the Whiz Kids were swept by the Yankees in the World Series.

Jim Bunning pitched the first perfect game in the National League in 84 years on June 21, 1964, against the Mets. But a stunning, complete collapse of the team in the final two weeks of that season cost the Phillies the pennant.

Rookie manager Dallas Green, a pitcher on the 1961 Phillies team that lost 23 games in a row, led the club out of the wilderness in 1980. The Phils won the division in the final weekend of the season in a head-to-head battle with Montreal, came from behind to beat Houston in the playoffs and then knocked off the Royals in the World Series.

The Phillies made it to the World Series again in 1983 but lost to the Baltimore Orioles in five games.

PICK OFF. To catch a runner off base as the result of a sudden throw from the pitcher or catcher. A good pick-off motion is essential to the success of a pitcher, and therefore many work hard at perfecting their throw to first. It comes naturally to a left-hander, but it is rare that a right-hander has a good pick-off move.

PINCH-HITTER. One batter substituted for another, so called because he is usually used in a pinch—when there are runners on base late in the game and a hit is needed. Men used as pinch-hitters are often players who are not noted for their fielding ability or older players unable to perform at peak efficiency if played daily.

Pinch-hitting is an art, and there have been many successful pinch-hitters. Johnny Frederick, for example, hit six pinch-hit home runs for the Brooklyn Dodgers in 1932. Dave Philley had nine pinch-hits in a row (a record) for the Philadelphia Phillies in 1958 and 1959. The single-season mark for pinch-hits is held by Jose Morales, who collected 25 for Montreal in

1976. The all-time pinch-hit king is Manny Mota, who delivered 150 pinch-hits for various National League teams between 1962 and 1982.

PINCH-RUNNER.   A runner who substitutes for a teammate who has already reached a base; the original runner is out of the game from that time on. A pinch-runner is used because he is faster than the man on base.

PITCH.   A ball delivered to the batter by the pitcher.

PITCHER.   The hurler, twirler, flinger, slinger, flipper, chucker, tosser, moundsman. By any name, he's the one who does the throwing.

PITCHERS' DUEL.   A close, low-scoring game that is dominated by the pitchers. Praised by old-time baseball fans as those good old pitchers' duels; complained about by modern fans as those boring pitchers' duels.

PITCHER'S RUBBER.   A rectangular slab of white rubber 24 inches long and 6 inches wide set in the ground on the pitcher's mound. The pitcher must have his foot on a part of the rubber when he starts his delivery.

PITCHOUT.   A pitch delivered wide of the plate on purpose when the catcher suspects that a runner intends to steal. It is thrown wide so the batter cannot reach it and so the catcher will have a clear path for his throw. The penalty for the privilege

of throwing a pitchout is that the pitch counts as a ball.

PITTSBURGH PIRATES.   The New York Yankees faced the Pirates in the seventh game of the 1960 World Series. The Yankees, winners of 18 previous Series, including a sweep of the Pirates in 1927, had come from behind in the ninth inning to tie the game at 9–9.

The 36,683 fans at Forbes Field were dreading the prospect of extra innings. They didn't have to worry. Leading off the bottom of the ninth, Pittsburgh's Bill Mazeroski hit Ralph Terry's second pitch deep to left. Home run! Jubilant fans circled the bases with Maz, celebrating the remarkable World Series triumph by the Pirates.

Pittsburgh has always had a rich tradition of slugging. The Pirates have won 20 league batting titles, including eight by Honus Wagner, four by Roberto Clemente, and three by Paul Waner. Ralph Kiner won or shared the National League home-run crown seven times and Willie Stargell won it twice.

Wagner, a lifetime .327 hitter, led Pittsburgh to pennants in 1901, 1902 and 1903, the year the Bucs lost the first-ever World Series to the Boston Red Sox.

They won their first World Series in 1909 against the Detroit Tigers, and did it again in 1925 against the Washington Senators. Two years later they were swept by the Yankees.

It took 33 years before they got into another World Series, but in between there were some glorious moments, including the game Harvey Haddix pitched in Milwaukee on May 26, 1959. He threw 12 perfect innings before losing to the Braves, 1–0, in the thirteenth.

It was a year later that the Pirates, with such stars as Bob Friend, Vernon Law, Dick Groat, Clemente and, of course, Mazeroski, downed the Yankees in the World Series.

With Clemente batting .341 during the season and .414 in the Series, and Willie Stargell winning the homer (48) and RBI (154) titles, the Bucs won another World Series, in seven games, over Baltimore in 1971.

The baseball world mourned on December 31, 1972, when, at age 38, Clemente died in a plane crash on a mercy mission to earthquake-ravaged Nicaragua.

The Pirates, maintaining their streak in postseason play, were led by Willie Stargell in 1979 when they bounced back from trailing three-to-one in games to defeat Baltimore in the World Series.

In 1990, paced by the hitting of Barry Bonds and Bobby Bonilla and the pitching of Doug Drabek (22-6), Pittsburgh won the National League East but was ousted in the playoffs by Cincinnati.

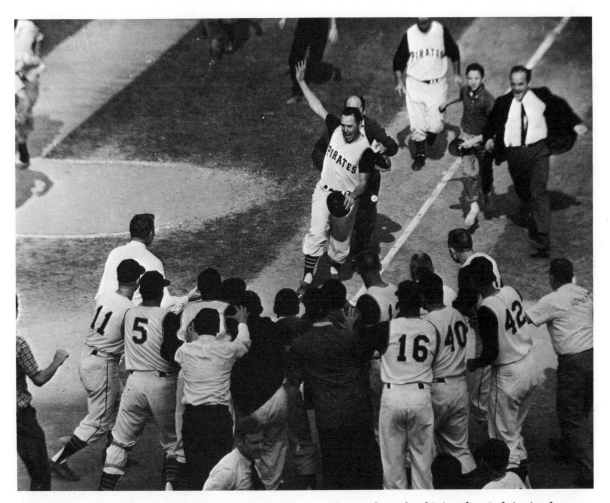

Followed by jubilant fans, the Pirates' Bill Mazeroski nears home plate after hitting the ninth-inning homer that won the 1960 World Series over the Yankees.

PIVOT. The pitcher's pivot foot is the foot that is in contact with the rubber as he delivers the pitch. It also refers to what the second baseman does as he takes a throw from another infielder and tries to complete a double play.

PLATOON. The practice of using two different men for one position, common in football and frequently used in baseball. The greatest believer in platoon baseball was Casey Stengel, who often had one team to play against right-handed pitchers, another against left-handed pitchers. Although the law of averages supports the idea that a left-handed hitter does better against a right-handed pitcher and a right-handed hitter does better against a left-handed pitcher, players like Babe Ruth, Joe DiMaggio, Hank Aaron, Stan Musial, Willie Mays, Rod Carew and Wade Boggs have never been platooned.

PLAYER REPRESENTATIVE. *See* Major League Baseball Players Association.

PLAYOFF. Since 1969 this term has taken on a new meaning. It is a series of games between champions of the Eastern and Western divisions in both leagues. The winner of the playoff is declared the pennant winner and represents its league in the World Series.

While baseball officially refers to this best-of-seven series as the National (or American) League Championship Series, it is more popularly known as the National (or American) League playoffs.

Originally a playoff meant an unscheduled game or series of games that was required when two (or more) teams were tied in games at the end of the regular season. The playoff was necessary to determine the pennant winner.

For the first 45 years of this century,

Celebrating the New York Giants' playoff victory over the Brooklyn Dodgers for the 1951 pennant: *(left to right)* third baseman Bobby Thomson, winning pitcher Larry Jansen and starter Sal Maglie.

there were no major-league playoffs, although there were five in the next 20 years.

In 1946 the Brooklyn Dodgers and the St. Louis Cardinals finished the season tied for first place in the National League. It was decided that they would play a series of three games, the winner of two of them to be crowned champion. The Cardinals defeated the Dodgers in the first two games, making a third game unnecessary.

The American League got into the act two years later when the Boston Red Sox tied the Cleveland Indians. They decided to play just one game to decide the winner. Cleveland defeated Boston and earned the right to represent the American League in the World Series.

All the National League's first four playoffs involved the Dodgers. In Brooklyn they lost to St. Louis in 1946 and to the New York Giants in 1951. In Los Angeles they beat the Milwaukee Braves in 1959 and lost to the San Francisco Giants in 1962.

The most memorable of all playoffs was the one involving the Brooklyn Dodgers and the New York Giants in 1951. Behind by 13½ games as late as August, the Giants stormed back to tie the Dodgers in the last days of the season. The Giants won the first playoff game and the Dodgers the second, setting up the third game as "sudden death."

Going into the last of the ninth inning, the Dodgers led, 4–1. The Giants began hitting Don Newcombe, the starting Dodger pitcher. A series of hits made the score 4–2, and the Giants had two runners on base with just one out. Dodger manager Charlie Dressen replaced Newcombe with Ralph Branca, and Giant Bobby Thomson hit Branca's second pitch for the most dramatic home run in baseball history. The Giants won the game, 5–4, and the right to play in the World Series, climaxing what has been romantically called the Little Miracle of Coogan's Bluff (Coogan's Bluff overlooked the Polo Grounds, where the game was played).

Since the Championship Series format began in 1969, a single-game playoff has been held to break first-place ties. In 1978 the New York Yankees defeated the Boston Red Sox, and in 1980 the Houston Astros beat the Los Angeles Dodgers.

POP FLY. A ball hit on a high fly to the infield, usually easily caught. Also called a pop-up and, when in foul territory, a foul pop.

PRESS BOX. The quarters assigned to reporters at the game, usually equipped with communication facilities. It is the place from which reporters view the game and write the stories that appear in the next day's newspapers. Press boxes have evolved from the old wooden boxes (still used in some minor-league parks) to modern, plush quarters.

PROMOTER. In its early years baseball got so much free publicity that all the owners had to do was to open the gates and the people would come. But when other professional sports and television began to compete for the entertainment dollar, many club owners realized they had to advertise their product, although a number clung to the old notion that baseball did not need promoting.

The most flamboyant and most successful promoter in the game was Bill Veeck, who owned, at different times, the St. Louis Browns, Cleveland Indians and Chicago White Sox and, not accidentally, set attendance records with each of them. Veeck used circus-type promotional stunts with unprecedented success. He gave away orchids to ladies and established a babysitting room so that young parents could go to the ballpark and not have to worry about what to do with their kids. His stunts were endless. His most famous one was using a midget, Eddie Gaedel, as a pinch-hitter in a regulation ball game.

Baseball's sideshows, as promoted by Veeck and others like him, are most common in the minor leagues and may feature anything from golf exhibitions to weddings at home plate. They may include fireworks, songfests, clown acts, foot races, beauty parades, giveaway shows and participation by the players in such events as hitting baseballs into the stands, throwing a ball into a barrel, heaving raw eggs at one another and milking a cow.

Veeck was scorned by his competitors, but many of his innovations, including an exploding scoreboard, are still used. To-

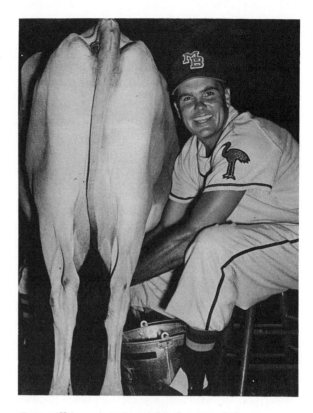

Cow-milking contests used to be one of the sideshows in the minor leagues.

Three-foot seven-inch Eddie Gaedel pinch-hit for the St. Louis Browns against the Detroit Tigers on August 19, 1951—a stunt conceived by promoter-owner Bill Veeck. The catcher was Bob Swift, and the umpire was Ed Hurley. Gaedel walked.

day most major-league clubs give away almost anything—from bats to gloves to tote bags to watches—to attract people to the ballpark.

PUCKETT, KIRBY. As living proof that good things do come in small packages, 5-foot 8-inch, 210-pound Kirby Puckett has done nothing but reward the Minnesota Twins for making him the third player drafted in the nation in January 1982.

Born on March 14, 1961, in Chicago, Puckett joined Al Simmons as the only right-handed hitters ever to collect 200 or more hits in as many as four straight years when he turned that trick in 1989. The Twin center fielder even seized the American League batting crown from Wade Boggs in 1989 with a .339 mark, which gave Puckett four straight years at .328 or above.

Puckett has also shown more power than most batting-title contenders. After going homerless in 557 at-bats as a rookie in 1984, he flexed his muscles in 1986, when he hit 31 homers and drove in 96 runs. This five-time All-Star unloaded 28 and 24 homers in the next two seasons.

This stumpy powerhouse tied an AL record with six hits against Milwaukee on August 30, 1987. He led the Twins to World Series glory that season when he hit .357 vs. the Cardinals. And in 1988, Puckett hit .356—the highest mark posted by a righty batter in the AL since Joe DiMaggio's .357 in 1941—and had 121 RBIs and scored 109 runs.

Kirby's excellence extends to his fielding, too. He led AL outfielders with 16 assists in 1984 and won four Gold Gloves in a row from 1986 to 1989.

PULL HITTER. One who consistently and effectively hits a ball down or close to the foul line—left field for a right-handed hitter, right field for a left-handed hitter. It is so called because the action of a right-handed hitter leaves him pointing in the direction of left field when he has followed through. If a right-handed hitter hits to right field or a left-handed hitter to left field, it is called hitting to the opposite field or pushing the ball, a very useful device if done successfully. One who can hit the ball well to all fields is called a spray hitter.

PUTOUT. The retiring of an opponent by a defensive player.

Kirby Puckett's consistent hitting brought him the American League batting crown in 1989 and makes him a perennial candidate for more honors.

QUICK PITCH. Also, a quick return. A pitch thrown hurriedly with the obvious intention of catching the batter unprepared. If it is detected by the umpire—which happens rarely—a quick pitch is called a balk, entitling all runners to advance one base. If the bases are empty, it is called a ball.

imaginable. As Casey Stengel, the most famous baseball manager of all, used to say: "You can look it up."

The records on pages 126–128 are the major ones, for batting and pitching. (*See also* Statistician.)

RAINCHECK. A ticket stub good for future admission if fewer than 4½ innings have been played before the game is called. Rainchecks were first used in New Orleans in 1888. The word has been taken into general slang and means to turn down an invitation while expressing the hope that it will be good at a later date.

REGULATION GAME. A game that has come to a decision after the prescribed nine innings or more. Also, a game that has been called off, for whatever reason, after the losing team has been to bat five times. If it is called off before that time or if it is tied when it is called off, it is not a regulation game and must be replayed.

RECORDS. Baseball, more than any other sport, has hundreds of all-time records, covering every position and every category

RELIEF PITCHER. A substitute pitcher who replaces the starting pitcher or another relief pitcher. Relief pitchers fall into three basic categories—the mop-up man, the long man and the short man.

Batting

CAREER

Games Played	3,562	Pete Rose, Cincinnati, Philadelphia, Montreal (all NL), 1963–1986
Batting Average	.367	Ty Cobb, Detroit (AL), Philadelphia (AL), 1905–1928
At-Bats	14,053	Pete Rose, Cincinnati, Philadelphia, Montreal (all NL), 1963–1986
Runs Scored	2,245	Ty Cobb, Detroit (AL), Philadelphia (AL), 1905–1928
Hits	4,256	Pete Rose, Cincinnati, Philadelphia, Montreal (all NL), 1963–1986
Doubles	792	Tris Speaker, Boston, Cleveland, Washington, Philadelphia (all AL), 1907–1928
Triples	312	Sam Crawford, Cincinnati (NL), Detroit (AL), 1899–1917
Home Runs	755	Hank Aaron, Milwaukee-Atlanta (NL), Milwaukee (AL), 1954–1976
Runs Batted In	2,297	Hank Aaron, Milwaukee-Atlanta (NL), Milwaukee (AL), 1954–1976
Stolen Bases	938	Lou Brock, Chicago (NL), St. Louis (NL), 1961–1979
Bases on Balls	2,056	Babe Ruth, Boston (AL), New York (AL), Boston (NL), 1914–1935
Strikeouts	2,597	Reggie Jackson, Kansas City–Oakland, Baltimore, New York, California (all AL), 1967–1987

The mop-up man is usually considered to be the weakest or least experienced pitcher on the team. He comes in when the outcome of the game is no longer in doubt—that is, when his team is way behind.

The long man is usually an alternate starter who gets the call when the starting pitcher gets in trouble early in the game, within the first four innings. The long man is expected to pitch anywhere from five to seven good innings.

The short man is the famed fireman, the relief specialist whom no good team can do without. He comes in late in the game when the score is close and the situation is serious but not hopeless. He is the fireman because he is called in to put out the fire (an opposing team's rally).

The fireman is a vital member of the team, and he has gained great prominence in recent years, although his importance was acknowledged as far back as the mid-1920s, when Wilcy Moore and Firpo Mar-

---

SEASON

Games Played	165	Maury Wills, Los Angeles (NL), 1962
Batting Average (since 1900)	.424	Rogers Hornsby, St. Louis (NL), 1924
At-Bats	705	Willie Wilson, Kansas City (AL), 1980
Runs Scored (since 1900)	177	Babe Ruth, New York (AL), 1921
Hits	257	George Sisler, St. Louis (AL), 1920
Doubles	67	Earl Webb, Boston (AL), 1931
Triples	36	J. Owen Wilson, Pittsburgh (NL), 1912
Home Runs	61	Roger Maris, New York (AL), 1961 (162-game schedule)
	60	Babe Ruth, New York (AL), 1927 (154-game schedule)
Runs Batted In	190	Hack Wilson, Chicago (NL), 1930
Stolen Bases	130	Rickey Henderson, Oakland (AL), 1982
Bases on Balls	170	Babe Ruth, New York (AL), 1923
Strikeouts	189	Bobby Bonds, San Francisco (NL), 1970

GAME

At-Bats	11	14 players; last done by Julio Cruz, Carlton Fisk and Rudy Law (all Chicago, AL) and Cecil Cooper, Milwaukee (AL), May 8–9, 1984 (25 innings)
Runs	6	12 players; last done by Spike Owen, Boston (AL), August 21, 1986
Hits	9	John Burnett, Cleveland (AL), July 10, 1932 (18 innings)
Doubles	4	34 players; last done by Damaso Garcia, Toronto (AL), June 27, 1986
Triples (since 1900)	4	42 players; last done by Craig Reynolds, Houston (NL), May 16, 1981
Home Runs	4	11 players; last done by Bob Horner, Atlanta (NL), July 6, 1986
Runs Batted In	12	Jim Bottomley, St. Louis (NL), September 16, 1924
Stolen Bases (since 1900)	6	Eddie Collins, Philadelphia (AL), September 11 and September 22 (first game), 1912
Bases on Balls (since 1900)	6	Jimmie Foxx, Boston (AL), June 16, 1938; Andre Thornton, Cleveland (AL), May 2, 1984 (16 innings).
Strikeouts	6	Five players; last done by Cecil Cooper, Boston (AL), June 14, 1974 (15 innings)

Pitching

CAREER

Games	1,070	Hoyt Wilhelm, New York (NL), St. Louis (NL), Cleveland (AL), Baltimore (AL), Chicago (AL), California (AL), Atlanta (NL), Chicago (NL), Los Angeles (NL), 1952–1972
Innings	7,356	Cy Young, Cleveland (NL), St. Louis (NL), Boston (AL), Cleveland (AL), Boston (NL), 1890–1911
Victories	511	Cy Young, Cleveland (NL), St. Louis (NL), Boston (AL), Cleveland (AL), Boston (NL), 1890–1911
Losses	315	Cy Young, Cleveland (NL), St. Louis (NL), Boston (AL), Cleveland (AL), Boston (NL), 1890–1911
Saves	341	Rollie Fingers, Oakland (AL), San Diego (NL), Milwaukee (AL), 1968–1985
Strikeouts	5,308	Nolan Ryan, New York (NL), California (AL), Houston (NL), Texas (AL), 1966–1990
Bases on Balls	2,614	Nolan Ryan, New York (NL), California (AL), Houston (NL), Texas (AL), 1966–1990
Earned Run Average (3,000 or more innings)	2.06	Three Finger Brown, St. Louis (NL), Chicago (NL), Cincinnati (NL), St. Louis (FL), Brooklyn (FL), Chicago (FL), Chicago (NL), 1903–1916
Shutouts	110	Walter Johnson, Washington (AL), 1907–1927

SEASON

Games	106	Mike Marshall, Los Angeles (NL), 1974
Innings (since 1900)	464	Ed Walsh, Chicago (AL), 1908
Victories (since 1900)	41	Jack Chesbro, New York (AL), 1904
Losses (since 1900)	29	Victor Willis, Boston (NL), 1905
Saves	57	Bobby Thigpen, Chicago (AL), 1990
Strikeouts (since 1900)	383	Nolan Ryan, California (AL), 1973
Bases on Balls (since 1900)	208	Bob Feller, Cleveland (AL), 1938
Earned Run Average (300 or more innings)	1.09	Walter Johnson, Washington (AL), 1913
Shutouts (since 1900)	16	Grover Cleveland Alexander, Philadelphia (NL), 1916

GAME

Innings Pitched	26	Leon Cadore, Brooklyn (NL); Joseph Oeschger, Boston (NL), May 1, 1920
Runs (since 1900)	24	Aloysius Travers, Detroit (AL), May 19, 1912
Hits (since 1900)	26	Harley Parker, Cincinnati (NL), June 21, 1901; Horace Lisenbee, Philadelphia (AL), September 11, 1936
Strikeouts	21	Thomas Cheney, Washington (AL), September 12, 1962 (16 innings)
Strikeouts (9-inning game)	20	Roger Clemens, Boston (AL), April 29, 1986
Bases on Balls	16	Three players; last done by Bruno Haas, Philadelphia (AL), June 23, 1915

berry were the first of the great firemen. Marberry appeared in 64 games for the Washington Senators in 1926 and was so important to the team that they would delay the starting time so that when Firpo was ready to go to work, late in the game, shadows would have begun to descend and his fastball would be more effective.

Johnny Murphy of the New York Yankees was the leading fireman in the 1930s, but it wasn't until the early 1940s that Hugh Casey of the Brooklyn Dodgers and Joe Page of the Yankees began to get proper recognition for the rescue squad. Ace Adams appeared in 70 games for the New York Giants in 1943, and Jim Konstanty topped that for the Philadelphia Phillies in 1950, appearing in 74 games and winning the National League Most Valuable Player Award, a first for a relief pitcher. Konstanty's record was broken by Mike Marshall of the Los Angeles Dodgers, who pitched in 106 games in 1974.

Bobby Thigpen of the White Sox owns the major-league mark with 57 saves in a season (1990).

Hugh Casey saved many a Dodger starter as a fireman in the late 1940s.

In subsequent years there have been such outstanding relievers as Rollie Fingers (A's, Padres and Brewers), Sparky Lyle (Red Sox, Yankees, Rangers, Phillies and White Sox), Willie Hernandez (Cubs, Phillies and Tigers), Dan Quisenberry (Royals and Cardinals) and Goose Gossage (White Sox, Pirates, Yankees, Padres, Cubs and Giants).

Among the top current firemen are the White Sox' Bobby Thigpen, who set a major-league record with 57 saves in 1990; Dennis Eckersley (Indians, Red Sox, Cubs and A's); Dave Righetti (Yankees and Giants); John Franco (Reds and Mets); and Randy Myers (Mets and Reds).

RESERVE CLAUSE. The controversial clause binding a player to his team. It was an important part of baseball for more than 50 years until it was buried by agreement in the summer of 1976. The standard players' contract had said that a player signing for one year also agreed to play for the club the year after, if the club wanted him to. Since players always signed contracts each year before being permitted to play, the reserve clause was, in effect, a contract for life.

But through the agreement of 1976 and other modifications through the years, players who have completed six years of major-league service are eligible to become free agents when their contracts expire. (See also Free agent and Major League Baseball Players Association.)

RESIN BAG. A bag that is placed in back of the pitcher's mound that contains resin, a sticky substance, which the pitcher may rub on his hands in order to dry them, though he may not rub resin on the ball. Resin is the only thing the pitcher may rub on his hand, but that does not stop pitchers from trying (and succeeding, in some cases) to use such sticky substances as hair tonic, saliva and petroleum jelly. The purpose of resin is to keep the ball from slipping. It is also used at certain times by a batter when his hands perspire so much that gripping the bat is difficult. In recent years batters have switched from resin to a rag saturated with pine tar, another sticky substance.

RHUBARB. A baseball controversy or argument, particularly an explosive one, on the field. Red Barber, who was a distinguished broadcaster with the Cincinnati Reds, Brooklyn Dodgers and New York Yankees, began using the expression on the air in 1939 after picking it up from baseball writers Garry Schumacher and Tom Meany, who had heard the word used by a Brooklyn bartender to describe a barroom brawl. A variation, also used by Barber, was, "They're tearing up the pea patch."

RIBBY. Players' slang for a run batted in, derived from trying to pronounce its initials: RBI. (See also Runs batted in.)

RIGHT FIELD. The outfield territory beyond first base bordered on the right by the right foul line and on the left by the area covered by the center fielder. The outfielder who covers right field is called the right fielder.

ROBINSON, FRANK. It was on October 3, 1974, that Frank Robinson was named major-league baseball's first black manager. His job with the Cleveland Indians lasted less than three seasons, but he got another shot when he took over as man-

Billy Martin could always be counted on to provoke a rhubarb whether he was with the Yankees or any other team.

ager of the San Francisco Giants in 1981 and again at Baltimore in 1989, where he oversaw the Orioles' transformation from a last-place team to a contender that challenged Toronto for American League East honors until the next-to-last day of the season.

As a player, Robinson proved himself time and again. He is the only one to have won the Most Valuable Player Award in both leagues—with the Cincinnati Reds in 1961 and the Baltimore Orioles in 1966, when he won the Triple Crown (the league leader in batting average, RBIs and home runs). He also played with the Los Angeles Dodgers, the California Angels and the Cleveland Indians for a total of 21 seasons in which he hit 586 home runs and posted a lifetime batting average of .294. He was elected to the Hall of Fame in 1982.

An all-star outfielder, Robinson was born in Beaumont, Texas, on August 31, 1935, the youngest of 10 children.

ROBINSON, JACKIE. The abuse poured down on him, from the stands where fans cupped their hands around their mouths and shouted racial insults, and from the dugouts, where opposing players did the same thing. On the field Jackie Robinson, the first black man in organized baseball and the first of his race to make it to the major leagues, stood with his hands on his hips, trying not to show his emotions as his blood boiled inside.

After a few moments Robinson felt an arm around his shoulders. There beside him stood Pee Wee Reese, a native of Kentucky and captain of the Brooklyn Dodgers in that summer of 1947. Reese's gesture was symbolic, an eloquent statement of support for a man facing the greatest pressure and test of character imaginable.

Robinson had been carefully selected by Dodger owner Branch Rickey as the man

Jackie Robinson, the first black player in the majors, played for the Montreal Royals of the International League before joining the Brooklyn Dodgers in 1947.

who would shatter baseball's color line. "I'm looking for a ballplayer with guts enough *not* to fight back," Rickey told Robinson. To his credit, Robinson, one of the game's fiercest competitors, kept his pledge to Rickey and turned the other cheek to the abuse being heaped on him. His courage forced open the doors of the sport to blacks, who had been previously barred from the majors.

Robinson was born in Cairo, Georgia, on January 31, 1919, and was a four-sport college star at UCLA. Rickey plucked him out of baseball's Negro leagues in 1946 and changed the face of baseball forever.

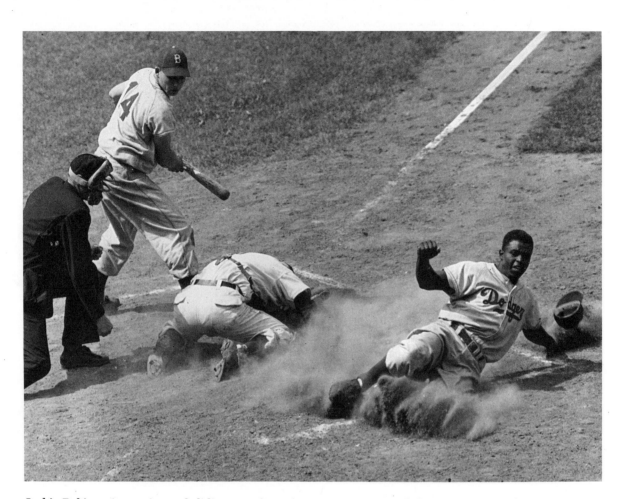

Jackie Robinson's running and sliding gave fits to his opponents. He stole home 19 times in his career.

In 10 seasons with the Brooklyn Dodgers, Robinson achieved a .311 batting average and hit over .300 six times. He played on six pennant winners and was the National League batting champion and MVP in 1949, when he batted .342. His basepath daring—taunting pitchers with fake starts—and clutch hitting made him the unquestioned leader of the Dodgers.

Robinson was elected to the Hall of Fame in 1962, his first year of eligibility. Ten years later, at age 53, he died of a heart attack.

ROOKIE. Also, a rook. A first-year player. Traditionally rookies are supposed to be innocent, and veteran players often take advantage of this by making them the butt of their inevitable gags. The most famous gag is to give the rookie a message to call a Mrs. Lyons. When the rookie calls the number given him, he finds he has reached the zoo.

Outstanding rookies are candidates for the Rookie-of-the-Year Award given in each league. They are chosen by the Baseball Writers Association of America, whose votes are based on best all-around performance. The award was begun by the National League in 1947 and by the American League in 1949.

ROSE, PETE. It was September 11, 1985, and the fans who filled Cincinnati's Riv-

Rookies of the Year

NATIONAL LEAGUE

Year	Player, Club
1947	Jackie Robinson, Brooklyn Dodgers
1948	Al Dark, Boston Braves
1949	Don Newcombe, Brooklyn Dodgers
1950	Sam Jethroe, Boston Braves
1951	Willie Mays, New York Giants
1952	Joe Black, Brooklyn Dodgers
1953	Junior Gilliam, Brooklyn Dodgers
1954	Wally Moon, St. Louis Cardinals
1955	Bill Virdon, St. Louis Cardinals
1956	Frank Robinson, Cincinnati Reds
1957	Jack Sanford, Philadelphia Phillies
1958	Orlando Cepeda, San Francisco Giants
1959	Willie McCovey, San Francisco Giants
1960	Frank Howard, Los Angeles Dodgers
1961	Billy Williams, Chicago Cubs
1962	Kenny Hubbs, Chicago Cubs
1963	Pete Rose, Cincinnati Reds
1964	Richie Allen, Philadelphia Phillies
1965	Jim Lefebvre, Los Angeles Dodgers
1966	Tommy Helms, Cincinnati Reds
1967	Tom Seaver, New York Mets
1968	Johnny Bench, Cincinnati Reds
1969	Ted Sizemore, Los Angeles Dodgers
1970	Carl Morton, Montreal Expos
1971	Earl Williams, Atlanta Braves
1972	Jon Matlack, New York Mets
1973	Gary Matthews, San Francisco Giants
1974	Bake McBride, St. Louis Cardinals
1975	John Montefusco, San Francisco Giants
1976	Pat Zachry, Cincinnati Reds
	Butch Metzger, San Diego Padres
1977	Andre Dawson, Montreal Expos
1978	Bob Horner, Atlanta Braves
1979	Rick Sutcliffe, Los Angeles Dodgers
1980	Steve Howe, Los Angeles Dodgers
1981	Fernando Valenzuela, Los Angeles Dodgers
1982	Steve Sax, Los Angeles Dodgers
1983	Darryl Strawberry, New York Mets
1984	Dwight Gooden, New York Mets
1985	Vince Coleman, St. Louis Cardinals
1986	Todd Worrell, St. Louis Cardinals
1987	Benito Santiago, San Diego Padres
1988	Chris Sabo, Cincinnati Reds
1989	Jerome Walton, Chicago Cubs
1990	Dave Justice, Atlanta Braves

AMERICAN LEAGUE

Year	Player, Club
1949	Roy Sievers, St. Louis Browns
1950	Walt Dropo, Boston Red Sox
1951	Gil McDougald, New York Yankees
1952	Harry Byrd, Philadelphia Athletics
1953	Harvey Kuenn, Detroit Tigers
1954	Bob Grim, New York Yankees
1955	Herb Score, Cleveland Indians
1956	Luis Aparicio, Chicago White Sox
1957	Tony Kubek, New York Yankees
1958	Albie Pearson, Washington Senators
1959	Bob Allison, Washington Senators
1960	Ron Hansen, Baltimore Orioles
1961	Don Schwall, Boston Red Sox
1962	Tom Tresh, New York Yankees
1963	Gary Peters, Chicago White Sox
1964	Tony Oliva, Minnesota Twins
1965	Curt Blefary, Baltimore Orioles
1966	Tommie Agee, Chicago White Sox
1967	Rod Carew, Minnesota Twins
1968	Stan Bahnsen, New York Yankees
1969	Lou Piniella, Kansas City Royals
1970	Thurman Munson, New York Yankees
1971	Chris Chambliss, Cleveland Indians
1972	Carlton Fisk, Boston Red Sox
1973	Al Bumbry, Baltimore Orioles
1974	Mike Hargrove, Texas Rangers
1975	Fred Lynn, Boston Red Sox
1976	Mark Fidrych, Detroit Tigers
1977	Eddie Murray, Baltimore Orioles
1978	Lou Whitaker, Detroit Tigers
1979	John Castino, Minnesota Twins
	Alfredo Griffin, Toronto Blue Jays
1980	Joe Charboneau, Cleveland Indians
1981	Dave Righetti, New York Yankees
1982	Cal Ripken, Jr., Baltimore Orioles
1983	Ron Kittle, Chicago White Sox
1984	Alvin Davis, Seattle Mariners
1985	Ozzie Guillen, Chicago White Sox
1986	Jose Canseco, Oakland A's
1987	Mark McGwire, Oakland A's
1988	Walt Weiss, Oakland A's
1989	Greg Olson, Baltimore Orioles
1990	Sandy Alomar, Jr., Cleveland Indians

erfront Stadium were there to see one thing—hometown hero Pete Rose break Ty Cobb's "unbreakable" record of 4,191 career hits. After five months of intense media pressure, Rose had finally tied the mark three days earlier in Chicago. Now, back in front of the people who idolized him, he was determined to break it.

And break it he did. In the first inning, Rose stepped to the plate against San Diego Padre right-hander Eric Show and at 8:01 P.M. lined a ball to left-center that Carmelo Martinez had no chance to catch. When the ball dropped in, Rose had his record, and a standing ovation from the crowd that had just witnessed history.

Rose had always been known as Charlie Hustle, a nickname he earned while play-ing for the Reds in a spring-training game against the New York Yankees in 1963. It was Hall of Famer Whitey Ford who hung the nickname on Rose when the rookie sprinted to first base after drawing a walk. "Hey, Charlie Hustle, take it easy," Ford teased. But Rose never took it easy, either as player or manager.

Born on April 4, 1941, in Cincinnati, Rose was a hometown hero for 16 seasons with the Reds, establishing many club records and helping his team win five divisional titles, four pennants and two world championships. He left as a free agent, and the Philadelphia Phillies, figuring his aggressive style was just what the club needed to become a winner, signed him in 1979, one year after he set a modern-day Na-

Pete Rose, whose headfirst slides typified the way "Charlie Hustle" played the game, scores against the Giants on July 30, 1972.

tional League record by getting a base hit in 44 consecutive games.

Rose had nearly 400 hits in his first two seasons with the Phillies, and his key defensive play in Game 6 of the 1980 World Series helped bring Philadelphia fans their first World Series title.

After a brief stay with the Montreal Expos in 1984, Rose returned to Cincinnati that August and was named player-manager. He concluded his magnificent career in 1986 with a batch of all-time records, including games played (3,562), at-bats (14,053) and, of course, hits (4,256).

Rose's story did not have a happy ending, though. He was suspended from baseball in 1989 by Commissioner A. Bartlett Giamatti for allegedly gambling on baseball games. In 1990 he was sent to prison for income-tax evasion.

RUBBER. The pitcher's plate. (*See also* Mound.)

RUBBER ARM. A pitcher who can work day after day and maintain effectiveness. Such a pitcher was Mike Marshall, a relief pitcher for the Los Angeles Dodgers, who set a major-league record by appearing in 106 of his team's 162 games in 1974.

In baseball history there have been 39 pitchers who have pitched and won two complete games in one day, the last being Emil Levsen of the Cleveland Indians in 1926. Four men performed that rubber-arm stunt twice, and another, Joe McGinnity of the New York Giants, did it three times in one month, earning him the nickname Iron Man.

RUBBER GAME. The deciding or odd game of a series that will break a tie in that series.

RUN. The score made by an offensive player who advances from the batter's box and touches first, second, third and home in that order. "Let's get some runs" is probably the most widely used and oft-repeated phrase in baseball.

The modern major-league record for most runs in a game is 49, made when the Chicago White Sox defeated the Philadelphia Athletics, 26–23, on August 25, 1922. The Boston Red Sox and the White Sox share the modern record for most runs by a team in a game at 29. The Red Sox made theirs against the St. Louis Browns on June 8, 1950; the White Sox against the Kansas City A's on April 23, 1955. In 1953 the Red Sox set a modern record by scoring 17 runs in a single inning.

RUNDOWN. The defensive act that attempts to put out a runner caught between bases.

RUNS BATTED IN. Also known as RBIs, or ribbies. Credit given to a batter for each run that scores when he makes a hit or is retired by an infield or outfield putout, or when a run is forced in because he becomes a base runner. However, an RBI is not credited to a batter if he hits into a double play. RBIs are the lifeblood of the offense and the most coveted statistic by hitters, even more than hits, homers or batting average.

All-time home-run champ Hank Aaron has the most career RBIs, 2,297. Babe Ruth shares with Lou Gehrig and Jimmie Foxx the record for having 13 years of 100 or more RBIs each year, although Hack Wilson of the Chicago Cubs holds the record for the most RBIs in a single season, 190 in 1930.

The following year Lou Gehrig set the American League record of 184. Jim Bot-

Before he became an outfielder, Babe Ruth was an outstanding pitcher with the Boston Red Sox.

tomley of the St. Louis Cardinals had 12 RBIs in one game in 1924, and nine players in modern times have knocked in six runs in an inning, including Jim Ray Hart of the San Francisco Giants in 1970 and Andre Dawson of the Montreal Expos in 1985.

RUTH, BABE. The bat sat back on Babe Ruth's shoulder as the pitcher began his windup. As the delivery was made, Ruth cocked the bat, dipping it in time with the pitch. Then he swung.

When he connected just right, the crack of the bat, wood smashing ball, commanded attention. The ball soared toward right field, and Ruth, the master of the dramatic, would watch it as it sailed for the seats. Then the Babe would break into his home-run trot, mincing steps on bandy legs that seemed strained to the limit carrying his top-heavy body.

The Babe was an American hero, a legendary character who sometimes seemed larger than life. In the 1920s, the Golden Age of Sports, no man dominated the scene as completely as Ruth. He had a gusto that captivated everyone.

Ruth, of course, was the greatest home-run hitter of his time, setting a career record of 714 and a single-season mark of 60 (in 1927). Both records were eventually broken, but they remain cherished numbers in baseball lore.

When Yankee Stadium was built in 1923, its inviting short right field was perfect for the left-handed Ruth. The Babe flourished there and hit the first home run in the stadium's history. He also hit the first All-Star Game homer in 1933, in Chicago.

Ruth hit 50 or more homers in a season four times and led his league in runs batted in six times. He finished his career with a .342 batting average.

George Herman Ruth was born in Bal-timore on February 6, 1895, and came to the majors in 1914 as a pitcher with the Boston Red Sox. In 1916 he posted a 23–12 record and led the league with a 1.75 earned run average. A year later he won 24 games and posted a 2.01 ERA. He set a record of 29⅔ scoreless innings in a row in the World Series and posted a 3–0 record and 0.87 ERA over two Series.

But Ruth was too good a hitter to remain a pitcher, which he proved after being sold to the Yankees. He was a charter member of the Hall of Fame and was mourned by millions when he died in 1948 at the age of 53.

RYAN, NOLAN. The A's' Rickey Henderson stepped into the batter's box. On the mound the Rangers' Nolan Ryan swung into his windup. Ryan kicked his left leg into the air, cocked his right arm and brought his body forward. His leg came down and he planted his foot forward as his arm came forward. The effect was like a slingshot, and the baseball hurtled toward the plate at nearly 100 miles per hour.

Henderson was overmatched, managing only a feeble swing as the ball flew by him. Suddenly, Arlington Stadium exploded. Ryan, who had spent his career doing what appeared to be impossible, had done it again. On August 23, 1989, he reached the almost unimaginable total of 5,000 career strikeouts.

To put that number into perspective, consider that a pitcher would need 25 seasons of 200 strikeouts to reach 5,000.

No pitcher in history has been able to match Ryan's endurance. Born on January 31, 1947, in Refugio, Texas, Ryan had one of his finest seasons in 1989, when at the age of 42 he won 16 games for the Rangers and struck out 301 batters. Already the all-time record holder with five no-hitters, Ryan carried bids for another into the eighth inning five times, only to be denied. In 1990, however, he was successful, pitching his sixth no-hitter on June 11 against the A's. Three weeks later he won his 300th game. By the end of 1990, Ryan had amassed 302 career victories (and 272 defeats), a record 5,308 strikeouts and a host of other major-league records that are unlikely to be broken.

Ageless Nolan Ryan has set marks for strikeouts and no-hitters that may never be broken.

SABERHAGEN, BRET. Someday, many, many years from now, Bret Saberhagen will tell his grandchildren about the year he had at age 21 in 1985. This is a tale that should begin with the words "Once upon a time . . ."

After showing little hint of greatness in a 10–11 rookie season with the Kansas City Royals in 1984, Saberhagen blossomed overnight. On September 30, 1985, the right-hander defeated the California Angels to become the fifth-youngest 20-game winner in American League history. His 20–6 record and 2.87 ERA reflected the remarkable control and poise that prompted his selection as the third-youngest Cy Young Award winner in history. However, his story was just beginning as the regular season ended.

On the World Series stage against the St. Louis Cardinals, Saberhagen was magnificent. He gave up one run in 18 innings in two complete-game victories, including an 11–0 win in Game 7. And, within a span of 36 hours, Bret became a father for the first time and won the World Series MVP award.

Saberhagen, born on April 11, 1964, in Chicago Heights, Illinois, fell off dramatically in 1986, as injuries limited him to a 7–12 mark. He won 18 games in 1987 and 14 in 1988 before recapturing his 1985 form in 1989. That was when he led the AL in wins with a club-record 23, ERA at 2.16, complete games with 12, innings with 262.1 and winning percentage at .793. Ap-

Right from the start, Kansas City's Bret Saberhagen proved his mastery on the mound.

ally. It occurs only when a batter has hit a ball far enough so that a runner may score from third base after the catch. The batter gets an RBI and is credited with a sacrifice (no official time at bat) only if the runner scores.

SAFE. A declaration by the umpire that a runner reached the base for which he was trying before the ball did. The umpire signals a runner safe by putting his hands down, palms parallel to the ground.

SAILER. A pitched ball that takes off—that is, it sails upward as it approaches the batter.

propriately, he won his second Cy Young Award.

SACRIFICE. A play in which the batter is out but is not charged with an official time at bat because he has succeeded in moving a teammate along on the bases at the expense of his turn at bat, whether intentionally or not. There are two types of sacrifices: the sacrifice bunt (sometimes called a sacrifice hit) and the sacrifice fly.

The sacrifice bunt is hit, usually under orders, to advance another runner. The batter deliberately gives up his time at bat to improve his team's chances of scoring. The sacrifice fly is rarely done intention-

ST. LOUIS CARDINALS. The cat-and-mouse game was on. Philadelphia pitcher Dick Ruthven stepped off the rubber and fired to first. The Cards' Lou Brock scampered back ahead of the tag. But as soon as Ruthven made his next pitch, Brock was off to the races.

It was, as it was so often with Brock, no contest. Sliding under Bob Boone's peg, Brock stole his 105th base of the 1974 season, breaking the record set by Los Angeles' Maury Wills in 1962. By the time he finished the 1974 season, Brock had swiped 118 bases. He retired in 1979 with a major-league career record of 938.

Aggressive base-running has always played a key role in the Cardinals' success. In the 1946 World Series against the Bos-

Pepper Martin, one of the Cardinals' Gashouse Gang in the 1930s, demonstrates his sliding technique.

ton Red Sox, Enos Slaughter scored all the way from first base on a single to give the Cardinals the championship. And the running of Brock and Curt Flood helped St. Louis defeat Boston again in the 1967 World Series. Then in the 1980s speedsters like Willie McGee, Ozzie Smith and Vince Coleman played major roles with one of the National League's most feared clubs.

The Cards won the 1982 Series by battling back from a three-games-to-two deficit to defeat the Milwaukee Brewers, and their success continued in 1985 and 1987, when they won pennants. Injuries to key players hurt the Cardinals in the World Series both those years, though, and they lost in seven games to the Kansas City Royals and Minnesota Twins, respectively. Still, just by making it to the World Series the Cardinals maintained their rich tradition.

In the 1926 World Series victory over the Yankees, pitcher Grover Cleveland Alexander had two wins and a save at the age of 39. Pepper Martin's 12 hits paced the Cards when they won the 1931 Series in seven games over Philadelphia. With Dizzy Dean becoming the last National

League pitcher to win 30 games and with Ducky Medwick, player-manager Frankie Frisch, Leo Durocher and Martin adding the fuel, the Cardinals' Gashouse Gang won a seven-game Series over the Tigers in 1934. St. Louis was world champion again in 1942, 1944 and 1946.

Despite the presence of Stan (the Man) Musial, a lifetime .331 hitter, St. Louis didn't win another pennant until 1964, when Brock, Ken Boyer, Curt Flood and Bob Gibson led the way to a seven-game triumph over the Yankees. And in 1967 they won the world championship again, over the Red Sox.

Gibson, an overwhelming right-hander, fanned 17 Detroit players in the first game of the 1968 World Series against Detroit, but the Cardinals lost in seven.

Peerless fielding has been his forte, but Ozzie Smith is also a wizard on the basepaths and a timely switch-hitter.

SAN DIEGO PADRES. After two games of the 1984 National League Championship Series, everyone but the most ardent San Diego Padre fans conceded the series to the Chicago Cubs. The Cubs had won the first two games by scores of 13–0 and 4–2, and they needed just one win in three games in San Diego to wrap up the series. And if the Padres did manage to come back and tie the series, didn't the Cubs have ace right-hander Rick Sutcliffe ready to pitch Game 5?

While all that was true, the Padres weren't quite ready to concede. In Game 3, Ed Whitson kept them alive by scattering five hits over eight innings in a 7–1 romp. The next night, first baseman Steve Garvey took over, knocking in five runs—two with a ninth-inning game-winning home run—as the Padres evened the series with a 7–5 victory.

Things looked bleak the next afternoon when Sutcliffe, who had not lost in three months, carried a 3–0 lead into the sixth inning. But the Padres battled back for two runs in the sixth, and then an error by Leon Durham and a bad-hop single by Tony Gwynn led to four more runs in the seventh.

Goose Gossage shut the door on the Cubs for the final two innings, and suddenly the Padres had become the first team in National League playoff history to overcome a two-games-to-none deficit. The Padres lost the World Series in five games to the Detroit Tigers, but that did not detract from what they had accomplished.

Named after the Pacific Coast League

As a Padre, Randy Jones won 22 games and the Cy Young Award as the National League's top pitcher in 1976.

rarely better than mediocre before their miracle comeback in the playoffs of 1984.

The most memorable near-achievement in club history belongs to Clay Kirby. He pitched eight innings of no-hit ball against the Mets in 1970, but was lifted for a pinch-hitter in the eighth with his team trailing, 1–0. The Padres lost the game and the relief pitcher blew the no-hitter.

SANDLOT. An informal field, such as a vacant lot, meadow or yard, on which youngsters play baseball. Before the establishment of Little League, just about every youngster in America played sandlot baseball. They were largely unorganized teams that rarely had uniforms and played on makeshift diamonds. In some places they were organized into teams, after a fashion, but most often a sandlot game would get started just as soon as a handful of boys had gathered.

entry that brought Minnie Minoso, Al Rosen and Ted Williams to San Diego during their minor-league careers, the Padres spent the years following their birth in 1969 wallowing in the second division.

The team had some bright moments (Nate Colbert belted five homers in a doubleheader in Atlanta in 1972, and pitchers Randy Jones and Gaylord Perry captured Cy Young awards), but the Padres were

SAN FRANCISCO GIANTS. It was known as the "Shot Heard 'Round the World." It happened in a playoff game in 1951, when New York Giant Bobby Thomson hit a ninth-inning home run off Brooklyn Dodger Ralph Branca to give the Giants a come-from-behind 5–4 victory and the National League pennant. Keyed by Rookie of the Year Willie Mays, the Giants had capped a comeback that saw them erase a 13½-game Dodger lead in the final six weeks of the season.

In 1962 the Giants' playoff lightning struck the Dodgers again, but this time the

Giants' home was San Francisco and the Dodgers' was Los Angeles. Trailing 4–2 in the ninth inning of the third game, the Giants rallied. Mays's bases-loaded single and Orlando Cepeda's sacrifice fly tied the game, and a walk forced in the winning run as the Giants captured their 18th National League pennant.

Pennant No. 19 didn't come until 1989, when sluggers Will Clark and Kevin Mitchell sparked the Giants to the National League West title and a playoff victory over the Chicago Cubs. But they were swept by the Oakland Athletics in the Earthquake Series.

The Giants' history dates back to the early 1900s. The club record book is dotted with Hall of Famers—John McGraw,

Will Clark's .333 hitting in 1989 was the second-highest in San Francisco history.

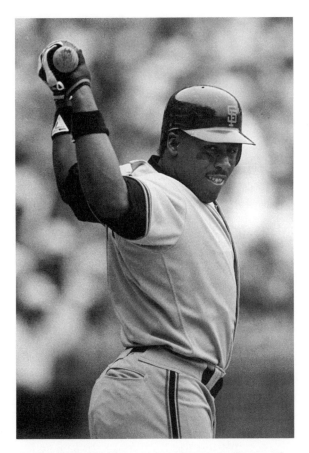

Kevin Mitchell's blasts (47) and RBIs (125) earned him the National League Most Valuable Player Award in 1989.

Frankie Frisch, Bill Terry (the NL's last .400 hitter back in 1930), Carl Hubbell (253 wins), Christy Mathewson (373 wins) and Mel Ott (511 homers).

Their heated rivalry with the Dodgers did not lessen after the teams went west in 1958. The Giants added Willie (Stretch) McCovey (521 homers) and pitcher Juan Marichal (243 wins) and were constant contenders in the 1960s and early 1970s.

SAVE. Credit given to a relief pitcher who finishes a game and protects a lead for another pitcher, who is credited with the victory. The rules grant a save to a pitcher who (1) pitches at least three innings and protects a lead, or (2) enters the game with the potential tying run either on base or represented by one of the first two men he faces, or (3) enters with a lead of no more than three runs and pitches at least one inning.

SCHMIDT, MIKE. The standard had been established in 1953, when Mike Schmidt was four years old. That was the year that Eddie Mathews blasted 47 home runs, a record for third basemen.

Twenty-seven years later Schmidt stood at home plate in Montreal's Olympic Stadium. It was the next-to-last game of the 1980 National League season, and the Eastern Division championship was at stake. Montreal and Philadelphia were locked in a head-to-head showdown. The teams had arrived at the final three games of the race in a tie for the lead.

Schmidt had driven in both runs in the opening game of the series and the Phillies won, 2–1. Now Philadelphia was one game away from the flag. But the Expos weren't surrendering quietly. The teams battled into the eleventh inning, tied at 4–4. Then Schmidt walloped a two-run homer, breaking the deadlock and delivering the deciding victory to the Phillies. It was his 48th home run of the season, an all-time record for third basemen, one more than Eddie Mathews had managed 27 years before.

By the time Schmidt ended his career on May 29, 1989, he had set many more records and established himself as perhaps the greatest all-around third baseman in the history of the game. In 2,404 games over 18 seasons, Schmidt batted .267 with 548 homers (seventh on the all-time list), 1,595 RBIs and 10 Gold Gloves for defensive excellence.

During his career, Schmidt, who was born on September 27, 1949, in Dayton, Ohio, led the Philadelphia Phillies to five division titles, two pennants and a world championship. He led the league in home runs eight times and was named Most Valuable Player three times.

His bat (548 home runs) and his Gold Glove made third baseman Mike Schmidt one of the most fabulous Phils in history.

SCORECARD. A printed card that helps spectators identify the players, giving their numbers and positions, and on which an account of the game can be recorded. Scorecards are sold in the stands, and the familiar cry of the scorecard huckster is, "You can't tell the players without a scorecard."

Scorecards date back to the 1800s, when

two young men named Harry Stevens and Ed Barrow sold scorecards in the ballpark at Wheeling, West Virginia, in the Tri-State League. Barrow went on to great success and Hall of Fame recognition as general manager of the New York Yankees. In 1890 Stevens went to New York to sell his scorecards and parlayed them into a multi-million-dollar concessions operation.

SCORING. At every major-league game there is an official scorer. Official scorers, usually baseball writers, are appointed by the league president. With the job goes a welcome fee from the league and some unwelcome abuse from disgruntled athletes, up to and including an occasional punch in the nose. Apart from the official scorer, who is responsible for deciding on hits and errors and other rulings associated with the statistics of the game, all baseball writers and broadcasters and many fans keep score in books or on scorecards.

Scorekeeping methods vary, but there are a number of basics, including the system of giving each position a number. The standard numbering code is: 1. pitcher, 2. catcher, 3. first baseman, 4. second baseman, 5. third baseman, 6. shortstop, 7. left fielder, 8. center fielder and 9. right fielder.

Fielding plays are recorded by number, with X often meaning a force play. Walks are B or W, an intentional walk is IW, strikeouts traditionally are K, or a backward K (И) for a called third strike. Base-path advances are noted by drawing the outline of a diamond, starting with home plate in the lower left corner or in the lower center and moving counterclockwise. A hit is usually a horizontal line (two lines for a double, three lines for a triple) crossed by a vertical or diagonal line to indicate the direction of the hit. A squiggly line indicates that a new pitcher has entered the game.

The accompanying score sheet (page 146) is taken from the final game of the 1989 World Series, showing how the Oakland Athletics completed a four-game sweep with a 9–6 victory over the San Francisco Giants.

Notice that in the first inning Oakland's Rickey Henderson led off with a home run. Carney Lansford then flied out to center, Jose Canseco hit a foul pop-up to first and Mark McGwire grounded out, shortstop to first base.

Oakland added three more runs in the second inning. Dave Henderson led off with a double and moved to third when Terry Steinbach flied to right. After Tony Phillips grounded out to second, Walt Weiss was intentionally walked. But pitcher Mike Moore spoiled the Giants' strategy by doubling to score both Henderson and Weiss.

Rickey Henderson followed with a single, scoring Moore to make it 4–0 and knock Robinson out of the game. Mike LaCoss relieved and walked Lansford. Canseco's single loaded the bases but LaCoss got McGwire to bounce into a force play, shortstop to second base.

The Athletics made it 7–0 with three runs in the fifth. Two came home on Terry Steinbach's triple and another scored on a double by Tony Phillips. Rickey Henderson's leadoff triple and Lansford's single produced another run in the sixth inning.

San Francisco got its first two runs in the sixth when Will Clark singled and Kevin Mitchell homered. And in the seventh inning against A's reliever Gene Nelson, Terry Kennedy drew a leadoff walk and Greg Litton homered, making it 8–4. Nelson got one out before being replaced by left-hander Rick Honeycutt. Candy Maldonado then tripled and scored on a double by Brett Butler. When Robby Thompson followed with a single, Butler scored to make it 8–6. Honeycutt retired

Scoring the fourth game of the 1989 World Series.

Clark on a fly to right and then Todd Burns, replacing Honeycutt, retired Mitchell on a fly ball to left.

The Athletics added a ninth run in the eighth on a single by Lansford and three walks, and the Giants went down in order in the ninth. When Dennis Eckersley retired Butler on a ground ball to second to end the game, the Athletics had their first world championship since 1974.

SCOUT. Expert assigned to gather information on rival teams or, if he is a talent scout, to recruit players. A bird dog, usually a part-timer, sniffs out talent and gives leads to the scouts.

SCRATCH HIT. A batted ball that results in a base hit, although it is not solidly hit, usually just slipping away from an infielder as it dribbles past him.

SCREWBALL. The pitch (not the person) is a ball rolling in a reverse spin off the outer side of the middle finger. Its action is the opposite of a curveball, breaking away from a left-handed hitter and toward a right-handed hitter when thrown by a right-hander, and breaking away from a right-handed hitter and toward a left-handed hitter when thrown by a left-hander. Sometimes called a reverse curve, it was made popular by Carl Hubbell, the

Giant left-hander, who used it when he struck out Babe Ruth, Lou Gehrig, Jimmie Foxx, Al Simmons and Joe Cronin in a row in the 1934 All-Star Game. Players often call it the scroogie.

The screwball was the favorite pitch of reliever Tug McGraw when he was with the New York Mets and Philadelphia Phillies, and also of Fernando Valenzuela of the Los Angeles Dodgers, who pitched a no-hitter during the 1990 season.

SEATTLE MARINERS. Since their birth as an expansion team in 1977, the Seattle Mariners have made few waves in the American League. Only twice in their 14 seasons have they finished as high as fourth, but Seattle entered the 1990s with a future superstar in outfielder Ken Griffey, Jr., and such other worthies as first baseman Alvin Davis and second baseman Harold Reynolds.

Seattle hasn't had many household names in its history, but there have been a few worthy of mention. Ruppert Jones had his following as the team's most dependable hitter in the early years, and Bruce Bochte hit .316 in 1979. In 1981 Tom Paciorek set the club hitting mark of .326.

There was excitement in Seattle in 1984 with the arrival of rookie pitcher Mark Langston and Davis, the first baseman, who became the American League Rookie of the Year. Langston proved a mainstay of the team until traded to the Montreal Expos early in 1989. Another important Mar-

iner was outfielder Phil Bradley, who batted .301 in a little over four seasons, 1983–87.

Clearly, Seattle fans can't treasure a rich past, but now they have a sweeter outlook, especially with young Griffey, who already has a chocolate candy bar named after him. And near the end of the 1990 season they could claim some major-league history all their own, when Griffey's father, Ken, Sr., joined the team. It was the first time that a father and son had played together. In addition, the Mariners finished the year with their second best record ever (77-85).

Mark Langston set club pitching records in his 5½ years as a Mariner.

Terrific Tom Seaver achieved everything a pitcher could want: the Cy Young Award (three times), five 20-victory seasons, a world championship (with the Mets) and a no-hitter (with the Reds).

SEAVER, TOM. Tom Seaver stepped up on the mound and peered in for the sign from catcher Don Werner. The runner took a cautious lead off first base. Seaver glanced over, his mind racing. It was the ninth inning. Cincinnati was leading, 4–0, and St. Louis hadn't made a hit all game.

Seaver had been this route before. He had pitched five one-hitters in his career. Three times he had carried no-hitters into the ninth inning only to have them broken up, once with two out and two strikes on the batter.

A no-hitter had been the one achieve-ment to escape Seaver, the right-hander with the classic delivery who was one of baseball's finest pitchers during the 1970s. He had won three Cy Young awards and been a 20-game winner five times. He had come close, but he had never managed that notable achievement, a no-hitter. Now he was on the verge again.

"I couldn't really think too much about the no-hitter because I was concentrating on winning the game," Seaver said. "My philosophy has been: If it happens, it hap-pens. If you pitch long enough, with good enough stuff, you are bound to pitch a no-hitter sooner or later."

So Seaver, unaffected by the pressure, proceeded to mow down the next three Cardinal batters in order—and did it at last. His no-hitter came on June 16, 1978— a year and a day after he had been traded to the Reds by the New York Mets.

Born on November 17, 1944, in Fresno, California, Seaver attended the University of Southern California, where he first at-tracted the attention of big-league scouts. When the Mets acquired his draft rights in 1965, it signaled the start of their de-velopment as a competitive club.

Seaver was Rookie of the Year in 1967. Among his many records, Seaver struck out 19 men in one game—including the last 10 in a row—in 1970, tying one major-league mark and setting another.

When he retired after the 1986 season with the White Sox and Red Sox, Seaver had a 311–205 won-lost record, a 2.86 earned run average, 3,640 strikeouts and 61 shutouts over a 20-year career.

SECOND BASE. The middle stop on the way around all four bases; the base a run-ner goes to after having reached first base. Second base, which is called the keystone, is in the middle of the diamond. The sec-ond baseman is responsible for the territory around and to the first-base side of second base.

SEMIPRO. One who receives money for playing but does it outside of organized baseball and not as his sole source of income.

SENIOR LEAGUE. Formed in the autumn of 1989, this league of eight Florida teams—officially known as the Senior Professional Baseball Association—was made up of players 35 and older, most of whom had major-league experience. The league gave former stars like pitchers Bill Lee and Jon Matlack and sluggers George Foster and Al Oliver a chance to play again, albeit at a slightly slower pace. The league played a 72-game schedule from late October to early February, plus playoffs.

SENT TO THE SHOWERS. An expression meaning a pitcher was ineffective and had to be replaced. Often he is said to have gone for an early shower. During the summer of 1965 New York City had a drought, and city officials appealed to citizens to save water. One young citizen at Shea Stadium had his own idea about how New York could help fight the water shortage. He made his suggestion in the form of a banner that read: "Save Water—Don't Send Met Pitchers to the Showers."

SEVENTH-INNING STRETCH. The period during a game when fans customarily stand up, stretch and show support for their team before it comes to bat in the seventh inning. Nobody knows how the tradition got started, not even veteran baseball writer Dan Daniel, the game's foremost historian. "It just grew, like Topsy," Dan said. "It probably originated as an expression of fatigue and tedium, which seems to explain why the stretch comes late in the game instead of at the halfway point."

SHAKE OFF. When a pitcher disagrees with the catcher's suggestion of which pitch should be thrown, he shakes off the catcher's signal with a prearranged signal of his own, usually by shaking his head or by flapping his glove back and forth.

SHOESTRING CATCH. The catch of a sinking line drive. This is done, usually by an outfielder, who grabs the ball just as it is about to fall or at the level of his shoelaces, so to speak. It is one of the most difficult and, consequently, one of the most spectacular catches in the game.

SHORTSTOP. The infield position between second base and third base (sometimes called the short field); also, the infielder who covers this position.

SHUTOUT. When one team fails to score at all in the course of a game. Also called whitewash or blank.

The record for shutouts in a career is 110, by Walter Johnson of the Washington Senators from 1907 to 1927. Grover Cleveland Alexander of the Philadelphia Phillies set the record for one season, 16 in 1916. And Orel Hershiser of the Los Angeles Dodgers pitched 59 shutout innings in a row in 1988—a record.

SIGNALS. When you see a third-base coach go through all kinds of gyrations, it does not necessarily mean he has ants in his pants. If he scratches his left ear, it may not be because he is itching; rather, he wants the man on first to try to steal second base on the next pitch. These are baseball signals used by the coach to tell the batters and runners what the manager wants them to do in a given situation. Signals are also given by the catcher to suggest to the pitcher what pitch should be thrown.

Signals are usually intricate enough so the opposing team can't understand them and can't tell what's about to happen. Sometimes signals are so complicated that they are missed by the player for whom they are intended—which may result in a fine. There is, however, no pattern to signals, and sometimes they are so simple they are difficult to detect.

Charlie Dressen was said to be the best at stealing the opposition's signals. There is a story about an All-Star Game when Charlie was sent to coach at third base.

"What signals are we using?" asked one player at a pregame meeting.

"Just use the signals you use with your regular team all season long," Charlie said. "I know them all."

The catcher signals before every pitch, and it is something of a baseball legend that the catcher's signals are one finger for a fastball and two for a curve. That is an oversimplification. The catcher actually works in a series. For example, he may arrange with the pitcher ahead of time that the real signal will be the second number he flashes. So he will flash four fingers, followed, for example, by two, two, three, one. Since the second signal is the one that counts, the pitcher knows the catcher wants a curveball, because the second signal was two fingers.

The catcher can change the code every inning if he chooses; but he usually keeps the same code and becomes more cautious and makes his signals more complex only

when there is a runner on second base, from where it is easy to see the catcher's signals.

SINGLE. A base hit on which only first base is legally and safely reached. In 1927 Lloyd Waner got the incredible total of 198 one-base hits for the Pittsburgh Pirates, a modern-day record. Pete Rose holds the record for singles in a career with 3,215.

SINKER. Either a pitched or a batted ball that breaks downward.

SLICE. To hit a line drive to the opposite field—that is, a right-handed hitter hitting to right field and a left-handed hitter hitting to left field.

SLIDE. In order to make a smaller target for the fielder and to make sure not to overrun the base, a runner going into a base will often slide, or "hit the dirt." Without breaking stride, he drops to the ground a few feet from the base. Some players slide on their bellies and go in head first, but the most common slide is feet first, with the player sliding on his side directly into the base. One of the prettiest and most exciting plays in baseball is the hook slide, in which the runner slides with his body flung away from the bag and hooks the bag with his trailing foot. This is done when the fielder has already received the ball and is waiting for the runner and a conventional slide would be useless.

SLUGGER. A powerful hitter. Usually the third, fourth or fifth batter in the lineup.

SLUGGING PERCENTAGE. A method of determining a batter's effectiveness in making extra-base hits. The batter's times at bat are divided into his total bases (carried to three decimal places). For example, if a batter hits a home run (4 bases) in 4 at-bats, his slugging percentage would be 1.000. The maximum slugging percentage is 4.000, a home run every time at bat. In 1920 Babe Ruth had a remarkable slugging percentage of .847 on 388 total bases in 458 at-bats. For his career, Ruth had a slugging percentage of .690 on 5,793 total bases in 8,399 at-bats.

SLUMP. A long period of ineffectiveness, usually by a batter, but also by a team, a pitcher or a fielder.

SMITH, OZZIE. Countless hitters have walked slowly back to the dugout, shaking their heads in disbelief at some piece of defensive larceny perpetrated by perhaps the greatest fielding shortstop of all time.

Though other shortstops may have been more valuable than Ozzie Smith for their offensive impact, none could challenge the Wizard of Oz's ability to reach a ball in the hole or make a leaping catch or turn a lightning pivot. In 1989, the St. Louis Cardinals' nine-time All-Star notched his 10th Gold Glove in a row, breaking Luis Aparicio's major-league record for a shortstop.

According to manager Whitey Herzog, Smith saved the Cards approximately a run a game by making plays no one else could. It was no coincidence that the Cards won a world championship in 1982, the year they obtained Ozzie from the San Diego Padres.

This switch-hitter became even more valuable, blossoming into a tough out (.303 with 75 RBIs in 1987) and a stolen-base threat (57 steals in 1988 and 464 in 13 seasons in the majors).

Smith, who was born on December 24, 1954, in Mobile, Alabama, and attended Cal Poly-San Luis Obispo, was at his peak in the 1985 playoffs against the Dodgers. Ozzie batted .435 and had the game-winning homer in the ninth inning of the decisive Game 5 en route to being named MVP of the playoffs.

Whatever else, the first and last name in shortstop defense is, and may well always be, Ozzie Smith.

SNIDER, DUKE. Edwin Donald (Duke) Snider hasn't swung a bat for the Dodgers since 1962, but the 389 home runs and 1,271 RBIs he hit for them starting in 1947 still stand as club records.

Counting his last two years, when he played for the New York Mets and the San Francisco Giants, Duke rammed a total of

Home runs—407 of them—boomed Duke Snider into the Hall of Fame. He's hitting a three-run pinch-hit homer against the Pirates on September 15, 1961.

407 home runs. Duke is one of only two National League players to have hit 40 or more homers in five straight seasons. He played in six World Series, and he slammed four home runs in both the 1952 and 1955 Series.

Born in Los Angeles on September 19, 1926, Duke was a graceful center fielder who rivaled his New York counterparts, Yankee Mickey Mantle and Giant Willie Mays.

He was elected to the Hall of Fame in 1980.

SONGS. Baseball is America's favorite sport. Even songs have been written about it. The most popular is "Take Me Out to the Ball Game," which has long been baseball's theme song. It was written at the turn of the century by Jack Norworth and Albert Von Tilzer, and did as much for baseball as it did for its authors. Songs have been written about individual players—the most famous was "Joltin' Joe DiMaggio," which was a hit record just before World War II. Other songs have glorified Jackie Robinson, Willie Mays and Mickey Mantle.

SPAHN, WARREN. The lanky pitcher swung into his windup, hands high over his head. As Warren Spahn brought his hands forward, he kicked his right leg high in the air. That kick was his trademark, the flourish at the end of the signature of one of the finest left-handers in baseball history.

No southpaw ever won more games than the 363 Hall of Famer Spahn recorded in his 21-season National League career, all but one season with the Boston and later Milwaukee Braves.

He didn't win his first game until age 25, after three years of combat service in

Warren Spahn pitched one of his two no-hitters when he was 40 years old.

World War II. He made up for lost time fast, winning 20 or more games in 13 seasons over a 17-year period, including six seasons in a row from 1956 to 1961. He pitched no-hitters in 1960 and 1961, the second one at age 40. In eight seasons he either led or tied for the lead in victories, and he was the National League earned-run-average leader three times.

Spahn, who was born in Buffalo, New York, on April 23, 1921, was not an overpowering pitcher, but he was a master of control, setting up hitters and nipping the corners of the plate.

Ironically, one of the few seasons in which Spahn failed to win 20 games was 1948, when he and Johnny Sain helped the Boston Braves win the pennant. That was the year the fans coined the saying, "Spahn and Sain and pray for rain." What this saying revealed was that Spahn and Sain were the team's only reliable pitchers and that if it rained, the team would be spared having to use one of its less-talented pitchers.

SPIES. Every so often there is a rash of newspaper stories telling of teams being accused of planting spies in scoreboards or buildings beyond center field to steal the signals of the opposition catcher and pass them on to the batter by various prearranged signals. Usually the accusations are laughed at, denied and then forgotten. However, the Chicago White Sox were exposed for spying not by the opposition but by one of their own players, Al Worthington, a pitcher of high principles who threatened to quit the team if the Sox did not stop spying. They stopped.

SPITBALL. A ball moistened on a small spot, either with saliva or perspiration, that sails or sinks in an unpredictable manner. For this reason the spitball (or spitter) is an illegal pitch. The spitball used to be a great weapon for the pitcher, but in 1920 baseball ruled against the spitball as well as the emery ball (one side of the ball was roughed up with emery paper), the talcum powder ball (one side of the ball was made slick by adding talcum powder) and the resin ball.

However, all recognized spitball pitchers then in the major leagues were permitted to continue to use the pitch without penalty for the rest of their major-league careers. Burleigh Grimes, the last of the legal spitball pitchers, pitched until 1934. Although the spitball has been illegal for half a century, it is generally believed that about 25 percent of modern-day major-league pitchers sometimes use it.

When Don Drysdale of the Los Angeles Dodgers was accused of throwing a spitball, his only defense was, "My mother told me never to put my dirty fingers in my mouth."

Among the common expressions ballplayers use to say a pitcher threw a spitball are: "The bottom dropped out of that one," "That was a wet one," "He loaded that one up" or, to the umpire, "Give him a bucket."

SPLIT-FINGER FASTBALL. The so-called "pitch of the 1980s" is a fastball thrown with the index and middle fingers on either side of the ball. This gives the ball the appearance of a straight fastball until the last split second, when the ball dips sharply. Taught by Roger Craig, first as pitching coach of the Detroit Tigers and then as manager of the San Francisco Giants, it has been used with great success by the Tigers' Jack Morris, Ron Darling of

Houston's Mike Scott has been known for his mastery of the split-finger fastball.

the New York Mets and Mike Scott of the Houston Astros. The split-finger, or splitter, became baseball's most talked-about pitch in the 1980s.

SPRING TRAINING.   *See* Cactus League, Grapefruit League.

SQUEEZE PLAY.   A bunt with a man on third and less than two out. If the base runner starts for home as soon as the ball is being delivered, it is called a suicide squeeze. If he breaks for the plate after the ball has been bunted, it is a safety squeeze. In either case it is a difficult play, but a very effective weapon if properly done.

STARGELL, WILLIE.   The ball jumped off Willie Stargell's bat, cutting through the night sky on a high arc—a rainbow shot labeled from the moment he hit it, bound for the Baltimore bullpen. It was to become a two-run homer, the deciding blow in the seventh game of the 1979 World Series, leading the Pittsburgh Pirates to the world championship.

It was entirely fitting for Stargell to strike the winning home run that season. Captain of the team, emotional leader of the Pirate family, he had spent the year distributing tiny gold stars to his teammates, saluting important contributions to the club's success. But no one contributed more than Stargell, who scored a stupendous sweep that year, sharing the regular-season MVP award with Keith Hernandez of the St. Louis Cardinals and then winning the playoff and Series awards by a wide margin.

Stargell was born on March 6, 1940, in Earlsboro, Oklahoma, and spent his entire big-league career with the Pirates. He holds two important batting records: four extra-

Willie Stargell's two-run blast won the 1979 World Series for the Pirates.

base hits in a single game four times and 90 extra-base hits during the 1973 season. That was the year he led the league with 44 homers and 43 doubles.

He finished his 21-year career in 1982 with 475 homers, 1,540 RBIs and a .282 batting average.

The years he would remember most would be 1979, when at the age of 38 he lifted his team to the championship, and 1987, when he was elected to the Hall of Fame in his first year of eligibility.

STARTING PITCHER.   The pitcher chosen to start the game. He is officially in the game once his name has been presented to the umpire-in-chief, and he must complete pitching to at least one batter unless he suffers an injury that, in the judgment of the umpire, is serious enough to sideline him.

STARTING ROTATION. The order in which a manager uses his starting pitchers, subject to change if one member is in a slump or another is pitching exceptionally well. Ideally, most teams use a five-man rotation, with the fifth starter sometimes working out of the bullpen early in the season, when there are fewer games.

STATISTICIAN. The person who keeps records on the game. There are many amateur statisticians, including newspaper reporters and fans, but each team and both leagues employ official statisticians. The Elias Sports Bureau keeps statistics on every game for both leagues, and the statistics are printed by MLB-IBM Information Systems.

Allan Roth revolutionized the use of statistics for ballclubs when he worked for the Dodgers in Brooklyn and Los Angeles. He recorded every pitch to every batter and kept massive records that were invaluable to the team. If the manager wanted to know how a particular player batted for a season against left-handed pitchers with a count of no balls and two strikes on him, for example, Roth could produce the answer almost immediately.

STEAL. A stolen base. It is credited to a runner who advances a base without benefit of a base hit, a fielder's choice or an opponent's error. Speed is important, but good base stealers are also skilled at taking a lead, getting a jump on the pitch and sliding. In 1915 Ty Cobb of the Detroit Tigers stole 96 bases, which stood as the record until Maury Wills of the Los Angeles Dodgers stole 104 in 1962. Then Lou Brock of the St. Louis Cardinals stole 118 bases in 1974.

But Rickey Henderson left them all in the dust in 1982 when he broke Brock's record with 130 stolen bases. Entering the 1991 season, Henderson had 936 stolen bases—just two short of Brock's all-time record of 938.

STENGEL, CASEY. *See Casey.*

STENGELESE. A foreign language not taught by Berlitz. It was the unique double-talk of longtime manager Casey Stengel, who fractured the English language and charmed his audience in the process.

An example of Stengelese: "No manager is ever gonna run a tail-end club and be popular because there is no strikeout king that he's gonna go up and shake hands with and they're gonna love ya because who's gonna kiss a player when he strikes out and I got a shortstop which I don't think I coulda been a success without him if ya mix up the infield ya can't have teamwork and it's a strange thing if ya look it up that the Milwaukee club in the morning paper lost a doubleheader and they got three of my players on their team and you can think it over. . . . Now ya ask what's wrong with Drysdale and he's pitched too much and I didn't make a success with my pitching staff because they had a bad year all along with myself and . . ."

Is that clear?

STEWART, DAVE. The Dodgers drafted him as a catcher in 1975, but Dave Stewart was quickly turned into a pitcher. Initially, it may have seemed the wrong decision, because he was 0-5 in his first season in the minors at Bellingham, Washington. In two years he had turned it around—17-4 with Clinton, Iowa (AA)—and by 1981 he was in the majors.

But the 6-foot 2-inch, 200-pound Stewart took a circuitous route—Los Angeles, Texas and Philadelphia—before attaining stardom with the Oakland Athletics. Until 1987, his first full year with Oakland, Stewart had never won more than 10 games in a big-league season. And he considered quitting the game after the Phillies released him in the spring of 1986.

The transformation began under Athletics' manager Tony LaRussa, and Stewart, master of the fastball and forkball, put together three 20-victory seasons, capped by his winning the World Series MVP award in 1989, when Oakland swept the Giants to win the world championship.

The steady and dependable Stewart was a 20-game winner again in 1990 (22-11), and he twice beat the Red Sox in the playoffs en route to the World Series. But the Cincinnati Reds vanquished Stewart (twice) and Oakland, taking four straight for the championship.

More than a gifted pitcher, Stewart is known for his community contributions to Oakland, where he was born, about a mile from the Coliseum, on February 19, 1957. After the earthquake struck during the 1989 Series, he made daily visits to the victims, and he donated 20 percent of his World Series check to earthquake relief.

Released by the Phillies, Dave Stewart landed with the A's—and wound up as a World Series MVP.

STOLEN BASE. *See* Steal.

STREAK. A batter is on a streak when he has hit safely in a number of games in a row. A team is on a winning (or losing) streak when it has won (or lost) a number of games in a row. A hitter is said to be a streak hitter or streaky if he does most of his hitting in clusters.

The most famous hitting streak was by the Yankees' Joe DiMaggio, who batted safely in 56 games in a row in 1941, a record many observers feel will never be equaled. Pete Rose hit safely in 44 games in a row as a Cincinnati Red in 1978 to set the modern record in the National League.

The longest winning streak by any team was by the New York Giants, who won 26 straight games in 1916. The longest losing streak was 23 defeats in a row by the Philadelphia Phillies in 1961.

STRETCH. *See* Windup.

STRIKE. A pitch that passes through a prescribed zone. (*See* Strike zone.) Whether a pitch is a ball or a strike is determined by the umpire.

A strike can be achieved in the following ways:

1. The pitch is swung at by the batter and missed.
2. The pitch enters the strike zone and is not swung at.
3. The pitch is fouled by the batter when he has less than two strikes.
4. The pitch is bunted foul.
5. The pitch touches the batter as he swings at it.
6. The pitch touches the batter when he is leaning into the strike zone. It doesn't matter if he has or hasn't swung at the ball.

Note: A strike of another sort has been introduced to baseball—by the umpires (when they went on strike to improve their lot in 1979) and by the players (when they struck in 1980, 1981 and 1985). The club owners' counterpart to the strike is the lockout. (*See also* Major League Baseball Players Association and Lockout.)

STRIKEOUT. When a batter is sent back to the dugout, charged with three strikes. Sometimes called whiffing or fanning a batter, it is the ultimate in effectiveness for a pitcher. Nolan Ryan holds the record for having struck out the most batters in one season (383, while he was with the California Angels in 1973). Roger Clemens of the Boston Red Sox set a record by striking out 20 Seattle Mariners in a nine-inning game in 1986. Tom Cheney of the old Washington Senators holds the record for strikeouts in an extra-inning game with 21. It took Cheney 16 innings to achieve his record.

The umpires call strikes on batters; they also call strikes on major-league baseball, as they did in 1979, when they struck for a better contract.

STRIKE ZONE. That space over home plate that is between the batter's armpits and the top of his knees when he assumes his natural stance. A pitch must be thrown in that zone to be called a strike if it isn't swung at by the batter.

SUBMARINE. An underhand delivery. A difficult pitch to throw, since the pitcher throws from a raised mound. Submarine pitchers are a vanishing breed. One of the most devoted practitioners was Kent Tekulve, who appeared in a record 1,050 games as a reliever from 1974 to 1989. Tekulve taught the submarine delivery to Dan Quisenberry, who set an American League record with 238 saves between 1979 and 1988. Others who have used the delivery with effectiveness have been Ted Abernathy (Cubs, Braves and Reds) and Terry Leach (Mets, Royals and Twins). Ballplayers used to say, in describing Abernathy's motion, "He comes from out of the ground."

SUN FIELD. That part of the outfield where the sun shines most, making the position more difficult to play. The most notorious sun fields in baseball are left field at Yankee Stadium and center field at Oakland Coliseum.

SUPERSTITION. Baseball has bred many superstitions, including the belief that finding a hairpin brings a base hit, spotting a wagonload of barrels or hay gives good luck, a pitcher who strikes out the first batter will be sure to lose, the man who leads off an inning with a triple will stay on third base without scoring and the player who makes a sensational fielding play will be the first to come to bat the following inning.

Most superstitions are out of date, but some live on—ballplayers and managers still wear the same shirt or tie throughout a winning streak, avoid number 13 (or else make a point of wearing it) and insist on touching or not touching a certain base when they go on and off the field. Sparky Anderson, one of the best managers in baseball history and the first one to win a World Series in each league, takes no chances. He refuses to step on the foul lines when he goes out to talk to a pitcher. The foul line aversion is shared by many players, as well.

Leo Durocher, when he coached at third base, always made certain to erase with his spikes the chalk markings that bordered the coaching box. An almost uni-versal superstition among players is their avoidance of any reference to a no-hit game if a pitcher is in the process of pitching one, although many pitchers who are not superstitious will take pressure off by mentioning their own no-hitter.

Somebody once asked Babe Ruth if he had any superstitions. "Just one," the Babe said. "Whenever I hit a home run, I make certain I touch all four bases."

SUSPENDED GAME. If a game in progress cannot continue (say, because of rain or an electrical failure or an earthquake), it will be suspended—that is, stopped, with play to be resumed at a later date—if the following conditions apply: at least 4½ innings have been played, and the score is tied or the visiting team is ahead and the home team hasn't had an equal number of outs. In the American League, there is a 1 A.M. curfew, meaning that no new inning can start after 1 A.M. (See Called game.)

SWINGING BUNT. A ball hit by the batter that dribbles slowly. It's not meant to be a bunt, but after a full swing, the ball travels no farther than a bunt.

SWITCH-HITTER. A batter who swings from either side of the plate, hitting left-handed against right-handed pitchers and right-handed against left-handed pitchers. At one time switch-hitters were rare, and for years the only truly successful ones were Frankie Frisch and Red Schoendienst. Then along came Mickey Mantle to switch-hit with such amazing success that switch-hitting became the vogue. Pete Rose became the first switcher to achieve 3,000 base hits. During the 1965 World Series the Los Angeles Dodgers presented an infield in which all four members—Wes Parker, Jim Lefebvre, Maury Wills and Jim Gilliam—were switch-hitters.

TABLE-SETTERS. The leadoff and second batters, often pesky hitters who reach base in front of the 3-4-5 hitters, the middle part of the batting order and the most productive hitters.

TAG. The action of a fielder in touching a runner with the ball, with his hand or with his glove holding the ball to register an out.

TAG UP. When a fly ball is hit, a runner on base can tag up, meaning he can try to advance to the next base after the ball is caught. He must, however, have his foot on the base until the fly is caught before attempting to advance.

TAKE. To let a pitched ball go by without swinging. When a coach wants a batter to let a pitch go, he gives the take sign. Youngsters often think "taking a pitch" means swinging at it, but in professional baseball the meaning is just the opposite.

TATER. Ballplayers' slang for a home run, arrived at by a long process. Origi-

nally, tater, slang for potato, meant a baseball, just as pill, apple and seed did. Later, a home run was a long tater. Then it was shortened to tater.

TEXAS LEAGUER. A looping fly ball that drops safely just beyond the infield and just in front of an outfielder. So called because before the turn of the century the parks in the Texas League were particularly small. Puny hits of this and other kinds are also known as sea gulls, dying swans, bloopers, bleeders, banjo hits and scratch hits.

TEXAS RANGERS. They've had a Billy Martin in their past and they have a Nolan Ryan in their present. Winning seasons have been rare, but the Rangers gave new hope to their fans in 1989 with the play of Ruben Sierra and Julio Franco on offense and the ageless Ryan making them American League contenders as late as August. The team set a franchise mark by drawing 2,043,993 fans to Arlington Stadium, and a high point in the season came when Ryan reached the 5,000-career-strikeout mark.

It was a glorious time for a franchise that began in 1961 as the Washington Senators, taking that name after the original Washington Senators moved to Minnesota and became the Twins. In 1972 the franchise moved to Texas and became the Rangers. After two disastrous years Martin

The Rangers' Jeff Burroughs was American League MVP in 1974, when he batted .301, hit 25 home runs and drove in 118 runs.

took over as manager in 1974 and guided the Rangers to 86 wins, just four less than the world champion Oakland A's. The Rangers were paced by league MVP Jeff Burroughs, Rookie of the Year Mike Hargrove and pitchers Fergie Jenkins (25 wins), Jim Bibby (19 wins) and Steve Foucault (69 games, 12 saves, 2.25 ERA).

One of their finest years came in 1977 when youngsters Jim Sundberg and Bump Wills led the team to a club-record 94 victories and second place in the American League West.

The Rangers, often picked to finish near the top of the division, were a disappointment as the 1970s came to a close. Not even the hitting of Al Oliver, who batted .319 or better in three straight seasons from 1978 to 1980, could make a difference.

THIRD BASE. The base to which the runner heads after having reached second base safely. It is located diagonally to the left of home plate and is 90 feet away from home and 90 feet away from second base. The player who covers third base is the third baseman.

THUMBED OUT. To be banished from a game by an umpire for any of a number of reasons, the most common of which is disputing a call. A ballplayer thrown out of a game is said to have been thumbed, given the thumb, chased, ejected. Joe Garagiola tells a story about his arguing with an umpire and growing so angry that he threw his catcher's mask 20 feet into the air. "If that mask comes down," said the umpire, "you're out of this game."

TOE PLATE. A piece of leather (previously metal) sewn to the pivot shoe of a pitcher to protect the shoe. It is necessary because the pitcher drags his pivot foot after making his pitch.

TOOLS OF IGNORANCE. The catcher's equipment: mask, chest protector and shin guards. They are so called because a catcher is so prone to injury that it is said that only the ignorant would choose such a position.

TOP. The first half of an inning, as in the top of the ninth. Also used in newspaper headlines to mean one team defeating another. For example, "Dodgers Top Cardinals, 4–3."

TORONTO BLUE JAYS. The experts snickered when the American League announced it had awarded a franchise to Toronto in 1977. After all, there was no guarantee that baseball would succeed in a city more interested in hockey. But the skeptics weren't laughing in 1989, when the Blue Jays not only won the American League East title but also drew a league-record 3,375,373 fans. The spacious new Skydome was an attraction, but the lure

was the appeal of the emerging Blue Jays, who had developed into one of baseball's best clubs in the late 1980s.

The Blue Jays finished in last place in each of their first five seasons, but gradually their farm system started to produce some stars. Pitchers Dave Stieb and Jim Clancy combined for 25 victories in 1980 and became the backbone of the staff as the team matured.

In the mid-1980s, the Jays' outfield of George Bell, Lloyd Moseby and Jesse Barfield was regarded as baseball's finest, and when Tony Fernandez arrived for good in 1985, Toronto had one of the top fielding shortstops in the game. That talent helped the Blue Jays to win 99 games and their first division championship in 1985.

In 1989, with Bell, Fred McGriff and late-season catalyst Mookie Wilson leading the offense and Dave Stieb and Jimmy Key setting the pace on the mound, the Blue Jays held off the Baltimore Orioles to capture their second divisional title. Alas, in the playoffs they ran into a buzz saw called Oakland.

The Blue Jays' George Bell was the American League MVP in 1987. That year he slugged 47 home runs and drove in 134 runs while batting .308.

TOTAL BASES. The total number of bases credited to a batter on his base hits—a single giving him one base; a double, two bases; a triple, three bases; and a home run, four bases. Babe Ruth's 457 total bases (85 singles, 44 doubles, 16 triples, and 59 home runs) made in 1921 are a record for one season. In 1954 Joe Adcock of the Milwaukee Braves made 18 total bases in one game on four home runs and a double.

TRADING DEADLINE. That time of year after which teams are no longer allowed to trade players, although players may be sold through waivers after that date. August 1 has been the trading deadline in recent years. (*See also* Waiver.)

TRIPLE. A three-base hit. Also a three-bagger. The triple is the rarest of base hits, combining power and speed on the part of the hitter. It is not surprising, therefore, that the record for three-base hits for a career is 312, less than half the record for home runs. The records for three-base hits in each league, coincidentally, were set in the same year—1912. J. Owen Wilson smacked 36 triples for the Pittsburgh Pirates that year to establish the National League record, and Joe Jackson of the Cleveland Indians set the American League record (tied two years later by Sam Crawford of the Detroit Tigers) with 26. Crawford holds the career record of 312.

TRIPLE CROWN. If a player leads his league in batting average, runs batted in and home runs, he wins the Triple Crown. There is no trophy for it, but it is one of baseball's rarest honors. Since 1910, only nine men have won it—two of them twice. The nine: Jimmie Foxx, Athletics, 1933; Lou Gehrig, Yankees, 1934; Rogers Hornsby, Cardinals, 1922, 1925; Chuck Klein, Phillies, 1933; Mickey Mantle, Yankees, 1956; Joe Medwick, Cardinals, 1937; Frank Robinson, Orioles, 1966; Ted Williams, Red Sox, 1942, 1947; and Carl Yastrzemski, Red Sox, 1967.

TRIPLE PLAY. The act of retiring three men in one sequence, rare in any form but especially if it is an unassisted triple play, only eight of which have been made in the majors. In 1927 two were made on successive days, one by Jimmy Cooney of the Chicago Cubs and the other by Johnny Neun of the Detroit Tigers.

TRIPLE STEAL. All three base runners stealing a base on the same play.

Mel Allen was the most popular New York Yankee broadcaster.

TV AND RADIO. Baseball broadcasters have added their own pet expressions to the game. Red Barber contributed "sittin' in the catbird seat" to describe a team or player in a position of advantage, and "squeaker" for a close game. Exclamations like Mel Allen's "How about that?" and Phil Rizzuto's "Holy cow!" are frequently mimicked when something odd or sensational happens.

Barber and Allen were the first of the well-known baseball broadcasters. In later years ex-ballplayers moved into the field with extraordinary results. When Frankie Frisch called the New York Giant games, he used to repeat his favorite expression, "Oh, those bases on balls!" Dizzy Dean rambled delightfully along about outfielders who "throwed" the ball and runners who "slud" into third.

Following the lead of Frisch and Dean and Waite Hoyt in Cincinnati, ex-players took the airwaves by storm. Rizzuto, Jerry Coleman, Ralph Kiner, Tony Kubek, Joe Garagiola, Bill White, Don Drysdale, Bob Uecker, Tim McCarver, Richie Ashburn, Tom Seaver, Johnny Bench, Joe Morgan and Jim Palmer became regulars behind the microphone.

Baseball went on the air in 1921, when Graham McNamee broadcast the World Series between the Giants and the Yankees over the radio. The Chicago Cubs instituted regular-season broadcasts in 1924, with Hal Totten at the microphone.

Television entered the field in 1939, with Barber doing the commentary on a game between the Dodgers and the Reds in Brooklyn. Today television is big business for ballclubs, and every team in the major leagues and some in the minors broadcast and telecast at least some of their games.

The addition of cable television and competition between the networks to buy the rights to telecast games brought hundreds of millions of dollars into major-league baseball in the late 1980s.

TWEENER. A ball hit between two outfielders (up the alley), usually a double or triple, sometimes an inside-the-park home run.

TWI-NIGHT. A one-admission doubleheader consisting of a twilight game (starting at about 6:00 P.M.) and a night game immediately following the twilight game. (*See* Doubleheader.)

UMPIRE. One of the officials who administer the rules. Umpires have been called arbiters, men in blue, Blind Toms and worse. Usually there are four umpires for a game, one at home plate (he is the umpire in charge of the game, calling balls and strikes as well as any play at home) and one each at first base, second base and third base. For All-Star Games, playoffs and the World Series two umpires are added, one down each foul line. Assignments for these prestige events are made on a rotating basis, so that all umpires eventually get a chance to be a part of them.

The umpire is a much-abused individual, yet any player will admit the game would be a joke without strong and cou-

Tony Kubek *(left)* and Joe Garagiola, both former players, were longtime announcers for NBC-TV's *Game of the Week.*

rageous umpires. That was the way it was until the 1920s, when along came a stern individual named Bill Klem, who gave the umpire new stature and respect. Klem is most famous for his comment: "I never made a wrong call in my life."

Like a player, an umpire starts out in the minor leagues and is scouted by the major leagues. The good ones make it to the big leagues.

An umpire's life is a lonely one. While a player spends half his season in his home ballpark, the umpire is almost always on the road during the season. He must stay at hotels other than the ones the players stay at, and he must never be seen associating with players.

Umpires' salaries have risen dramatically in recent years, thanks to a strong umpires' union. Rookie umpires make around $40,000 per season, plus expenses, while 20-year veteran umpires can make over $100,000.

UNIFORM. The players' whites, grays, flannels or monkey suits. The New York Knickerbockers wore the first uniforms in 1849. For years the uniforms were standard—white ones for the home team and gray ones for the visiting team—and all uniforms were made of flannel. With the start of night baseball, the Cincinnati Reds and the Brooklyn Dodgers experimented with a satin uniform for night games. Most teams these days wear double-knit or polyester uniforms, which stretch. Permanent numbers on the back of uniforms were first displayed by the 1929 New York Yankees. This answered the need for player identification. Without numbers, a scorecard wasn't much help.

UP. The team at bat or the player at bat. Traditionally, the game begins when the home-plate umpire cries, "Batter up!"

Emmett Ashford became the first black umpire in the majors in 1966.

VICTORY PARTY. It is traditional that the team that wins the pennant or the World Series celebrates with a victory party in the clubhouse after the winning game. The highlight of the party is the uncorking of champagne, most of which is poured on the players' heads instead of into their

The Oakland A's have a victory party in 1974 after winning their third straight World Series. Announcer Joe Garagiola is on the left, Reggie Jackson in the center and manager Alvin Dark on the right.

mouths. Often the players continue the victory party long after they leave the clubhouse, sometimes with disastrous results.

After one pennant-clinching, the Yankees continued their celebration on the train returning to New York. Pitcher Ryne Duren got into a playful mood and smashed a cigar in the face of Ralph Houk, then a Yankee coach. Houk became manager some years later, and early in his first season Duren was traded.

The Pittsburgh Pirates clinched the 1960 pennant and kept their party going on the

bus back to the hotel from the ballpark. Another playful guy innocently tugged at the foot of Vern Law, the Pirates' ace pitcher, and accidentally sprained Law's ankle. The ankle was still sore when Law pitched in the World Series. Favoring the ankle, he put added strain on his pitching arm and developed a sore arm that almost ended his career.

Oakland's clubhouse celebration after its 1989 World Series triumph over San Francisco was without champagne. Sober in the aftermath of the earthquake that had hit during the Series, management and players alike felt this was not a time for the bubbly.

WAGNER, HONUS. To baseball card collectors, shortstop Honus Wagner is the biggest name of all. A model of clean living in his playing days of 1896–1917, Wagner demanded a tobacco company's baseball card of himself be withdrawn from the market because he didn't want to be associated with smoking. The card, which had only limited distribution and therefore is a collector's item, is now worth more than $100,000 (in mint condition).

Wagner, who was born in Mansfield, Pennsylvania, on February 24, 1874, was the finest shortstop of his time. He compiled a lifetime average of .327 and won eight National League batting titles in 12 years, all with the Pittsburgh Pirates. In 1936 he was among the first group of players selected for the Hall of Fame. He died in 1955.

WAIT OUT. When a batter waits for a type of pitch he prefers to hit. In waiting out a pitcher, the hitter will often try to foul off strikes until he receives his favorite pitch or forces the pitcher to walk him.

WAIVER. The means by which a team can sell a player or send him to the minor leagues after the opening day of spring training. The team places the player's name on a waiver list and he becomes available to the other clubs. If none of the other teams—which select in the reverse order of their standing—claim him, the player may be sent to the minors. If, however, the player is claimed, his team must either remove his name from the list and keep him or sell him to the claiming team for the waiver price of $25,000. After the trading deadline (August 1), a player cannot be sent from one team to another without first being cleared through waivers.

WALLY PIPP. To say this to a player is to remind him that if he sits out a game, he may never get his job back. It comes from Wally Pipp, a Yankee of the 1920s. Pipp, the regular first baseman, got sick on June 1, 1925. His place was taken by a young man named Lou Gehrig, who did not miss a game thereafter until May 2, 1939. Gehrig played in a record 2,130 games in a row, and, of course, Wally Pipp never got his job back.

WASTE ONE. When the count on the batter is strongly in the pitcher's favor, the pitcher might waste one (throw one deliberately out of the strike zone) with the hope of getting the batter to swing at a bad pitch.

WHIZ KIDS. The name given to the Philadelphia Phillies of 1950, who surprised everybody by winning the National League pennant. Not one of the starting players had yet reached his 30th birthday, thus the name Whiz Kids, a variation of "Quiz Kids," a popular radio show of the time that featured a panel of child prodigies.

WILD PITCH. A legally delivered ball thrown so high or so wide of the plate that it cannot be handled by the catcher and results in a base runner moving up one or more bases. It is charged against the pitcher as simply a wild pitch, not an error. There can be no wild pitch if there is no runner on base or if a runner does not advance.

It is interesting to note that the most wild pitches made in an inning was four, by two men, including Walter Johnson, one of baseball's greatest pitchers, which gives rise to the thought that a little wildness is a good weapon because it may make batters afraid to dig in at the plate.

WILD THROW. A fielder's erratic throw that enables a runner or runners to advance one or more bases. Unlike the wild pitch, a wild throw is scored as an error even if it is by the pitcher.

WILLIAMS, TED. It was the final home game of an otherwise unmemorable 1960 season for the Boston Red Sox. Yet it had special meaning because, at age 42, Ted Williams, perhaps the greatest pure hitter in baseball history, was retiring. This would be his last appearance at Fenway Park, where he often feuded with the critical fans.

On this day Williams gave the critics something to remember him by and put a fitting end to a Hall of Fame career. In his final at-bat he sent a huge home run over Fenway's right-field fence, a final exclamation point to a truly remarkable career.

Williams was born on August 30, 1918, in San Diego, California, and came to Boston to stay in 1939, breaking in by winning the league RBI crown with 145 and hitting .327. A year later he raised his average to .344. In 1941 he wrote baseball history, soaring to a .406 average. Fifty

years later, no other player had come within 16 points of that accomplishment.

Going into the final day of the 1941 season, Williams's average stood at .3996 and manager Joe Cronin offered to keep him on the bench to protect the .400 he had before a doubleheader against the Philadelphia A's. Williams would have none of that. He played in both games and tacked the final six points onto his average with six hits in eight at-bats.

That was the first of six batting titles for Williams. Twice—in 1942 and 1947—he won the Triple Crown, leading the league in batting, home runs and runs batted in.

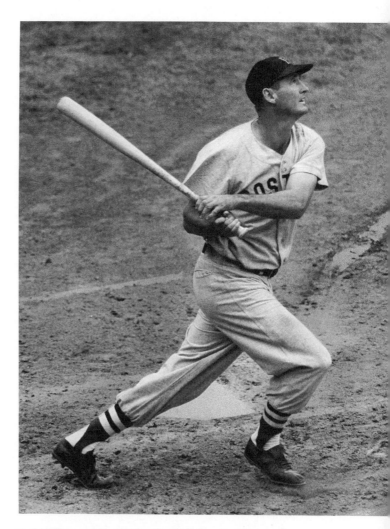

Ted Williams hit .406 for the Red Sox in 1941, and nobody has hit .400 since then.

He was passed over for the MVP award in both of those seasons and also in 1941, his .406 season, when Joe DiMaggio won it for hitting in a record 56 straight games. Williams did win MVP crowns in 1946 and 1949.

When he won the 1958 batting title with a .328 average, he was 40 years old, the oldest man ever to be a batting champion. He finished with a career average of .344 and that farewell Fenway Park homer gave him 521, third highest in history at the time.

WINDUP.   One of the two legal pitching positions, the other being the stretch position. A pitcher winds up when there are no runners on base, or runners are on third, or second and third, or the bases are loaded. He stretches at all other times. The stretch is a short windup and insures against a potential base stealer taking too big a lead.

With his bat and his charisma, Dave Winfield has been a compelling force on the baseball scene, with the Padres, the Yankees and the Angels.

WINFIELD, DAVE.   A fierce competitor, he was blessed with such diverse athletic gifts that he was drafted by football's Minnesota Vikings and basketball's Atlanta Hawks in addition to baseball's San Diego Padres. But Dave Winfield opted for the diamond, going directly from the University of Minnesota to the majors without spending a single day in the minors.

The best of his eight solid years in San Diego was 1979, when he batted .308 with 34 homers and a league-leading 118 RBIs. In 1981 he took his RBI bat and rifle arm to the Yankees as a free agent. Although the 6-foot 6-inch, 220-pound right fielder gave Yankee owner George Steinbrenner no legitimate cause for complaint, it was Steinbrenner who labeled him "Mr. May" in the wake of a 1-for-22 World Series flop in 1981, meaning that Winfield could do well in the spring but not in October. But Winfield has proved himself as "Mr. Consistency" during his illustrious major-league career.

As a Yankee, Winfield produced six seasons with at least 100 RBIs and tied Roger Maris for seventh on the all-time club homer list with 203, including a single-season high of 37 in 1982. In the 10 seasons prior to 1989, which Winfield missed due to back surgery, he led all major leaguers with 1,017 RBIs. His 21 homers for the California Angels in 1990 gave him a 17-year career total of 378.

A seven-time Gold Glove winner, he was an All-Star every year from 1977 through 1988.

WINNING PITCHER. The pitcher credited by the official scorer, according to the rules, as the winner of the game. It is what all pitchers strive for.

In the case of a starting pitcher, he must pitch at least five complete innings to receive credit for a victory. A relief pitcher, on the other hand, may pitch to only one batter and still be the winning pitcher if, while he is in the game, his team goes ahead and stays ahead.

WORLD SERIES. A tape of the previous game's action was showing on screens all across America, with ABC announcers Al Michaels and Tim McCarver describing the details. Suddenly, the picture started to scramble a little, and as it got worse Michaels said to his confused viewers, "I'll tell you what, we're having an earthquake." With that, ABC lost its transmis-

The Yankees' Reggie Jackson connects for a two-run homer off Burt Hooton of the Dodgers in the fourth inning of Game 6 of the 1977 World Series. Jackson followed it up with two more homers, tying Babe Ruth's Series record of three in a game. The Yankees won the game, 8–4, and the championship. With a total of five home runs, Jackson also set a Series mark.

Boston's Carlton Fisk is welcomed home after his game-winning blast in the 12th inning tied the 1975 World Series against Cincinnati at three games each. But the Reds won the seventh game and the championship.

sion from San Francisco's Candlestick Park. It would be 10 days before the 1989 World Series—known forevermore as the Earthquake Series—resumed, and the Athletics went on to sweep the Giants.

That the fall classic did resume maintained a tradition that had started in 1903, when the champions of the National and American leagues met to determine the champion of baseball. The best-of-seven series (in some early years it was a best-of-nine) has been held every year since then, except for 1904, when John McGraw, manager of the lordly New York Giants, refused to let his team play the upstart Boston Red Sox of the new American League.

The World Series operates on an alternating schedule, opening in the American League city one year and in the National League city the next. After two games the Series shifts to the other team's park for the third, fourth and, if necessary, fifth games. If more than five games are needed to determine a winner, the Series goes back to the first park.

Among the most memorable Series have been: the underdog Cincinnati Reds shocking the Athletics with four straight victories in 1990; Kirk Gibson's dramatic two-out, two-run homer in the ninth inning that sent the Dodgers on their way to an upset of the Athletics in 1988; the Mets rallying for three runs with two out in the

Champions

Year	A. L. Champion	N. L. Champion	World Series Winner
1903	Boston Red Sox	Pittsburgh Pirates	Boston, 5–3
1904	no World Series		
1905	Philadelphia Athletics	New York Giants	New York, 4–1
1906	Chicago White Sox	Chicago Cubs	Chicago (AL), 4–2
1907	Detroit Tigers	Chicago Cubs	Chicago, 4–0–1
1908	Detroit Tigers	Chicago Cubs	Chicago, 4–1
1909	Detroit Tigers	Pittsburgh Pirates	Pittsburgh, 4–3
1910	Philadelphia Athletics	Chicago Cubs	Philadelphia, 4–1
1911	Philadelphia Athletics	New York Giants	Philadelphia, 4–2
1912	Boston Red Sox	New York Giants	Boston, 4–3–1
1913	Philadelphia Athletics	New York Giants	Philadelphia, 4–1
1914	Philadelphia Athletics	Boston Braves	Boston, 4–0
1915	Boston Red Sox	Philadelphia Phillies	Boston, 4–1
1916	Boston Red Sox	Brooklyn Dodgers	Boston, 4–1
1917	Chicago White Sox	New York Giants	Chicago, 4–2
1918	Boston Red Sox	Chicago Cubs	Boston, 4–2
1919	Chicago White Sox	Cincinnati Reds	Cincinnati, 5–2
1920	Cleveland Indians	Brooklyn Dodgers	Cleveland, 5–2
1921	New York Yankees	New York Giants	New York (NL), 5–3
1922	New York Yankees	New York Giants	New York (NL), 4–0–1
1923	New York Yankees	New York Giants	New York (AL), 4–2
1924	Washington Senators	New York Giants	Washington, 4–2
1925	Washington Senators	Pittsburgh Pirates	Pittsburgh, 4–3
1926	New York Yankees	St. Louis Cardinals	St. Louis, 4–3
1927	New York Yankees	Pittsburgh Pirates	New York, 4–0
1928	New York Yankees	St. Louis Cardinals	New York, 4–0
1929	Philadelphia Athletics	Chicago Cubs	Philadelphia, 4–2
1930	Philadelphia Athletics	St. Louis Cardinals	Philadelphia, 4–2
1931	Philadelphia Athletics	St. Louis Cardinals	St. Louis, 4–3
1932	New York Yankees	Chicago Cubs	New York, 4–0
1933	Washington Senators	New York Giants	New York, 4–1
1934	Detroit Tigers	St. Louis Cardinals	St. Louis, 4–3
1935	Detroit Tigers	Chicago Cubs	Detroit, 4–2
1936	New York Yankees	New York Giants	New York (AL), 4–2

Year	A. L. Champion	N. L. Champion	World Series Winner
1937	New York Yankees	New York Giants	New York (AL), 4–1
1938	New York Yankees	Chicago Cubs	New York, 4–0
1939	New York Yankees	Cincinnati Reds	New York, 4–0
1940	Detroit Tigers	Cincinnati Reds	Cincinnati, 4–3
1941	New York Yankees	Brooklyn Dodgers	New York, 4–1
1942	New York Yankees	St. Louis Cardinals	St. Louis, 4–1
1943	New York Yankees	St. Louis Cardinals	New York, 4–1
1944	St. Louis Browns	St. Louis Cardinals	St. Louis (NL), 4–2
1945	Detroit Tigers	Chicago Cubs	Detroit, 4–3
1946	Boston Red Sox	St. Louis Cardinals	St. Louis, 4–3
1947	New York Yankees	Brooklyn Dodgers	New York, 4–3
1948	Cleveland Indians	Boston Braves	Cleveland, 4–2
1949	New York Yankees	Brooklyn Dodgers	New York, 4–1
1950	New York Yankees	Philadelphia Phillies	New York, 4–0
1951	New York Yankees	New York Giants	New York (AL), 4–2
1952	New York Yankees	Brooklyn Dodgers	New York, 4–3
1953	New York Yankees	Brooklyn Dodgers	New York, 4–2
1954	Cleveland Indians	New York Giants	New York, 4–0
1955	New York Yankees	Brooklyn Dodgers	Brooklyn, 4–3
1956	New York Yankees	Brooklyn Dodgers	New York, 4–3
1957	New York Yankees	Milwaukee Braves	Milwaukee, 4–3
1958	New York Yankees	Milwaukee Braves	New York, 4–3
1959	Chicago White Sox	Los Angeles Dodgers	Los Angeles, 4–2
1960	New York Yankees	Pittsburgh Pirates	Pittsburgh, 4–3
1961	New York Yankees	Cincinnati Reds	New York, 4–1
1962	New York Yankees	San Francisco Giants	New York, 4–3
1963	New York Yankees	Los Angeles Dodgers	Los Angeles, 4–0
1964	New York Yankees	St. Louis Cardinals	St. Louis, 4–3
1965	Minnesota Twins	Los Angeles Dodgers	Los Angeles, 4–3
1966	Baltimore Orioles	Los Angeles Dodgers	Baltimore, 4–0
1967	Boston Red Sox	St. Louis Cardinals	St. Louis, 4–3
1968	Detroit Tigers	St. Louis Cardinals	Detroit, 4–3
1969	Baltimore Orioles	New York Mets	New York, 4–1
1970	Baltimore Orioles	Cincinnati Reds	Baltimore, 4–1
1971	Baltimore Orioles	Pittsburgh Pirates	Pittsburgh, 4–3
1972	Oakland A's	Cincinnati Reds	Oakland, 4–3
1973	Oakland A's	New York Mets	Oakland, 4–3
1974	Oakland A's	Los Angeles Dodgers	Oakland, 4–1
1975	Boston Red Sox	Cincinnati Reds	Cincinnati, 4–3
1976	New York Yankees	Cincinnati Reds	Cincinnati, 4–0
1977	New York Yankees	Los Angeles Dodgers	New York, 4–2
1978	New York Yankees	Los Angeles Dodgers	New York, 4–2
1979	Baltimore Orioles	Pittsburgh Pirates	Pittsburgh, 4–3
1980	Kansas City Royals	Philadelphia Phillies	Philadelphia, 4–2
1981	New York Yankees	Los Angeles Dodgers	Los Angeles, 4–2
1982	Milwaukee Brewers	St. Louis Cardinals	St. Louis, 4–3
1983	Baltimore Orioles	Philadelphia Phillies	Baltimore, 4–1
1984	Detroit Tigers	San Diego Padres	Detroit, 4–1
1985	Kansas City Royals	St. Louis Cardinals	Kansas City, 4–3
1986	Boston Red Sox	New York Mets	New York, 4–3
1987	Minnesota Twins	St. Louis Cardinals	Minnesota, 4–3
1988	Oakland A's	Los Angeles Dodgers	Los Angeles, 4–1
1989	Oakland A's	San Francisco Giants	Oakland, 4–0
1990	Oakland A's	Cincinnati Reds	Cincinnati, 4–0

Giants' Willie Mays against Vic Wertz of the Cleveland Indians in 1954.

Two of baseball's rarest rarities popped up in the World Series—an unassisted triple play by Bill Wambsganss of Cleveland in 1920 and Don Larsen's perfect game for the Yankees against the Dodgers in 1956.

The Reds' Billy Hatcher doubles in the first inning of the second game of the 1990 World Series against the Oakland A's. It was his fourth consecutive hit, and he added three more in the game for a Series record of seven hits in a row.

X. Used in box scores, this means something out of the ordinary. For instance, if a runner has reached first base on a call of catcher's interference, the box score will read X—Henderson. At the bottom of the summary a line says: X—reached first on catcher's interference. In baseball standings an X before a team in the listing means that the club has won its division title.

bottom of the 10th inning to shock the Red Sox in 1986; Babe Ruth's pointing finger, which may or may not have predicted the home run that followed against the Chicago Cubs in 1932; Brooklyn's Mickey Owens's failure to hold a third strike in 1941, opening the gates for a Yankee comeback and ultimate victory over the Dodgers; and two unbelievable catches—by Al Gionfriddo of the Dodgers against the Yankees' Joe DiMaggio in 1947 and by the New York

YASTRZEMSKI, CARL. The ball wended its way past Yankee Willie Randolph's vacuum-cleaner glove at second base. Carl Yastrzemski limped down the first-base line, favoring an aching Achilles tendon.

But for those 90 feet between home plate and first base, the pain took a back seat in this game in 1979. And when the man they called Yaz pulled in safely at first, he had achieved his 3,000th hit, a milestone in itself but all the more significant because he thus became the first player in the American League ever to combine 3,000 hits and 400 home runs.

Red Sox fans exploded with a roar of approval for the left fielder who had followed in the footsteps of the legendary Ted Williams at Fenway Park.

Yastrzemski was born on August 22, 1939, in Southampton, New York, the son of a Long Island potato farmer who was determined that his son would get an education. In 1958, after his freshman year at Notre Dame, Yaz signed a $100,000 bonus contract with the Red Sox. But he pledged to complete the courses necessary for his degree. And eventually he got his diploma at Merrimack College near Boston.

Yastrzemski came to the Red Sox in 1961 following Williams's retirement. But it wasn't until 1967 that Yaz won the fans over with a remarkable year in which he became baseball's last Triple Crown winner. He batted .326, with 44 home runs and 121 runs batted in, leading the league in all three departments. In the final two games of the season, when the Red Sox won their Impossible Dream pennant, Yaz had seven hits in nine at-bats as Boston beat Minnesota to clinch the flag.

The batting title was the second of three Yastrzemski would win in his career. He retired following the 1983 season with an American League–record 3,308 games played, 3,419 hits, 452 home runs and 1,844 RBIs. He was elected to the Hall of Fame in 1989, his first year of eligibility.

YOUNG, CY. In 1890 a young pitcher warming up against a wooden outfield fence in Canton, Ohio, did enough damage to cause someone to remark that it looked "like a cyclone hit it."

A sportswriter picked up the phrase and so Denton True Young was dubbed "Cy." He was born in Gilmore, Ohio, on March 29, 1867, and nobody has come close to matching some of the records Young compiled in his 22 seasons in Cleveland, St. Louis and Boston.

His 511 victories are 95 more than Walter Johnson's second-best total. He also holds the mark for complete games (750) and innings pitched (7,356). Young, who pitched three no-hitters, was elected to the

Cy Young pitched the most victories in baseball history—511.

Hall of Fame in 1937. In 1955, shortly after he died, baseball named its top-pitcher award in his honor.

The Cy Young Award is given by the Baseball Writers Association of America to the best all-around pitcher in each league. Until 1967 there was only one award—to the top pitcher in the majors.

YOUNT, ROBIN. It takes a special talent and maturity to rise through the minor leagues in less than one year, at age 18. Then again, Robin Yount always has been special.

A prized first-round draft choice in 1973, Robin reported to Milwaukee in 1974, after only 64 minor-league games, as that rarest

Cy Young Award Winners

(Before 1967 only one pitcher won an overall major-league award.)

Year	Player, Club	Year	Player, Club
1956	Don Newcombe, Brooklyn Dodgers	1962	Don Drysdale, Los Angeles Dodgers
1957	Warren Spahn, Milwaukee Braves	1963	Sandy Koufax, Los Angeles Dodgers
1958	Bob Turley, New York Yankees	1964	Dean Chance, Los Angeles Angels
1959	Early Wynn, Chicago White Sox	1965	Sandy Koufax, Los Angeles Dodgers
1960	Vernon Law, Pittsburgh Pirates	1966	Sandy Koufax, Los Angeles Dodgers
1961	Whitey Ford, New York Yankees		

NATIONAL LEAGUE

Year	Player, Club
1967	Mike McCormick, San Francisco Giants
1968	Bob Gibson, St. Louis Cardinals
1969	Tom Seaver, New York Mets
1970	Bob Gibson, St. Louis Cardinals
1971	Ferguson Jenkins, Chicago Cubs
1972	Steve Carlton, Philadelphia Phillies
1973	Tom Seaver, New York Mets
1974	Mike Marshall, Los Angeles Dodgers
1975	Tom Seaver, New York Mets
1976	Randy Jones, San Diego Padres
1977	Steve Carlton, Philadelphia Phillies
1978	Gaylord Perry, San Diego Padres
1979	Bruce Sutter, Chicago Cubs
1980	Steve Carlton, Philadelphia Phillies
1981	Fernando Valenzuela, Los Angeles Dodgers
1982	Steve Carlton, Philadelphia Phillies
1983	John Denny, Philadelphia Phillies
1984	Rick Sutcliffe, Chicago Cubs
1985	Dwight Gooden, New York Mets
1986	Mike Scott, Houston Astros
1987	Steve Bedrosian, Philadelphia Phillies
1988	Orel Hershiser, Los Angeles Dodgers
1989	Mark Davis, San Diego Padres
1990	Doug Drabek, Pittsburgh Pirates

AMERICAN LEAGUE

Year	Player, Club
1967	Jim Lonborg, Boston Red Sox
1968	Denny McLain, Detroit Tigers
1969	Mike Cuellar, Baltimore Orioles
	Denny McLain, Detroit Tigers
1970	Jim Perry, Minnesota Twins
1971	Vida Blue, Oakland A's
1972	Gaylord Perry, Cleveland Indians
1973	Jim Palmer, Baltimore Orioles
1974	Jim Hunter, Oakland A's
1975	Jim Palmer, Baltimore Orioles
1976	Jim Palmer, Baltimore Orioles
1977	Sparky Lyle, New York Yankees
1978	Ron Guidry, New York Yankees
1979	Mike Flanagan, Baltimore Orioles
1980	Steve Stone, Baltimore Orioles
1981	Rollie Fingers, Milwaukee Brewers
1982	Pete Vuckovich, Milwaukee Brewers
1983	LaMarr Hoyt, Chicago White Sox
1984	Willie Hernandez, Detroit Tigers
1985	Bret Saberhagen, Kansas City Royals
1986	Roger Clemens, Boston Red Sox
1987	Roger Clemens, Boston Red Sox
1988	Frank Viola, Minnesota Twins
1989	Bret Saberhagen, Kansas City Royals
1990	Bob Welch, Oakland A's

of birds—a shortstop who could hit. He struggled defensively at first, committing a league-high 44 errors in 1975, but his hard work paid off in 1976 as he led American League shortstops in double plays and total chances.

Meanwhile, young Yount's offensive production rose steadily. In 1980 he hit .293 with 23 homers and 87 RBIs and was named an AL All-Star for the second time. The best was yet to come for this talented right-handed hitter, who was born on September 16, 1955, in Danville, Illinois.

In 1982 Yount led the Brewers to an AL pennant with one of the greatest years ever by a shortstop—a .331 average, 29 homers, 114 RBIs and a league-leading 46 doubles—and he was honored as the league's MVP. Although Milwaukee lost the World Series to the St. Louis Cardinals in seven games, Yount hit .414 with a homer and six RBIs.

Converted into a center fielder in 1985, Yount mastered that position, too. And, in 1989, when he hit .318 with 21 homers and 103 RBIs and collected his second MVP trophy, it marked the sixth time he had hit .300-plus and the third time he had driven in more than 100 runs.

No wonder Milwaukee fans were jubilant when, as a free agent who could have gone anywhere, he decided to remain a Brewer and signed a three-year contract in 1990 that would pay him $9.6 million.

ZIP. Another word for a shutout, used mainly in newspaper headlines. Newspaper headline writers like the word because it is the shortest way to say "shutout."

Index

Page numbers in **boldface** refer to illustrations.